SWANAGE

PIER

Railway Hotel

Drill Hall

Mowlem Institute

Royal Victoria Hotel

TRAMWAY

Grove Hotel

Coastguard Station

St. Aldhelm's Ch.

247
137·240

239
3·520

240
1·779

245
20·796

SWANAGE PAST

SWANAGE PAST

David Lewer and Dennis Smale

Phillimore

2004

First edition 1994

Published by
PHILLIMORE & CO. LTD
Shopwyke Manor Barn, Chichester, West Sussex, England

© David Lewer and Dennis Smale, 1994, 2004

ISBN 1 86077 311 7

Printed and bound in Great Britain by
THE CROMWELL PRESS
Trowbridge, Wiltshire

*We dedicate this book to our families,
and to all those lovely Do'set Folk, both past and present,
who have encouraged and guided us over the years.*

Contents

List of Illustrations

Frontispiece: Swanage Seafront, *c.*1893

ix

Acknowledgements

Due to the wealth of interest, encouragement and co-operation extended to us over the years and the goodwill generated for the project, it gives us great pleasure to acknowledge the assistance received from the following, past and present:

Ray Aplin, Martin Ayres, Hazel Bailey, Richard Bartelot, Hubert Beavis, John Beavis, Walter Bishop, Jean and John Bowerman, William Bradford, Jim Bradford, Mrs John Bradley, David Bragg, Miss Brotherton OBE, Basil Buckland, Tony Buffery, Brian Bugler, Joan and Pat Burgess, John Burry, David Burt, Kenneth Burt, Anne and Bill Carter, Peter Chadwick, Ron and Brenda Chappell, Eddie Corben, Sister Liam Cummins, Edward and Moreen Curtis, Mr and Mrs John Curtis, John Dean, Sue Dodd, Dorset Archaeology & Natural History Society, Dorset Central Library, Dorset Record Office, Helen Dunman (née Muspratt), Durlston Country Park, Margaret Emms, David Florence, Phil Francis, Peter Gibb, Leslie Gibbons, David Glassock, Arthur Hancock, Peter Hancock, David Hames, Edwin and Pat Hardy, George Hardy, Jack Hardy, Llew Hardy, Ron Hardy, David Haysom (Curator, Swanage Museum), Frank Haysom, Treleven Haysom, Walter Haysom, David Henstridge, Mark and Rachel Helfer, Christine Hercock (née Burt), Jack Hixson, Charlie Hooper, David Hunt, Chris Kaye, Anne King, Eric Long, David Lovell, Phyllis Mapley, Bet and Jim Mitchell, John Patrick, Audrey Pembroke, Stan and Inger Purser, Eric Roberts, the Revd Andy Roberts, Reg Saville, Donald Simpson, Fred Smale, John Smale, Chrissy Smith, Peter Smith (of Westport House, Purbeck District Council), Tony Sparkes, Harry Spencer, Mary Spencer-Watson, Mick Stainer, Cyril Suttle, Swanage Library, Swanage Town Council, the Rector of Swanage, Harry Tatchell, Dr William Tudor-Thomas, Sidney Tringham, Catherine Turner, Charlie Turner, Mr and Mrs N. Viney, Geoff Varney, Sue Weeks, William Whatley, Graham White, George Willey.

David Lewer would like to thank especially David Haysom, Curator of Swanage Museum, for reading the proofs, also a momentous thank you from Dennis Smale in appreciation of his two secretaries, Janny his wife, and Liza his daughter, for typing his relevant section of the book and all the correspondence this task has produced, as well as the encouragement from his sons Keith and Mark, 'Go for it Dad'. He would also like to acknowledge the following, whose work has contributed so greatly to the book: photographers Walter Pouncy (1844-1918), William Powell (1882-1973), and his father Thomas Powell (1860-1921), Lucien Levy, George Henry Cox (1875-1955), Helen Muspratt, Ray Hibbs, Sidney Tringham, T.J. Wilkes, Sydney Newbery, Aero Pictorial Ltd, artists T. Webster, H. Gastineau, W.A. Miles, R.R. Reinagle, Philip Brannon, J.W. Gibbs, Alfred Dawson, Walter Field, Leonard Patten, Frank Richards, Francis Newbery and Phyllis Mapley.

Both authors are deeply indebted to the following for permission to use these illustrations: Jean and John Bowerman, 17; William Bradford, 75-6; Tony Buffery, 4; Brenda and Ron Chappell, 58, 70; Edward and Moreen Curtis, 2, 6, 33, 45-6, 54, 65, 68-9, 80-81, 83-6, 89, 96; Mr and Mrs John Curtis, 24-7, 61-2, 94, 101; Dorset County Museum, 29, 44, 74; Dorset Record Office, 10, 30; Mrs Dunman (née Muspratt), 19, 99; the Field family, 18; Hastings Museum, 3; Edwin and Pat Hardy, 53, 107; David Haysom, 112, Treleven Haysom, 38; Chris Kaye, 72, 110; Ken and Molly Miller, 49; John Mowlem & Co. plc, 36; Dr and Mrs Purser, 9; Royal Commission on Historical Monuments, 39; Tony Sparkes, 100; St Mary's Parish Church, 40; Swanage Cottage Hospital, 119-20; Swanage Town Council, 43, 63; Swanage Museum, 15, 41-2, 47, 67, 73, 102-3, 105, 111; Wessex Water, 117. All the other photographs were provided by David Lewer and Dennis Smale.

Scene of the geological discoveries at Swanage.

Introduction

In attempting a history of a parish there is one important point to bear in mind, and that is – change! It is unwise to refer to a house, for instance, as being 'next to the post office': the Swanage post office has been moved at least four times. 'By the railway station' – that nearly disappeared, but now, with its new lease of life, it is still there and likely to survive. Perhaps 'next to the church' might be thought safe, but on the other hand St Aldhelm's was demolished after only a short life.

Even in a full-length book with more than a hundred illustrations we cannot give a complete picture of one parish, but we can tread warily along the path and invite the reader to come with us to enjoy the fascinating journey which is the unfolding of a local history. Occasionally we may even come upon some hitherto unknown nugget to add to our pile of information. There are markers on the way, early ones often broken or lost, then becoming more frequent as we come nearer to the present: objects to be noticed in the landscape, or information to be found in surviving documents now carefully preserved in record offices. Then there are the increasing number of books and maps, and finally the overwhelming evidence that arrived with the coming of newspapers and photography. The reminiscences of local inhabitants should also be remembered. My old friend Captain Alfred Dewar, of the Admiralty Historical Section, said to me many years ago, 'History is what happened yesterday', when he encouraged my interest in the subject. Insofar as quotations have been freely made from numerous books and records, I would echo John Playford's words (1658), 'The work as it is, I must confess, is not all my own, some part thereof was Collected out of other men's Works, which I hope will the more Commend it.' William Masters Hardy's *Old Swanage* (1910, 2nd edn) is so often quoted here that references are marked WMH. John Mowlem and his nephew George Burt are also frequently mentioned and are usually marked JM and GB.

A history without illustrations is not very attractive, and the reading of it may be hard going. A picture book with only brief captions affords easy going but lacks depth. Together, however, they can make a valuable contribution to knowledge and form an enhanced volume, for which we hope this one will qualify.

Co-author, Dennis Smale, is much more than the photographer for our book, though he is highly accomplished in that field. He has contributed to the text both by being extremely knowledgeable about geology, landscape and history, and by being aware, as I am, of the often amusing idiosyncrasies of Purbeck folk. Together we offer both local people and the town's many visitors the story of *Swanage Past*.

DAVID LEWER

Note to the Second Edition

When in 1994 Dennis Smale and I arrived at the Swanage bookshop there was a queue of some fifty people waiting for us to sign our new book, *Swanage Past*. Many of our local friends, and visitors too, were eager to read more about the town's history. It continued to be a popular book, and last year it ran out of print.

Since its first publication, many new residents have moved to Swanage, some for a happy retirement in this gem of the Isle of Purbeck. No doubt they and other new visitors will look for an interesting book on the subject. A second edition has given us the opportunity to correct a few errors, rearrange existing and add new illustrations, and to include an extra chapter to bring the book up to date. We thank our publishers and you, the reader, for enabling us to see *Swanage Past* in the bookshops once again.

D.J.L. and D.J.T.S.

I

Rocks and Dinosaurs: The Scene is Set

Where to begin? Perhaps with the dinosaurs, because they still arouse such interest, not least with our children, who often these days know more about them than their parents.

We are told by geologists that the dinosaurs ('terrible great lizards') roamed 'Jurassic Purbeck' some 130 million years ago. A time-span such as this means little to us, yet that is recent history compared with that of life on earth or with the earliest rocks since the cooling of the planet.

The Isle of Purbeck, in fact only a peninsula,[1] draws many students of geology, as well as holiday visitors, due to its compact structure and consequently varied and attractive landscape. The disposition of the strata from south to north, following the cliff face, begins with the Jurassic deposits of Kimmeridge Clay and is overlaid by the Portland Beds running from Chapman's Pool to Tilly Whim Caves and Durlston Head. Above the Portland stone come alternate beds of Purbeck stone and clay, forming Durlston Bay and the southern plateau. Burr stone and the celebrated Purbeck 'marble' lie downhill and northward together with the reefs of Peveril Point. In Durlston Bay the Cinder Bed makes the junction with the newer Cretaceous rocks.[2] The extensive Wealden sand, grits and clay form the valley and Swanage Bay, then narrow bands of Greensands and Gault follow, lying beneath the almost vertical Chalk which forms the impressive Purbeck Hills which run from Ballard and Nine Barrow Down, through Corfe Castle, to Worbarrow Bay.[3]

1 Dinosaur footprints at Suttle's quarry, Herston, 1963. These were later removed and are now exhibited at the Natural History Museum, South Kensington.

North of the ridge beyond Swanage are bands of Reading beds and London clay, but the extensive Studland heaths are composed of thick beds of Bagshot sands: recent Eocene deposits (albeit some 50 million years ago) forming, with Poole Harbour, the southern borders of the Hampshire Basin. Blown sand forms the dunes of Studland Bay.

2   Jimmy Trim ploughing Gannetts Field above Beach Road (now Shore Road) with Beach Cottage beyond. The cliffs of the Weald, Gault, Greensand and Chalk are a mirror image of Worbarrow Bay.

All these layers of rocks deposited during hundreds of millions of years have gradually formed Purbeck: over time part of Europe, then separated from it, sunk beneath the waves, raised up again, convulsed, tilted, denuded, flooded, sunbaked, and frozen, for time out of mind. Forests grew up, and wondrous plants, fishes, birds, insects and animals appeared – and dinosaurs.

'Footprints on the sands of time'

So far no complete fossilised dinosaur has been found in Britain, but bones have occasionally been discovered in the Isle of Wight. A cast of a skeleton is exhibited in the Natural History Museum at South Kensington, and the fascinating Dinosaur Museum at Dorchester explains much in detail.[4] *Iguanodon* stood some fourteen feet high and was probably herbivorous, while *Megalosaurus* was thought to be carnivorous. Footprints of both have frequently been found in the Middle Purbeck beds at Swanage.

Even before geology was much understood, the old-time quarrymen underground were familiar with these footprints, often revealed in the stone ceiling above the excavations. 'Arr, 'e's bin thar a-weay aforre!' was the comment. Purbeck stone is much less homogeneous than Portland and was originally a mud laid down unevenly in lagoons some 150 million years ago. It preserved numerous such relics of fossil fish, turtles and small crocodiles. J.B. Delair, an eminent authority, remarked that perhaps no region in the British Isles yields such abundant and continuous tracks of fossil footprints as are found in the Purbeck beds.[5]

In 1933 J.B. Calkin, a local archaeologist, recorded and published a group of 14 footprints of an *Iguanodon* track uncovered in Suttle's quarry at Herston.[6] In 1962 a double track of 26 footprints was traced there for a distance of 70 feet. Experts from the British Museum visited the site and in the following year extended the excavation. These

3 (left) Samuel Husbands Beccles (1814-90)

4 (right) W.R. Brodie (1830-76). Note his geological hammer, for, though only an amateur geologist, he has been credited as the first discoverer of air-breathing mammalian in the world, at Durlston Bay, Swanage in 1854.

tracks showed a longer and narrower footprint than the earlier ones and were believed to be those of a *Megalosaurus*. The discoveries were subsequently removed to London.

Another important find occurred in the summer of 1981 when Mr D.W. Selby at Townsend was excavating into the hillside to construct a garage for his bungalow. Seventeen tridactyl (three-toed) footprints were revealed, covering an area of 120 square metres, 'which clearly show the animal walked on its hind legs, placing one foot in front of the other'. Eventually there were 170 recognisable footprints, the majority being tridactyl, thought to be of both *Megalosaurus* and *Iguanodon*. Archaeologists spent several weeks on the site measuring, photographing and recording the finds, and the majority of the slabs were removed to Dorchester Museum where they are displayed to great advantage. A few of these footprints may be seen recessed in the courtyard wall at the Swanage Tithe Barn Museum. Here also is a splendid ammonite fossil 2ft 6in. in diameter. Smaller specimens are often found embedded in the Purbeck-Portland stone. People have incorporated them in the walls of their houses.

Then, suddenly, about 60 million years ago the dinosaurs disappeared. This remains a mystery, though there have been several theories to explain the puzzle: that there was a severe change of climate, or even that a giant meteor hit the earth and wiped out these large animals. At all events the boundary between the Chalk and the later Tertiary beds has been called 'probably the most important break in British geological history'. On land the dinosaurs were replaced by mammals; in the sea, the ammonites did not survive. 'During this break in deposition the seas withdrew and the chalk was lifted and warped.'[7]

Dirt Diggers

On the southern plateau the total thickness of the Purbeck beds at Swanage was estimated to be three hundred and eighty feet. The lower beds (160ft) contain a variety of marls, shales and sandy limestone. The middle beds, of about the same thickness, include the various layers of building stone quarried up the south hill; the upper beds (60ft) include the Burr stone used for building Corfe Castle, and the narrow bands of the famous Purbeck 'marble' that consists of freshwater limestone and tiny fossilised snails (*viviparus*).

The prominent 'Dirt' bed, about a foot thick, occurs at the junction of the Middle and Lower Purbecks, and its exploration, just before the publication of Darwin's *The*

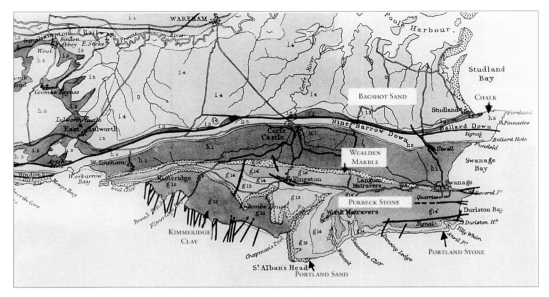

5   Damon's Geology Map of Purbeck, 1884, which is still considered the definitive example of its kind.

Origin of Species (1859), caused considerable excitement. The earliest specimens were obtained in 1854 by W.R. Brodie[8] and Charles Wilcox, a local surgeon, when a fossilised mammal jaw was discovered here. In 1856, encouraged by Sir Charles Lyell and Sir Richard Owen (who coined the term dinosaur), S.H. Beccles[9] carried out an extensive exploration in Durlston Bay. *La Belle Vue Restaurant* (later *Tilly Whim Inn* and since demolished) is thought to have been built (1870) close to the cutting which uncovered what is known as the Mammal Bed. Beccles was granted £150 from the Royal Society and rented a house at 4 Victoria Terrace in the High Street, Swanage. The work lasted for nine months and he employed 11 labourers who are shown, together with top-hatted Beccles, in the etching which appeared with an extensive report in the *Illustrated London News* of 26 December 1857.[10] Beccles 'extracted remains of no less than 27 species of marsupial animals, about 16 of which were then entirely new to science ... these are almost the only mammals known to have existed before the Tertiary period'. Many of the fossils discovered by Beccles were described, with illustrations, by Prof. Richard Owen in the *Monographs of the Palaeontographical Society*. One shows him caricatured, presiding at a dinner with an extraordinary assemblage of prehistoric – and not so prehistoric – animals. Owen described a tiny dinosaur jaw, now displayed in the Dorchester Museum, which had been discovered by Charles Wilcox; after the publication it went missing for a century until it was rediscovered at Encombe House in 1981.

Henry Willett, of Brighton, repeated Beccles' experiment in 1880 in the hope of finding more specimens but, after digging for 10 days and the fine sifting of the dirt bed, only one was found and that only a 1½ in. fragment from the lower jaw of a tiny marsupial, *Triconodon mordax,* though interesting in that it had only *three* molar teeth instead of the usual *four*![11]

The Cinder Bed, a little higher and found between the Middle Purbeck upper and lower building stones, is about eight feet thick and is made up almost entirely of crushed oyster shells. A quantity of gypsum in Durlston Bay was used commercially for a time and was mentioned for sale at 16s. per ton in 1852.

6   Ballard Cliff from Sheps Hollow, 1797. It is thought that the original name was Shett's Hollow (Saxon).

Landslides and Slumps

'Durlston Bay is a cartographer's nightmare … the cliffs are undergoing constant erosion, burial, overgrowth and landslips. The cliff-top above the new coastal protection works receded 25m between 1982 and 1988.'[12] The cliffs themselves are unstable because of the dip and pitch of the Purbeck beds, the many faults and underground water. Soon after the construction of the zigzag path by George Burt [of whom more later] in the 1870s there was a major landslip, which obliterated much of his work. Landslides continued to occur from time to time and a major one in November 1960 uprooted trees, which fell to the beach. The path was again blocked and a bungalow undermined and abandoned.[13] In 1987 there was more slumping further north when rocks and debris slid down to the sea, threatening a recently-built block of flats. A costly scheme involved the dumping of thousands of tons of boulders below to form an angle of repose. This unfortunately masked the view of the interesting strata. The hard rocks of Peveril Point are more resistant to the sea despite the attack on the south side by the waves. Intensely crumpled reefs can be clearly observed, especially at low water. 'The structure is a sharp syncline with minor and still sharper folds within it.'[14] These contain beds of broken shell limestone (Burr) and Purbeck marble as well as clays and shales.

Swanage Bay

Buildings mask the junction between the Purbeck and Wealden series. Here is the outfall of the Swanage Brook and, inland, an area of alluvium. Northwards the valley contains ridges of sandy grit and beds of clay suitable for brick-making. Excellent firm sand forms the beach at the southern end of the bay, but northwards comes shingle, then pebbles and finally chalk boulders below Ballard Cliff, barring any further close view except from the sea.

   Round the bay, weak cliffs of sand and clay become taller, and here again the face is unstable. Alternate periods of high rainfall, drought and frost have taken their toll, as have underground springs and the sea waves themselves. Despite a sea wall, more groynes and isolated attempts at defences, there have been more falls from the cliffs. Following the prolonged drought of 1976, and heavy winter rainfall later, there was major slumping along the entire cliff-line with extensive mud-flows. The northern promenade was completely blocked. It was cleared, but more recently there have been further heavy cliff falls, and property above remains threatened.[15]

Beyond the end of the sea wall, Sheps Hollow gives access from the low cliff to the shingle beach. Slumping has again taken place in this incised valley, and the footpaths have had to be diverted. Further north Punfield Cove marks the junction of the Wealden strata with the Greensands, Gault and the towering Chalk. It is especially interesting as it affords the scene of complicated rock beds together with a great variety of fossils. 'It marks the northern limit of the Wealden sands and clays which were laid down under predominantly freshwater conditions in the Lower Cretaceous period about 120 million years ago.'[16] There has been much slipping of the beds around the pond area which is at present overgrown. A sandy limestone called the Punfield Marine Band contains fossilised shells two inches long or more, ornamented with spiral ribs. Bored fossil wood is common, and also remains of crustaceans.

The chalk was formed in a deep sea. The Upper Chalk, more than a thousand feet thick and extremely hard and pure, contains few fossils or flints. The strata of Ballard Down and Godlingston Hill is almost vertical, following the famous Purbeck 'thrust' fault at Ballard Cliff. This runs inland where it meets another major fault running through Ulwell from Swanage Bay. Here, at Forked Down, the strata have been forced out of line, thus forming the pass between the hills and the road to Studland. The chalk forming the northern lower slope towards Studland is in contrast almost horizontal. It is surprising to learn that the Portland and Purbeck beds are completely missing north of this great fault, a fact confirmed by recent oil drilling on the heath.

Upheaval

The Eocene period lasted for about 20 million years. The seabed continued to sink, forming the Hampshire and London basins. The climate and vegetation became sub-tropical and life, both in the seas and on land, began to acquire a modem aspect. The Bagshot beds form a large area of the Dorset heaths, and from them comes the pure clay used to make the renowned local pottery. Near Studland the Agglestone, a prominent anvil-shaped block weighing 500 tons, is an isolated outcrop of coarse grit. It tipped at an angle in September 1970. Once it was thought that the Devil at the Isle of Wight aimed the Agglestone at Corfe Castle but it fell short! The Puckstone nearby is a smaller but similar feature of the heath.

Passing through the 12 million years of the Oligocene period, which was more temperate with shallow seas and land, we come to the Miocene time. Around 25 million years ago, the folding of the earth became intense, and the Alps and the Pyrenees were created. Africa was on the move northwards, putting tremendous pressure on Europe. Although southern England was on the margin of the action folding did occur, forming a great arch: the Purbeck anticline, whose apex stretched from east to west and was much steeper to the north than to the south. The pressure of the rocks can be seen best in Stair Hole at Lulworth, at Worbarrow or, only from a boat, at Ballard Cliff where the northern horizontal chalk appears to have been forced over the vertical beds; but there are differing opinions as to the reason for this phenomenon.

The Solent River

A river system began to develop from west to east through the Hampshire Basin in Miocene times and, with tributaries flowing from the south, the work of breaching the chalk ridge began. But sea levels rose and fell in later periods, and the Ice Ages released a vast amount of water from time to time when the glaciers melted, though these themselves did not reach the south coast. At one time the great Solent river flowed northward of the Isle of Wight into the sea from Spithead, but when the sea rose again it was left with the outfall of the Itchen, Test, Avon and Stour rivers, and the developing Poole Harbour from the Frome and Piddle, now flowing on either side of Wareham.

In comparatively recent times, the sea finally broke through the chalk barrier from both north and south, leaving Old Harry rocks in Purbeck, 15 miles from the Needles in the Isle of Wight. The erosion continues, with the sea attacking weak points in the chalk and forming caves, which then become arches, until eventually a whole section of cliff falls. Old Harry's wife collapsed to half her height during the storm of 1896, at the time when the Foreland (Handfast Point) was joined to the cliff. Parson's Barn, a great cavern near the Pinnacles, fell only a few years ago.

Purbeck Streams and Springs

Erosion has also continued inland. In former periods the southern face of the Purbeck anticline extended much further into the Channel, and the chalk overlaid the Wealden and Purbeck beds. From the highest point, streams flowed south and north. Two of the latter resulted, after erosion, in the formation of the hillock of Corfe Castle, where the Corfe River and a tributary, the Byle brook, flow on either side of it until they unite on their journey north into Poole Harbour. However, at the eastern watershed in the present Purbeck valley at Harman's Cross, a stream rises nearby and flows eastwards down to Swanage Bay. It has no

7 Old Harry Rocks and the chalk Pinnacles, with Swanage in the distance.

official title but some call it the Swan brook.[17] A tributary to it rises in Godlingston Wood and another flows down from Langton Matravers. From Herston to the sea the brook meanders across the alluvial flood-plain, the 'Whistles', though it is constricted by a low hill as it approaches the sea, the narrow crossing giving rise to severe flooding during storms and high tides. The only other stream of any size is that at Ulwell below Ballard Down.

The former mill there was renowned for its pure water, and the brook still spills across the sand into the sea at the north end of Shore Road.

At the foot of the limestone hillside there is a line of springs which flow into the Swanage brook and which clearly gave rise to the future settlement. These springs maintain their supply and vary little. They appear at Herston, Newton, Carrant's Court, above Church Hill, which provided the town pump and mill pond, at the Old Rectory and Tithe Barn, Frogwell below the High Street, and at Spring Hill, which fed the brewery. Near the pier, at Boil Well, a plentiful supply of pure water gushes into the sea, which was invaluable for the sailors of old when landing from their monkey-boats: hence the name of the Monkey Beach.

Tides and Climate

'The coastline is defined and controlled by the sea, its waves and tides.'[18] Waves are largely independent of tides but are made by the 'fetch' or distance the wind has been over the sea. There is a double tide in both Swanage and Durlston bays. Even at spring tide the rise between high and low tide is no more than about six feet, and at neap tide, four feet or even less. Spring tides come a few days after new and full moons. Flood tide runs to the east, ebb tide to the west. Small boats should be kept within the bay and not beyond the pier because the tides are very strong off Peveril Point: as the Danes found to their cost.

A curious book appeared in 1890, edited by John Braye and entitled *Swanage - its History, Resources as an Invigorating Health Resort, Botany and Geology*. The report on health was contributed by L. Forbes Winslow MB,[19] who wrote that 'Purity of the water and purity of the air are two undeniable facts associated with the name of Swanage.' He enthused about the climate of Swanage and said of Durlston, 'at "Sunnydale",[20] can be seen many rare plants, flowers in full blossom even in the coldest part of the year'. Professor Letheby, he said, found the water was in every way similar to that at Burton-on-Trent. Swanage Pale Ale from the local brewery was said to be equally as good as Burton beer.

An amusing anecdote relates that on 6 December 1881 a large herring, caught in Swanage Bay, was hung up in the Meteorological Society's station in Durlston Park, 178 feet above sea level. It was taken down in May 1884 and found to be 'without the least decomposition … The herring is now perfectly sweet, and nothing but skin and bone. Mr Burt will show it to anyone with pleasure.' One suspects that George Burt had the book published to advertise Swanage and, in particular, the attraction of his domain, which is now the Durlston Country Park.

Typically there are 31 inches' rainfall yearly, less than the average for Dorset, and thunderstorms are rare. 'Sunny Swanage' deserves its name: a solar bar cuts across the south coast embracing only Portland Bill, Durlston, Ventnor and Beachy Head as the sunniest spots; Swanage beach is not far behind. Nevertheless the climate is bracing in contrast to relaxing Bournemouth. Normally sheltered from the prevailing winds, Swanage shows a different face when a strong north-easterly gets up.[21] The bay is then exposed to rough seas and the shore liable to be swamped. Snow is rare, yet there have been spectacular, though short, blizzards as recorded in past photographs.

And so we come to the landscape, so dependent on geology and climate. Some parts of Swanage changed little before the arrival of man: the chalk downs, though covered with bushes and scrub,[22] and the limestone cliffs, not yet quarried. Swept by the southwest gales, the plateau was as yet undivided by the characteristic drystone walls. In the valley, apart from the swampy flood plain, there were many more trees than now, with tangled oaks, ash, thorn and ivy, on the rough grassy slopes before farmland and hedges had come into being. How strange to imagine the waves breaking upon a shore deserted except, perhaps, for a fox chasing a polecat, or a seagull swooping upon fish.

2

Settlers and Invaders:
Britons, Celts, Romans, Saxons and Normans

Until some fifty thousand years ago Purbeck was still connected to Wight, while the South Hampshire area lay on the north bank of the river Solent. In Purbeck evidence of early man in the Old Stone Age is rare. These primitive people were nomadic hunters and many of their flint tools were preserved in terrace gravels laid down by the great river and its tributaries. In the Middle Stone Age, when the ice had finally retreated, hunting and fishing increased, and many microliths (flakes of flint used to tip arrows or sharpen primitive tools) have been found in Purbeck. In 1931 road widening at Ulwell revealed flint tools and a small gathering-pit containing periwinkles, cockles and limpets.[1]

In the New Stone Age, from about 2500 BC, the inhabitants were herdsmen and, though still nomadic, began to till the land after a fashion, using flint or stone hand-axes and hoes to clear bushes and scrub to grow wheat and barley on the hills. A stone axe was found on Ballard Down and others have been discovered near Swanage.[2] By now the coastline had more or less assumed its present form. Neolithic men seem to have preferred the high chalkland and built earthworks there. The Britons buried their more important dead in long barrows, perhaps to contain the chieftain and his family. They can be seen mostly in areas west of Dorchester and in Cranborne Chase; the only one in Purbeck is on Nine Barrow Down above Ailwood Farm, about half a mile west of the Swanage parish boundary.[3] As usual, it was aligned east-west and is linked with several round barrows of later date. Thomas Hardy, in *The Hand of Ethelberta,* describes his heroine on a donkey ambling along the chalk ridge on her way from Swanage to Corfe Castle 'through a huge cemetery of barrows, containing human dust from prehistoric times'.

The Bronze Age

The stone circle at Rempstone,[4] just south of the B3351 road, consists of Studland ferruginous sandstone and was probably erected by the Bronze-Age 'Beaker folk' who invaded Britain about 1800 BC. They raised the round barrows on the chalk ridge, later named Nine Barrow Down, prominently seen from the valley ever since. These were burial chambers of the more important folk, the dead usually being laid on their side in a crouched position, sometimes with 'grave goods' such as their characteristic pottery and drinking-beakers. One of these trussed skeletons, with handled cup, was found in the round barrow on Ballard Down above the waterworks at Ulwell which was the site of an obelisk erected in 1892. The so-called Giant's Grave and Giant's Trencher on Godlingston Hill were excavated in 1851 and 1857 by the Revd J.H. Austen, who found nothing, and it is doubtful whether either was in fact a barrow. There were five small 'bowl' barrows on Ballard Down, which were later levelled by the plough. In them were found burial urns of the 'collared' type, used before the rite of cremation replaced inhumation. Below, to the north, in Studland parish are Thorny Barrow, Fishing Barrow and King Barrow near the Foreland. During this period sheep were kept for weaving wool, and barley was grown on the higher land. Around 1000 BC a large number of immigrant Celts arrived using ploughs, who introduced settled farming. Bronze tools and weapons became more common.

The Iron Age and the Celts

From the fifth century BC Hengistbury, at the mouth of the Stour and Avon, became a busy port when trade increased with Normandy, it being a short Channel crossing from the Cotentin peninsula. Though most of these primitive ships arrived safely at the Hengistbury harbour, a few must have found their way into the bays of Studland or Swanage, blown by easterly gales. In Purbeck needles, burnished tools and weaving combs made of bone were preserved in the limestone soil.[5] Kimmeridge shale was worked in prehistoric times, and in 1946 excavation displayed flint lathe-tools, worked flakes, and slabs of unworked shale.[6] Ornaments and armlets of this material were widely worn, and many examples have been found abroad. Carbonised grains of wheat and oats were found in local storage pits. The inhabitants would have lived in round huts of wattle and daub, with a central hearth and a thatched roof. Objects of daily use included spindlewhorls, loomweights and rotary querns for grinding corn.

About 450 BC Celts using iron crossed the Channel, some landing at Lulworth Cove, others in Poole Harbour. They overran the Bronze Celts whose weapons could not compete with iron. Christopher Taylor[7] has suggested that lower land was not unfavourable to prehistoric man, and there was a concentration of sites in the clay valley of the Isle of Purbeck. However, the Celts built many hill-forts on the higher chalklands to guard against another threatened invasion from Gaul. The fort of Flowers Barrow above Worbarrow Bay was constructed on the ridgeway track extending eastwards to Ballard and westwards towards the great fort of Maiden Castle, which became the capital of the Durotriges tribe. Later another tribe, the warlike Belgae, invaded Dorset and captured Maiden Castle. They had wheeled ox-drawn ploughs and war chariots. But the Durotriges survived and even struck their own primitive coins.

The beginning of Celtic society evolved from ancient clans. This led to the formation of small hamlets loosely linked by family dwellings following pastoral occupations. The people lived on the produce of their herds and, although the cultivation of arable soil increased, there was as yet little manuring and no rotation of crops. The management of the herds was communal, and the importance of ownership of land was yet to come. The local chieftain claimed his right through descent from the dim past. There were freemen and slaves, the latter probably descendants of the conquered Bronze Celts or earlier Britons, but all worked to maintain this rudimentary civilisation. Defence from attack by strangers was of first importance, and military men increased their power. From all this, the concept of the 'manor' began to appear. Land ownership was gradually accepted but as yet there was no organisation of the estate in which labour could be gathered round an economic centre, and many serfs lived alongside the free owners and free tenants. 'There was no settled system of hierarchical privilege and patronage. For the chief purpose of defence and of economic organisation the tribal grouping remained the principal scheme of society.'[8]

Where does this leave Swanage, the parish-to-be? The first essential for any permanent settlement was the provision of water, and here was a line of springs emerging from the limestone hills westwards from Peveril Point. It is probable that the first settlements were here, forming the hamlets which would become Swanage, Newton and Herston. There were other springs coming from the chalk, and here the hamlets of Whitecliff, Ulwell and Godlingston came into being. They were little more than small groups of huts built of wood and thatch. Later there were small areas of cultivation around these settlements, particularly where the soil was suitable, but for the rest there was extensive pasture and then vast areas of 'waste': thick woods below the downs, and the marshy lagoon stretching a mile inland from the sea.[9] Such might have been the scene when the Romans arrived in Dorset soon after the invasion of AD 43 in which Vespasian took Maiden Castle after fierce fighting with the Celts.

The Romans

'The area was amongst the first in southern England to come within the sphere of peripheral trade with Rome via Gaul in the first century BC.'[10] Perhaps the local people were not so surprised to see Romans at first hand. Quarrying and manufacturing in Purbeck was already known to the Romans before the invasion, so the new masters soon continued these activities with the Celtic labourers. Four centuries of comparative peace imposed on warring Celts resulted in the increase of population and extension of agricultural land. Although the Romans were here so long, their civilisation remained essentially urban; it overlaid that of the Celts but did not destroy it. For one thing, after the conquest, there were generally few Romans in any rural area; the Celts continued to be the backbone of the workforce and kept their own language. The most lasting reminders of the Romans after they had left were their roads and cities which survived in some degree until after the Dark Ages.

In the second century AD Hengistbury was abandoned in favour of the new Roman port established within Poole Harbour, near Hamworthy. From here a road led north to a fort and depot near Wimborne and then on to the great junction of Roman roads near prehistoric Badbury Rings, making in three directions for Old Sarum, Bath and Dorchester. From the Hamworthy port it was easy to approach Purbeck by sea to Swanage or up the river to Wareham, where there was substantial occupation, and Stoborough, on the south side of the Frome, where there were pottery kilns.

Before long, modest 'villas' made their appearance in the countryside, mostly not far from the new roads but sometimes on the site of native farmsteads where the British gentry retained their connections with the land. 'Most probably they were still chiefly resident on their estates, and many ordinary farmers shared their prosperity.'[11] In the second century more villas were built: some occupied by retired Roman soldiers who, where it had been compulsory for the legionaries, could read and write. 'The curious persistence in Britain of forms of Latin indicative of educated speech but tending to be peculiar to this island does suggest that the native aristocracy remained a significant element in society.'[12]

Discoveries

Centuries later, with Roman England forgotten, the remains of demolished villas were occasionally unearthed, revealing relics of sophisticated and practical buildings, with their mosaic floors and under-floor heating arrangements. Fewer than twenty villas are known in Dorset but of these several have been discovered in Purbeck, including those at

8   Skeleton discovered at Ulwell in 1982.

East Creek (1869),[13] Brenscombe (1962)[14] and Bucknowle (1975),[15] all near Corfe Castle.[16]

In Swanage it was said that Roman remains were found in the vicinity of Whitecliff, and it was supposed that the farm was built on the site of a villa, but there was no firm evidence. In 1877, however, two stone-lined graves or cists were discovered on the cliff nearby.[17] Romano-British farm buildings of a simpler type were discovered in 1940 at Woodhouse over the hill in Studland; extensive excavations were continued there from 1952 to 1958.[18] In 1961 David Henstridge of Swanage discovered a collection of Roman coins below the sand at the foot of the *Grand Hotel*. The British Museum identified most of them as third and fourth centuries AD, but others as third century BC from Chios, Carthage and Crete. Among the designs they show a sphinx, an eagle, a bull, a nymph, and a harp. The varied provenances and dates remain a puzzle.

Many Romano-British graves have been found in Swanage. In 1953 a grave from around AD 150 was discovered in Atlantic Road. It was constructed with slabs of local stone and contained, besides the skeleton, three dozen large iron nails (probably the only remains of a wooden coffin) and a brooch. Near the edge of the cliff of Durlston Bay a Roman burial-ground was discovered.[19] W.M. Hardy related how eight skeletons were found in June 1904 when he was building a house near *La Belle Vue Restaurant*. At least four were buried in cists and contained roughly-made black-ware vessels. More cists, now obliterated, were discovered at Herston. But the most impressive local discovery was that at Ulwell. During building work at the recently named Shepherd's Farm in 1949, three burials in cist graves and a Roman roof tile were found. Then in 1982 further building necessitated digging northwards into the hillside, and as a result an extensive Romano-British cemetery was revealed containing 57 inhumations. Some were in simple earth graves, others in stone cists. There was only one 'grave good': a small iron knife. The skeletons were of men, women and children, and all were facing east, but it is uncertain whether it was a Christian cemetery. It was used over several generations and continued into the seventh century. There was no evidence of a contemporary settlement nearby, yet Ulwell lies ideally placed between the chalk gap and Swanage Bay, and it is thought there might be the remains of a seventh-century settlement beneath the modern village. [20]

Mention should be made of the discovery of bones in the old Rectory garden 'near the well' reported in 1881 to the local doctors Jumeaux and Delamotte. They pronounced the bones to be human and condemned the water to be on the safe side. This area was 'a very ancient place of interment, apparently for Christian people, from the manner in which the bodies were buried, though of unknown date. They were recently discovered by the Revd R.D. Travers MA in his garden while digging to discover the source of a spring.'[21] In the 1950s Cyril Parsons, while working in the approach to the tithe barn, found a number of skulls, 'and with characteristic dry humour, displayed some of them on the low wall there'.[22] Then in 1993 a few more bones were unearthed below the south wall of the Barn Museum when the ground was being excavated for its new office. Alongside was an old stone-lined drain still in operation.

Roman Quarrying

This subject raises some questions:[23] how extensive was the quarrying, where did it take place, what material was worked and for what purpose was the product used? It seems that local quarrying did not take place on a vast scale, as there is very little Roman construction visible, and what there is to be seen is in Dorchester.[24] We know that there were pavements and hypocausts beneath, but little stone appears to have been used in building villas, though Roman roof tiles were common. Large numbers of pestles and mortars were fashioned for trade, and for these both Purbeck marble and other stone were used. The most popular use of the marble was for decorative internal work, and for memorial inscriptions in particular, as externally the material did not weather well. Examples have been found in London, Colchester, St Albans, Cirencester, Silchester, Chichester and Dorchester. Chester and Caerleon produced military examples. The villa at Fishbourne, near Chichester, used Purbeck marble extensively and there is evidence that most of the working took place close by.

It would be reasonable to assume that the marble would be quarried at easily accessible sites, and the first would be at Peveril where plenty of stone could be extracted near the surface. It could also be exported conveniently from Swanage Bay when the weather was favourable. It is possible that the Romans quarried marble further inland along the outcrop line, but, if so, evidence of it was obliterated by later medieval works. The marble might have been sent away via Poole Harbour. It is fairly certain that the marble was worked at Norden, but the variety of design and lettering of inscriptions suggests that the final work was done by letter cutters at the delivery sites. There are some forty inscriptions listed, the greatest number being at Silchester, followed by Colchester. Purbeck marble seems to have been used frequently until about AD 150, after which it gradually declined until its reappearance in medieval times.

The end of Roman Rule

It seems that Christianity had little hold on Britain before the fourth century, but with Constantine's conversion and its acceptance as the state religion, it spread in both town and country. This was a 'golden age' for Roman Britain. There was a wealthy Christian community in Dorchester, and in some villas, notably at Hinton St Mary and Frampton, there were representations of Christ in mosaics. Lead baptismal fonts were used, many of them in rural areas, but the Romano-British cemeteries in Dorset do not indicate whether or not the burials were Christian.

But soon Britain experienced the first of the barbarian invasions. Looting and killing took place, particularly near the coast, and discipline broke down. Although civil authority was restored, foreign tribes came to stay and began to be accepted into the Roman armies. But the collapse of Roman rule throughout the West was imminent, and early in the fifth century Britain was left to look after itself. Coinage ceased, the soldiers were no longer paid and the Roman army was withdrawn. The pottery industry suddenly ceased. However, there is no evidence that the villas had come to a violent end and 'at least until the 440s, something survived in Britain that was like "post-Roman" or "post-imperial" life.'[25]

The Dark Ages

The Germanic hordes who descended were illiterate, so the fifth and sixth centuries afford little evidence apart from objects from graves in pagan cemeteries. Christianity had gone underground. Of the tribes, the Jutes occupied the Isle of Wight while south Hampshire was invaded by the West Saxons. It is suggested that they fanned north and west and came up against the formidable Bokerly Dyke before breaking through the defences into Dorset. It is probable that Purbeck was the last area of Dorset to be taken. There was considerable resistance by the Britons and a major victory led by the legendary King Arthur, 'possibly the last chieftain to unite the former Roman province before it collapsed finally into a patchwork of British and Anglo-Saxon states'.[26] The battle was at Mons Badonicus, said to be the site of Badbury Rings. There is a story that it was on Studland heath that Sir Bedevere cast Excalibur into the sacred lake of Little Sea, that 'magic mere'.[27] But then Little Sea was, in early times, an inlet from Studland Bay. Other semi-legendary chieftains, Cerdic and Cynric, arrived in Wessex in 495, the traditional date.

The Anglo-Saxons were non-urban but chieftains needed meeting places and may have used some of the old Roman towns for this purpose. It is thought that Dorchester just survived in this way. Kingship continued to be important and larger settlements became more usual, yet by Domesday the population had halved since Roman times.[28] At what time England was divided is uncertain, but land settlements are more likely to have been Romano-British than Saxon. The boundaries may have developed from districts formed around a royal manor house, sometimes a king's *tun*, and later named Kingston, where tithes were exacted and paid, laws were made and justice was done. Thus the 'manor' may have originated from very early times, and when Saxon kings granted away lands they later became post-Conquest 'demesnes'.

While the shires were finally fixed in the 10th century, the hundreds, nominally holding a hundred families, had been formed very much earlier. In Purbeck there were two roughly equal hundreds: Hasler to the west and Ailwood (or Rowbarrow) to the east, which contained the later parishes of Corfe Castle, Kingston, Worth Matravers, Langton Matravers, Swanage and Studland. Ailwood stands below the Down of the same name. Rowbarrow, the later name for the hundred, probably means Rough Barrow and it is thought that it was the gathering place where, at first in the open, agreements, decisions and transactions took place. Hutchins writes (I, 629):

> Near Tapers or Talbot's hill in Woolgaston and south of it, is a lane called Rowbarrow Lane, and in a ground near it the Hundred court was formerly held. It is about a mile SW from Aylwood which formerly gave name to this hundred.

Christianity

The reappearance of Christianity in Britain came with St Augustine's mission to Kent in 597 and his enthronement as first Archbishop of Canterbury four years later. In 635 Cynegils, King of Wessex, was baptised by Birinus, a missionary who became the first bishop of the West Saxons. During his mission to Dorset, St Aldhelm founded the church at Sherborne, where it became the See in 705 with himself as first bishop. At Wareham he founded the church of Lady St Mary, built in the eighth century; both nave and aisles survived until 1841 when they were unfortunately demolished for rebuilding.

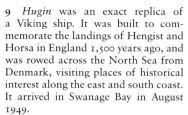

9 *Hugin* was an exact replica of a Viking ship. It was built to commemorate the landings of Hengist and Horsa in England 1,500 years ago, and was rowed across the North Sea from Denmark, visiting places of historical interest along the east and south coast. It arrived in Swanage Bay in August 1949.

By the eighth century 'minsters' had been established, ranging from houses lived in by monks under a Rule to small communities of pastoral priests. At first these minsters or 'mother churches' were few, each serving large areas such as Wimborne Minster and probably Wareham. There was a church at Winfrith before the Conquest serving the west part of Purbeck, Hasler hundred, and another for Ailwood in the east. F.P. Pitfield[29] suggested the ancient, though seemingly remote, church of Studland. However, David Hinton made an interesting and more convincing proposal for Kingston as the minster.[30]

St Aldhelm was said to have built a church 'two miles from the sea, close to Wareham, where also Corfe Castle is prominent from the sea'; this account was written by William of Malmesbury about 1125. Several parishes have claimed the site, one of them being Worth Matravers with its ancient church near St Aldhelm's Head. Thomas Bond, in his history of Corfe Castle, made out a case for the Saxon herringbone stone wall still standing on the west end of the Castle hill.[31] But Laurence Keen has shown[32] that it was probably at Kingston that St Aldhelm founded his church as it seems that most of these minsters were on royal, or formerly royal, estates. One such would have included Kingston/Corfe, the 1086 16-hide Shaftesbury Abbey property. The abbess of Shaftesbury owned Kingston in the 11th century, out of which she conceded the castle site to King William. Kingston remains a part of the civil parish of Corfe Castle though the ecclesiastical parish is now linked with Worth and Langton Matravers. Kingston old church was rebuilt in 1833 and there is little evidence of its medieval state. No former plan was made, and the only remaining structure is a round arch built into the later external west wall which was illustrated by Hutchins.

The eighth century was comparatively peaceful and English villages were beginning to develop. Then in 789 without warning three Norwegian ships raided Portland before withdrawing. In 836 Danish 'Vikings' (called 'pirates' by the natives) landed at Charmouth and defeated Egbert of Wessex, sailing off after plundering the land. But a real invasion by the Danes was imminent following their conquest of East Anglia in 869.

Alfred the Great

With Alfred and the rise of the House of Wessex, Swanage at last comes into the picture. When Alfred became king in 871 the Danes attacked Wessex. He was not yet able to drive them out and had to buy them off. But they returned after five years, having overcome Mercia, and took Wareham as a base. In 877 it appears that the Danes were sailing west for Exeter, when their fleet was wrecked on Peveril ledges, and the mystery has never ceased to engage the attention of historians and everyone else. In 1862 John Mowlem erected a granite column on the Swanage shore, the inscription on the base reading, 'In commemoration of a great naval battle fought with the Danes in Swanage Bay by Alfred the Great, AD 877.' Was there any battle? The *Anglo-Saxon Chronicle* recorded that the Danes were caught in a great storm at sea off Swanage and 120 ships were lost. Ernest Oppé of Worth Matravers spent much time investigating the matter. In his research he referred to the *Anglo-Saxon Chronicle*, Asser's *Life of Alfred*, quoted by Archbishop Parker in 1574, and to W.H. Stevenson's *Life* in 1904. A painting by Colin Gill depicting the great sea battle was added in 1928 to a series of murals in the Palace of Westminster, 'a consummation of error for which there is no reasonable defence'.[33] No doubt the Swanage people flocked to Peveril to watch the spectacle of the wrecks and drowning Vikings. But were all the ships sunk, all the men drowned, and were there no Saxon vessels off shore? Another account said that there was a thick mist rather than a storm. Everyone would have liked to believe in the victory at Peveril, but the evidence is against it, if only because it is quite clear that Alfred was as yet powerless at sea and had years of struggle on land ahead. Soon, however, he was able to build longboats with 60 oars each, much bigger than those of the Danes.[34] Naval engagement or no, Alfred defeated the Danes on land in 878. The Danish leader Guthrum accepted baptism and they left Wessex. It was a near thing, like the cakes perhaps.

Alfred was then able to build fortified towns laid out in measured grids as at Winchester, Chichester and Wareham. These 'burhs' became thriving centres for trade as well as for defence. Alfred died in 899, greatly revered and having been a just and wise king. He wrote books, learned Latin and encouraged education. He 'remains the outstanding figure of early English history'.[35]

Durlston and Durl

Mrs Panton, as the author of E.S. Harman's *Handy Guide to Swanage*, included this entertaining story:

> Perhaps one of the most interesting of local legends is that from which we obtained an account of the origin of the terms 'Old Harry Rocks', the 'Whitenose Rock', 'St Alban's Head' and 'Durlstone Head'. It is recorded that in the days of King Alfred, among those who joined the English army to fight the Danes were two brave and handsome young men from 'Swanawyc' (Swanage), the one named Beorhtric, or Beorht, a clever stonemason, and the other named Martin, who was surnamed Ceoles (signifying a boat) because of his skill as a sailor. With the Danish forces who occupied Swanage and Wareham in those days was Earl Harold, a chief, who had a beautiful daughter, Gytha, called for her grace and fairness, 'Gytha of the white neck'. Martin Ceoles was at length almost tempted by the love which Gytha showed towards him to give his adhesion to the Danes, when suddenly the apparition of the blessed St Aldhelm appeared and besought him to be true to his country. So he proceeded to the shore and called the saints to help him to destroy the posts which, on the morrow, were to afford anchorage to the Danish fleet. Getting no answer from the heavenly spirits he called upon the 'Spirits of the Rocks and Seas', and lo! there appeared a gigantic white object, a spirit which took the form of a huge horse, and was supposed to haunt the caves of our shores. This visitor announced its name as 'Durl', and promised assistance on one condition. that Martin would pray to St Aldhelm to grant that it might be permitted to live peacefully for ever among the rocks. The promise was given, and away to work went the sea monster, dragging the huge posts, by means of his long tail, out of their strongholds. The Danish fleet arrived on the following day in a storm, but there was no anchorage, and most of the vessels were wrecked.
>
> Earl Harold, Gytha, Beorht and Martin escaped in one of the Danish vessels, but his lordship appears to have become very wroth with Martin for what he had done the night before, and we are

told that he flung an axe at him; but at that moment the vessel gave a lurch and went down with all on board. Martin found himself subsequently being conveyed through the water on the back of Durl, who flung him ashore at the feet of St Aldhelm, and 'galloped off with a snort of satisfaction'. The shipwrecked heathen strangers were transformed into rocks, to which their names, in a corrupted form, are now attached: 'Earl Harold and his wife' are now always called 'Old Harry and his wife'; the 'White Neck' has been changed to the 'White Nose'; and the rock dedicated to St Aldhelm is now always called 'St Aldhelm's Head'.

A pretty tale!

The derivation of Durl or Durdle is generally accepted as meaning an arch, as seen at Durdle Door near Lulworth Cove. It is said that there was a similar stone arch and 'blow hole' in Durlston Bay before later rock falls.

The Royal House of England

Alfred was succeeded by Edward the Elder, Athelstan and Edmund whose reigns were dominated by the reconquest of the Danelaw in the north-east. Following the murder of Edmund in 946 the royal house of Wessex became the royal house of England.[36] In the north and east, struggles continued, but under Edgar (959-975) Wessex remained peaceful and the law was kept, enabling trade to flourish. The English counties were finally fixed, each supervised by aldermen, later sheriffs, and the hundreds were organised into tithings, being groups of 10 households. Edgar designed new silver pennies, and all coins were minted in the 'burhs', of which Wareham had two. He also established many new monasteries under Benedictine rule, replacing secular priests with monks, but many of the old minsters continued. Art flourished but nearly all their fine monasteries were later rebuilt by the Normans. Edgar was finally crowned and anointed in Winchester in 973 but died two years later. His elder son, Edward the Martyr, became king but was murdered in March 978 at Corfe gate, almost certainly by his stepmother's henchmen in favour of her own son, Ethelred.

There followed an unhappy period when the Danes attacked again, led by their king, Sweyn. Finally, after the death of Edmund, who had succeeded Ethelred and held only Wessex, Cnut the Dane became King of all England in 1016. In general the English landowners were not displaced, and many of the earls became very wealthy. Godwin, earl of Wessex, dominated these last years of the Saxon kingdom. The saintly Edward the Confessor, who became king in 1042, married Edith, daughter of the earl, but there was no issue. On his deathbed in January 1066, Edward named Earl Harold, Godwin's son, his successor, whereupon he was elected, anointed and crowned. But Halley's comet appeared in April and both the King of Norway and Duke William of Normandy were waiting for the chance to invade England. Norway moved first and in September defeated the northern earls at York. Harold and his army hurried north, won a handsome victory at Stamford Bridge and the Norwegian king was killed. But meanwhile William set sail for Sussex and his army landed at Pevensey without opposition. Harold quickly marched south with his exhausted soldiers and arrived at Senlac on 13 October to take battle against the Normans next morning. The fight continued all day, and at one point Harold, with better luck, could have won. But he and his two brothers were killed and the battle was lost.

Duke William was anointed and crowned king of England in Westminster Abbey on Christmas Day 1066. Skirmishes aside, this brought centuries of invasions, and the threat of invaders, to an end. Napoleon and Hitler each considered trying, but both thought better of it.

3

Domesday; The Parish; Manors South of the Brook

It is remarkable how quickly William conquered the country, but after the initial harassment of Kent, the taking of Dover, Canterbury, Winchester and finally London, everything was organised promptly. With him were 470 'compagnons' at the battle, and there were many more Norman nobles following, all anxious to he granted land in return for their loyalty to William, who was assured of 4,000 knights. Saxon owners were before long replaced by the French, though a few thanes survived as landholders. Otherwise he did not need or wish to alter the existing Saxon manors, but he had to know all the details of the great changes made since the Conquest for updating taxation.

Domesday

'How was the great share-out accomplished?' asks Ralph Arnold,[1] and goes on to answer the question. In Domesday about a fifth of England was kept by the king, about a quarter by the Church, and nearly half held by knight-service tenure by the greater Norman nobles. 'About 50 per cent of this was granted to 11 men of the "inner ring" of the lay and clerical magnates who had made the Conquest possible and who were closely related to the Conqueror and to one another.' There were some important new owners of land (held of the king) in Purbeck. One of these was Robert of Mortain, the Duke's half brother, who was the largest landholder in the country after the king, having holdings in 19 counties and some eight hundred manors, and ranked as a baron. In Purbeck he held land in Creech, Stoborough, Tyneham and Studland. Another was Ida, Countess of Boulogne, who held land in Swanage. Her husband the Earl was brother-in-law of Edward the Confessor and William's cousin. Hugh fitzGrip, also called Hugh of Wareham, was Sheriff of Dorset; his wife, too, held much land in Swanage for herself and for her husband who died before Domesday. Serlo of Burcy had large holdings in Somerset and Dorset and held Whitecliff in Swanage; his daughter married William of Falaise. Roger Arundel, one of William's 'compagnons', held Worth Matravers and land at Herston.

By 1086 Domesday Book was completed, the whole undertaking done within 12 months. The surveyors had to find out: the name of the place, who held it before 1066, and who had it now; how many hides and ploughs there were; how much woodland, meadow and pasture; how many mills and fishponds; how much had been added or taken away, and what the total value came to; how many villagers, cottagers, slaves and freemen lived there. 'The Domesday Book describes Old English society under new management.' A hide was ploughland assessed for taxation, varying in extent, but on average reckoned as 120 acres. A virgate was a quarter of a hide, between twenty-five and thirty acres. A furlong was a strip of arable land in an open field, roughly 220 yards long. 'Plough' was the term given to the amount of land that a team of eight oxen could plough in a day. Meadow was common land for hay, and pasture for grazing.[2]

'The Survey finally took the form of a shire-by-shire directory of landowners, the entries being listed under the names of the holders of estates.' It was based on the Saxon hundreds and, as we have seen, Swanage and the associated manors were within Rowbarrow.

The Isle of Purbeck, in the shire of Dorset, was called *Purbicinga* in 948, *Porbi* or *Porbiche* in Domesday, and later *Purbic*. The derivation is uncertain, possibly from the Celtic *Porbuch*, a cattle pasture. OE *pur* may have referred to bitterns of which it is said there were many; OE *becc* seems to suggest a point or headland (cf. Portland 'Bill'). The most likely suggestion for the second element of the name was made by the geologist W.J. Arkell, who considered the 'hog's back' of the Purbeck chalk hills and wondered if they were so prominent that they were eventually used to refer to the whole island.

Swanwich, Sandwich or Swanage

The derivation is also uncertain. The earliest recorded mention is in the *Anglo-Saxon Chronicle* (877) as *Swanawic*. Domesday gives two different spellings: Sonwic and *Suuanwic*. The name appears as *Swanewiz* in later Pipe Rolls. Ekwall suggests OE *Swān* 'herd' and *Wīc*, from Latin *vicus*, 'a dwelling, village or (dairy) farm', producing 'the swineherd's farm'. He adds, 'Swanage is on Swanage Bay, and a meaning "Swan Bay" may be tempting. But no OE *Wīc*, "bay" is known. A meaning "swannery" is possible, and perhaps preferable'. Fagerston also gives the derivation 'the swineherds' farm', but does not mention swans. AD Mills refers to herdsmen or swans.[3] There was a suggestion that the Abbess of Shaftesbury, who held Kingston and Peveril, might have had a swannery in Swanage.

Hutchins calls the place 'Swanwich, Sandwich, *vulgo* Swanage', the latter being an unfortunate version of the surely much preferred 'Swanwich'. 'Sandwich', although often used in the 18th century, and despite the sandy beach, is a corruption, for there is no doubt that the earliest forms of the name have 'swan' as the first element. The story of a Danish admiral named Sweyn having perished in the Bay can be dismissed as far as the name 'Swanage' is concerned.

In an article entitled 'Swanage as a Health Resort' in the *Medical Times* (quoted in the DCC, 5 November 1868), the writer says:

many liberties have been taken with the name, which in most maps is written Swanage, but as the oldest form is 'Swanwich', and as the preservation of old names may he of historical importance,

10 Extracts from Domesday Book, 1086, with references to *Suuanwic, Sonwic, Herestone, Witeclive,* and *Moleham.*

I shall take the liberty of spelling it 'Swanwich' until it becomes the fashion to write Harwich 'Harrige' or Norwich 'Norrage'.

The *Poole and Dorset Herald* had 'Swanwich' throughout 1847 and following years. Alas, it is now too late to alter the name.

The Parish Boundaries

At the Conquest the formation of the parishes was in its infancy. Thus Domesday Book followed the old hundreds and manors, though later the new parishes often coincided. There was no doubt about the eastern and southern boundaries of Swanage which were formed by the sea coast. On the west, the boundary with Langton Matravers ran from a point just east of Blackers Hole in the cliffs, due north in a straight line for some two and a half miles to the top of Godlingston Hill, except for a diversion near Gully eastwards along the road to Herston Cross, and then back at Alderbury barn. This 'bulge' was not straightened until 1933 when Swanage gained this area, which now includes the Middle School, at the expense of Langton.

The northern boundary would seem naturally to have been set along the top of Ballard Down, which was so, until we come to complications at the Ulwell gap. The whole of Godlingston Hill was included with Swanage but, until the Local Government Act of 1894, the parish also extended a further two miles north to Goathorn Farm and Drove Island in Poole Harbour, the tract across Godlingston heath being some half mile wide, cutting Studland parish into two. This is because it followed the manor of Godlingston.[4] Similarly, until the changes, Studland parish stepped between the hills at Forked Down gate and extended southwards as far as the modern brickworks and Godlingston cemetery.[5] At Ulwell the farm and mill were in Swanage, but Ulwell House was in Studland. All was straightened out, Studland lands were united and Swanage gained the Ulwell area. Currendon Farm, on the east side of the road branching off to Corfe Castle, also became part of Swanage parish.

Parish or no Parish?

The first mention of parishes in England was in AD 970, but many were not finally fixed until the 14th century. The church of St Nicholas, Studland, was built before the Conquest, St Nicholas, Worth Matravers, soon after, and St George, Langton Matravers, probably dates from the 14th century. Swanage did not become a parish in its own right until about 1500, being then only a chapel-of-ease of Worth Matravers. Why was this so? Swanage was clearly a vill (Norman) or township (OE), but at first it did not have a parish church of its own. But what was a parish? FitzHugh[6] says that it was 'a township under the administration of a single priest who was originally paid by tithes on the produce of the parochial area, and who was under the supervision of a bishop'. Tate[7] says that, ecclesiastically, 'a parish was the area of ground committed to the charge of one minister, and possessing a church with full rights of sepulture', citing Blackstone. It seems, then, that Swanage was not strictly a parish until it had its own priest at the end of the 15th century. The age of Swanage church and its tower is discussed later.

The Swanage Manors

Hutchins' third edition admits that it is difficult to distinguish the early manors in the records. 'The account we are able to lay before the reader of the various properties in Swanwich is far less clear and complete than could be wished.' We should repeat this plea, but perhaps we have unravelled one or two knots, or at least made some points clearer,

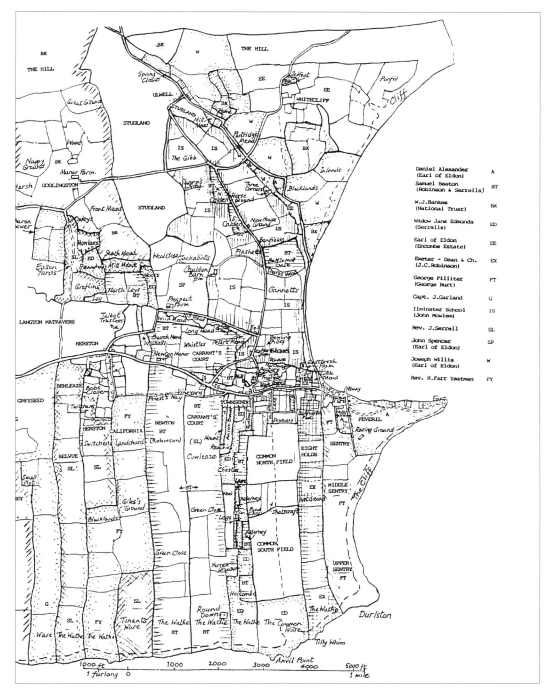

Daniel Alexander   A
(Earl of Eldon)

Samuel Beaton   BT
(Robinson & Serrells)

W.J.Bankes   BK
(National Trust)

Widow Jane Edmonds   ED
(Serrells)

Earl of Eldon   EE
(Encombe Estate)

Exeter - Dean & Ch.   EX
(J.C.Robinson)

George Filliter   FT
(George Burt)

Capt. J.Garland   G

Ilminster School   IS
(John Mowlem)

Rev. J.Serrell   SL

John Spencer   SP
(Earl of Eldon)

Joseph Willis   W
(Earl of Eldon)

Rev. H.Farr Yeatman   FY

11   The Swanage Tithe Map of 1839, reduced and adapted to show ownership, both at the time and later.

since Hutchins himself was no doubt scratching his head on this subject. Unfortunately for the tellers of the tales, Swanage was not a straightforward parish as some others were, with one manor house and the demesne surrounding it. Here we have the problem of more than a dozen 'manors' or independent farms, mostly with absent owners. However, with information from Domesday Book, Hutchins, the Tithe Map and other records, let us proceed from east to west, south of the Swanage brook, and then clockwise from west to east on the north.

The Brook, having been broader, it seems,[8] for much of its distance from the Bay to the boundary with Langton Matravers, makes an important demarkation between manors north and south of it. In addition, the boundaries are quite different in appearance: those on the limestone plateau are parallel and set out in straight lines, stretching from the Brook to the cliffs. Do these miles of drystone walls date from Saxon times? It seems unlikely that these thousands of tons of stone were placed there before the quarries were first excavated; it would have been much easier to use stone 'waste' in this way. But the date of these stone walls is a puzzle, though the boundaries themselves must have been fixed in ancient times. North of the Brook the present fields are irregular and, though enclosed at a later date, some of the hedgelines may denote the original manors or farms. Then comes the parish boundary along the chalk crest, and over the hill in Studland the terrain is quite different again, with the vast heath, where a few small enclosures here and there were anciently won from it, no doubt with great labour.

12   The Mill Pond old cottages with St Mary's parish church tower in the background, 1906. The boys appear to have been paddling. The cottages were rebuilt sympathetically after bomb damage.

Peveril

This small headland between Swanage and Durlston bays, including the Point and marble reefs, was from early times attached to the manor of Kingston in Purbeck. As such it belonged to the Abbess of Shaftesbury before the Conquest, when the manor paid tax for 16 hides. It was perhaps three square miles in extent and included lands in Corfe. Peveril or Peverel may have taken its name from Ranulph Peverell, who is said to have made his fortune by marrying a Saxon concubine of Duke William of Normandy and bringing up her son by the Duke as his own. William Peverell was said to have been the Conqueror's son; certainly by the early 12th century there were many Peverells.[9]

After the Reformation Encombe, as part of the manor of Kingston, was acquired by the Cullifords, and later by the Pitts, who rebuilt Encombe House in 1735. When John Scott, Lord Chancellor and First Earl of Eldon bought Encombe from William Morton Pitt in 1807, Peveril was excluded from the sale, and until the 1823 Chancery sale was on lease from the Dampier family.

Centry

In Domesday the land of the Countess of Boulogne was named *Sonwic*. Before the Conquest it paid tax for one hide and the third part of one virgate. There was land for one plough, and there was one villager (a class of peasant who held land). There were four acres of meadow. The value was 15 shillings. King William had never had the tax from the manor: Wulfera held it before 1066. This land appears to have been the south-east corner of Swanage, excluding Peveril. At an early date it was parcelled out into two farms. The first of these was Centry, later spelt 'Sentry', which was held by the prior of Frampton. The property was attached to a cell of Caen Abbey, and on the seizure of the possessions of alien religious houses in the reign of Henry V, the lands went to the Crown and were later given to the College of St Stephen, Westminster. Centaury, the modern Sentry Fields, is so written in 18th-century parish records. The cliff fields probably took the name from the profusion of the common centaury, a wild flower, still found in the Durlston Country Park, where it likes dry coastal slopes and can grow to the height of a foot.[10] Though sometimes called the 'manor of Swanwich', Centry does not seem to have possessed a manor house.

Eightholds

The second farm parcelled out by the Countess, situated to the west, was Eightholds (*vulgo* Eight Holes). It was a mile long and one field wide lying between parallel boundaries which ran north-south from the Brook to the coast at Tilly Whim. It was parcel of the manor of Winterborn Wast, Bockhampton and Swanwich, all in the possession of the Countess, and was held from her by the Priory of le Vast, a Cluniac priory in France. After its suppression it passed to Edmund Stafford, Bishop of Exeter; Queen Elizabeth gave it to the Dean and Chapter. Hence the names of Cluny, St Vast, Stafford and Exeter given to modern roads on the estate. It was subsequently leased from 1748 to William Taunton of Wracklesford whose descendants held it until the freehold was purchased from Exeter by Charles Robinson of Newton Manor in 1875. Taunton Road (formerly East Drove) formed the boundary with Sentry Fields.

Like Sentry, Eightholds was sometimes referred to as the Manor of Swanage, but again it was only one of the several farms. It had, however, a Court Baron attached, and the court rolls have survived.[11] The tenements or eight 'holds' were held of the 'Lord and Farmer of the Manor of Sandwich, Swantwich or Swanage' by various persons, on the usual system of 'three lives and the longest liver'. Each tenement had one-eighth part of Tilly Mead, the common Great Meadow, now covered by Commercial Road and King's Road East. South of the High Street, up Bullhouse Lane (now Mount Pleasant) was a close known as the Hides (the later Hedes Estate developed by Robinson) and, higher up, a large close called Inhooks in which there were a dozen or more quarry 'holes'; the six closes southwards to the sea were arable or pasture.[12] Presumably as there was no manor house the Court Baron was held in a building in the High Street within the manor boundary, perhaps in later times in the *Red Lion*! From evidence in a legal dispute it appears that William Taunton never attended, and it was left to his bailiff to transact the business.

The derivation of the name 'Tilly Whim' is uncertain.[13] It certainly does not mean 'Tilly's Folly'. A whim was a windlass to raise ore from a mine, as in Cornwall, but the word does not seem to have been generally used by the Purbeck quarrymen; the wooden crane for lowering the stone into boats was called a derrick or gibbet due to its triangular form. Chapel Lane leading from the High Street to the cliffs was earlier called Derrick Lane. Tilly might have been a personal name: Robert Tilly held Rollington at Domesday and there was a John Tilly listed in the 1664 Hearth Tax (Langton Matravers). Jane Tilly, 1740, is the only name in the Church registers before 1812, and there is no such name in the complete invasion census of 1803 nor in the general census of 1851. There is, however, a record of the name Tilly in a list of marblers in the 17th century. But it does not explain Tilly Mead being a mile north of Tilly Whim. Could Tilly be an adjective? J.E. Mowlem, citing Wright's *Dialect Dictionary*, gave 'tilly' meaning 'clayey' and 'whim' an obsolete form for brow of a hill. The first mention of Tilly Whim quarry appears to be in the inventory following the death of Alexander Melmoth, quarrier and merchant, in 1703. It is also mentioned in a lease of two quarries dated 13 September 1805 where it was stated that they had been used 'immemorially'.

The Common Fields

Sometimes called 'Celtic' fields, the Swanage Common Fields were the Saxon strip furlongs and lay west of Eightholds. The approach from the High Street was up Derrick Lane to the North Field which extended from the present Queen's Road to Russell Avenue; south of this, Shadscroft (or Shaltscraft) field lay where Scar Bank House now stands; the South Field extended from South Barn to the last stone wall before the descent to the Common Wathe (meaning water or spring) or Town Ware (meaning hill brow above the cliff), which was a sheep run and included the Howcombe valley and Anvil Point, now within the Durlston Country Park. By 1788 many of the strips were owned privately: WMH gives lists for South Field and Shaltscraft in 1795, when Dampier, Edmonds and Phippard owned the largest numbers and possessed the most sheep runs. He thought that a farmhouse west of the parish church was originally connected with the Common Fields. As some of these furlongs were 'glebe', perhaps it was the rector's private storehouse. In these fields there were also many 'quarrs'.

Townsend

There were several small closes north of the Common Fields in various ownership, but to the west was Townsend, a narrow and disjointed farm belonging to Thomas Cockram (d.1716). It was probably part of the lands of the wife of Hugh fitzGrip in Domesday times. The property came to the Edmonds family, some of whose monuments adorn the parish church. WMH says that the old farmhouse stood on the site of the *Black Swan Inn*, though the 1889 O.S. map shows the farmhouse behind it. In 1843 Sheffield Serrell of Durnford, Langton Matravers, bought Townsend and the adjoining Carrant's Court cowleaze to the west. By the time of the freehold sale in 1964 by his descendants, the 162 acres were known together as Townsend, which was not originally so. Here were some of the deepest quarries in Swanage.

Carrant's Court

Carrant's Court seems to have been one of the two principal medieval manors of Swanage, the other being Godlingston. The history of the manor is somewhat confused. The name comes from the family of Carent, one-time owners, and Hutchins says that this was no doubt the Domesday *Suuanwic* held by the wife of Hugh fitzGrip. It was let to Walter and, before the Conquest, Alward held it jointly. One and a half hides were taxed and there was one plough, a slave and one smallholder. There were seven acres of meadow, 20 sheep and five pigs. The value was 20s., later 25s.

This large domain was split into two portions in the 14th century and, according to Hutchins (3rd edn), 'the share which belonged … afterwards to Carent, is the manor which in process of time acquired the name of Carant's Court Manor, while the Talbots' share was the manor of Godlingston'. This may be the reason why Godlingston is not mentioned in Domesday though it was certainly a Saxon manor. Carrant's Court lands included many acres north of the Brook as well as southwards from the house and farm through the cowleaze to Court Wathe and the sea below Round Down.

The manor subsequently passed to Robert Rempston and then to the Malets who sold it in 1556 to Humphrey Walrond of Somerset. In 1587 he devised part of the

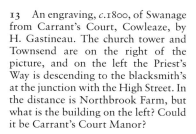

13 An engraving, *c.*1800, of Swanage from Carrant's Court, Cowleaze, by H. Gastineau. The church tower and Townsend are on the right of the picture, and on the left the Priest's Way is descending to the blacksmith's at the junction with the High Street. In the distance is Northbrook Farm, but what is the building on the left? Could it be Carrant's Court Manor?

estate, including the house, farm and cowleaze, to Alice Bond, widow of Denis Bond of Lutton, and William and John Bond, her sons, for their lives; later it was purchased by the family.

The original manor house itself is conjectural. It may have stood on the site of the present house called Ivydene on the west side of Court Hill (now called Court Road by the post office). Although the house is not ancient it retains some early worked stones, and is marked 'Court Farm House and premises' on the tithe map and also on the Chancery sale catalogue of 1823. WMH stated that Court farmhouse occupied the site of 'an old-world house pulled down in the mid-19th century'. So presumably this was it. Opposite the house was House Meadow, and the great barn and other buildings are clearly depicted on the 1889 O.S. map before their sad demolition, unfortunately without photographs. A view down Court Hill shows impressive stone pillars at the entrance on the right, and an 18th-century engraving of Swanage taken from the Cowleaze (illustration 13) shows on the left what surely must be part of Carrant's Court. There appears to be a house and not merely farm buildings.

14 The view looking down Court Hill to the north, *c.*1885. The original Carrant's Court house was possibly on the site of the later house, Ivydene, seen here on the left, although this is still open to conjecture. The Great Barn and farm buildings were across the road on the right. The house where John Mowlem was born is immediately behind the pony and trap. On his retirement and return to Swanage he improved the trough or pond opposite Ivydene, as he did the roads. On 14 October 1848 he wrote in his diary: 'It is strange indeed that 60 years have gone by and not a single improvement here, and God Almighty has spared my life to improve the place where I first drew breath.'

15 Children at the town pump, *c.*1900. All the buildings in the background have since been demolished, including the old school, just out of shot on the extreme left.

Denis Bond of Lutton, grandson of the original Denis Bond, held Carrant's Court in 1639 and wrote in his *Chronology*[14] for that year, 'The 27 December at 10 of the clock in the night, there was such a wind that it did blow downe diverse houses and several woods. I had at Carrans Cort blone downe 30 great ealmes which had in them 50 tunes of timber.' Denis Bond, son of John Bond, a merchant, was a Republican and a friend of Cromwell. They both died within a few hours of each other. Bond was buried in Westminster Abbey but at the Restoration was, with others of the same persuasion, 'ignominiously cast into a pit before the back door of one of the canons of Westminster'.

Court Hill was the highest part of the High Street going westwards from the town pump on Church Hill, where Court Hill post office was formerly situated, correctly named. At the junction of Priest's Way and the High Street was Parker's Stores, an ancient building and formerly a smithy, which was at the boundary of the Manor; this is clearly seen in an early engraving (illustration 13). On the west wall of Oxford Terrace, a later row of tenements to the east of the cowleaze, may be seen a reset cartouche which may just possibly be a relic of the old manor. Higher up is another terrace with an incised cornerstone: 'Carrants Court Place'. This is the only location in Swanage still retaining the name 'Carrant'; as we have seen, Court Hill, Court Farm and Cowleaze have all lost the original prefix. Indeed, the Cowleaze came to be called 'Townsend' quite inaccurately. Part of a third row of tenements, Alexandra Terrace, collapsed over an underground quarry.

In 1676 Denis Bond sold the Cowleaze to William Rose, rector of Swanage, who died in 1690. To pay for his debts his son, Thomas, sold this land to John Chapman in 1702. In this way it came to John Dampier, and in 1843 to the Serrells, as already described.

Newton

Newton, signifying a 'new' settlement, was the next manor west of Carrant's Court and was in Herston tithing. It was another narrow farm extending from the Brook to Newton Ware at the cliffs. The oldest part of the present house, much altered, was Elizabethan, with a stone fireplace in the kitchen. Newton probably had a Saxon origin and though not itself mentioned in Domesday, Herston was; *Nyweton* was mentioned in 1299. After the Conquest it became part of the Rempstone estates. In the reign of Mary it came into the possession of the Prior of St John of Jerusalem. Lewis Cockram, who also held Whitecliff, acquired it in 1597 and the family retained it until their demise in 1830. On a window-pane, scratched with a diamond, was an inscription: 'John Cockram/ April the 4th 1799/ Very cold Easterly wind, Swanage'. It was he, Captain Cockram, who refaced the east front in Purbeck ashlar and planted many elm trees there. 'He was a captain in the Militia, proud of his title, and smoked a long clay pipe in the winter evenings down at

16 The town pump, above Church Hill, 1906. The cottages near the church tower were demolished after a bombing raid during the Second World War. The house fronted by steps and railings bears the date 1793.

the *Anchor.*' He married his cousin, Sarah Cole, late in life, and there was no issue.

Newton stood on a knoll with former farm buildings that have since been swallowed up by houses in King's Road West and Morrison Road, named after the last farmer. The High Road here was known as Newton Knap (complete with ghost, of which more later). Newton Cottage on the south side of the road was built on a small plot taken out of the property.[15] It received a direct hit from a bomb in the last war, with casualties. In Newton cowleaze, south of the Priest's Way and in the fields towards the sea, there were many quarries.

Herston

In Domesday, Roger Arundel, one of William's 'compagnons', held his own land at Herston and was formerly held by Her in 1066 (Her's Farm). Before the Conquest tax was paid for two parts of a hide. There was land for half a plough and two and a half acres of meadow. The value was ten shillings. Godfrey Scullion, the embroiderer, held one virgate of land and four acres; his father had held them before. Herston lay west of Newton and in the 1811 O.S. one-inch map it is named Easton, one of several corruptions. Hutchins (3rd edn) says: 'In 1774 it contained more than 50 houses. It is now divided into several properties, held by different proprietors, the history of which is very difficult to trace ... About 171 acres which touch the western boundary of the parish now form part of Leeson farm in Langton, to which they adjoin.' This would include Greyseed (Greasehead), the post-war council housing estate, formerly intensively quarried. The 'manors' of Herston and Benleaze (Benlidge) belonged in 1788 to Elizabeth and Anne Serrell, 'Ladies of the Manor of Sandwich' (yet another). These lands extended from the turnpike road to the sea and included Belle Vue Farm on the Priest's Way, and many quarries. Hutchins says that Belle Vue, about 151 acres and formerly called Herston Farm, was usually occupied with Durnford Farm in Langton. This was probably the same as Benlidge and anciently belonged to the Rempstons, whence it passed to the Mompessons and was sold together with Durnford in 1721 to Samuel Serrell.[16] At Herston there were also ancient Common Fields.

California Farm, sometimes called Herston Farm, of about 124 acres lying between Newton and the Serrell estates, belonged to the Farr family. Hutchins (3rd edn) says that the old farmhouse in the hamlet of Herston was sold and a new house was erected and given the name California. This farm abounded in quarries from which came great quantities of stone for paving the footways of London and for building the docks at Portsmouth.

Finally the three fields known as Verney, 84 acres extending to the sea, were in the manor of Langton Wallis belonging to the Bankes family of Kingston Lacy.

4

Manors North of the Brook;
St Mary the Virgin, the Parish Church

We now turn inland, north of the Brook, where we first observe Prospect farm which was built in the early 19th century. The tithe map returns show four closes owned by the butchers John and James Spencer: Jackalints, Wool Close, the Cowleaze, and the house and garden. This property was a parcel of the manor of Langton Matravers and formerly belonged to the Farrs.

Moulham

To the west, and approached from Herston (Eason) Yards, is Moulham, part of the lands of the Countess of Boulogne. In Domesday Durand the carpenter held Moulham as one of the King's servants.[1] Three thanes held it before the Conquest and paid tax for one hide. There was land for one plough, with one cottager. A mill paid six pence, and there was one acre of meadow. The value was five shillings at that time, but it rose to 30 shillings. The increase is notable and is possibly the reason for Durand's fortunate engagement by King William at Corfe Castle.

> Though the descent cannot be proved, it is very probable that the de Moulhams were descendants of Durand, and that the latter had received the manor as a reward for building the wooden tower which no doubt preceded the existing stone keep. This probability is strengthened by the fact that in 1130 a person described as 'the carpenter of the castle of Wareham' was among those excused Danegeld in Dorset (Pipe Roll 31 Henry I, p.16), for Corfe was originally known as 'the castle of Wareham', and the sum of two shillings entered in his favour on the Pipe Roll would have been the exact amount due from the manor of Moulham. The name of the tenant in 1130 is unfortunately not stated, but there is every reason to suppose that he was the son or grandson of Durand and the ancestor of the de Moulhams of the following century.[2]

In the time of Edward I a tenement in Moulham was held by William of Moulham by the service of finding a carpenter to work in the great tower of Corfe Castle, for which he received 2d. a day, or his board. His family continued to hold their land by this service until their extinction in the reign of Henry V, but as late as 1568 there were lands in Moulham which were said to be held of the Queen 'as of her castle of Corfe, by the service of cleansing the gutters of the great tower of the said castle' (Hutchins).

There was some doubt as to the exact provenance of the Moulham manor, but on examining an early document[3] the land could be defined. The Latin deed was translated thus:

> 1448 3 November 27 Henry VI. Robt. Rempston, late of Godlynston, to Jn. Homme, clerk,[4] Walter Crawell, clerk, and Jn. Wymond. Gift. House with garden called Le Grofe at Moulham and meadows

and closes there, all of which are usually called Moulham, in the parish of Swanewych, and were formerly, inter alia, lands and tenements of Jn. de Moulham, son and heir of Wm. de Moulham.

Identified in the 1839 tithe map (see illustration 11) were Pennyhays (Piryhayes), Mill furlong (Mulfurlong), Brook furlong (Brokefurlong), Brook meadow or Moors (Brokefurlonggysmede), Withybed (Witheber) and Mowlam itself (Moulham). This close included a modern brickworks but it is now used as a caravan site. A meadow called Brodecroft and a close Cheddescroft were also listed. The close called Graflins bordering the Brook in 1839 is suggested as *le Grofe* and, if so, was the site of the house and garden, though of these there is now no sign.

It will be seen that the de Moulhams were no longer there by 1448 but, following a gap in the records, the family reappears in Studland, the first recorded direct ancestor of John Mowlem (1788-1868) being Alexander (b.1622).

Godlingston

Though not mentioned in Domesday, Godlingston is thought to have been a part of *Suuanwic*, the lands held by the wife of Hugh fitzGrip. North of the Moulham lands, and of Washpond Lane as it turns east, stands the manor house and farmstead, framed by Godlingston Wood and the hill above. The stream, which descends to Swanage Brook, rises from the wood, where the spring was called Tanswell in 1755 but St Ann's Well in 1655. A dam was constructed and the water diverted to serve the house, but it now flows down as originally. A new well was formed in 1982 and the pure water from very deep strata is now marketed as Godlingston Manor Springs. The tithe map shows a long pond on the west of the house.[5]

17 Godlingston Manor before the fire of 1871. Note the ground floor door to the ivy-clad, semi-circular tower, *c*.1300, which was later walled up.

Stepping into Godlingston Manor or wandering round the garden, one is strongly conscious of the past, as though something is about to happen: a face at a window, the creak of an opening door, a clink of armour. The remarkable semi-circular tower at the west has immensely thick walls and was probably a fortified stone house of around 1300, although it is believed by some to be one of a pair of towers at the entrance to a Saxon stronghold, possibly with a moat, where remains have been discovered. Within the enclosure would have been the house, built finally in the 16th and 17th centuries. The main building is long and low and contained a great hall but was considerably altered following the fire of 1871 when the east wing and farm buildings were burnt down: possibly intentionally, since the house was dilapidated, and there had been a suggestion to demolish it and build a 'brand new farmhouse', which aroused protests. Hutchins (1773) wrote 'here was anciently a chapel which now makes part of the house'. Philip Brannon made an arresting picture before the fire and the building on the east suggests that the chapel was there, although it may have been in the kitchen area.

There is an unusual trefoil stone arch forming the main entrance door, and formerly there was a similar one to the north passageway. The small door in the old tower is said to have been the only entrance and at high level. However, before the fire there was a normal door at ground level, though perhaps not ancient; it was removed and blocked with stone at the time of the alterations, as shown in comparable photographs.

The Saxon Godlyngton manor – the 's' crept in during the 14th century – covered some two thousand acres, stretching over the heath to Newton, Edward I's abortive new town on the shores of Poole Harbour. Stones and mounds on Godlingston Heath indicate a later boundary where the area eventually became part of the Rempstons' Corfe Castle estate, and the present extent of Godlingston farm is reduced to less than 500 acres.

The property seems to have come via the de Lincolns, Govis and Latimers to Alured de Talbot in the reign of Henry II, from whom it descended to the Rempstons. In the time of Edward VI Isabel, the heiress of the Rempstons, married John Carent. Fully described in Hutchins is a curious document[6] called the Godlingston Roll, written in Latin on parchment and believed not to be of later date than the early years of Henry VI's reign, which gives a complete account of the title of Robert Rempston to the lands of Godlingston. His title, it seems, had been disputed by one Stephen Mathewe, whose claims were finally settled by purchase.

There were a number of changes of ownership, which saw the Chaunterells and Poles until the recusant Welles family bought the manor in 1557. There they stayed until 1687. There is a small 17th-century brass to Henry Welles (d.1607) and his first wife Marie (d.1560) in Swanage parish church, which formerly had a Godlingston north aisle. The next owner was John Frampton whose descendant sold the manor in 1765 to John Bankes of Kingston Lacy. It remained in the family until 1981 when Ralph Bankes left all his property to the National Trust. It remains a working farm and so the house (Grade 1) is not open to the public.

There have been many tenant farmers over the centuries. During the mid-19th century Godlingston was farmed by Thomas Hunt and was also the home of Dr James Hunt when he was not in London. He was 'well-known as a Curer of Stammering. Describes the cures as effected in 20 minutes, but keeps the means a secret. Has been called a quack by medical men. A pity.'[7] He was admired by 'his most illustrious friend, the Revd Charles Kingsley', who found him in Swanage in the summer of 1857 and wrote the well-known eulogy in the *Illustrated London News,* describing the scenery of Swanage and Beccles' geological discoveries at Durlston.

Ulwell and Studland

Taylor marks 'Elwell' as a Saxon manor and part of Studland, but it was not mentioned in Domesday. It may have been, with Studland, part of the land of Count Robert of Mortain; it was he who rebelled in 1088 but was pardoned and died in 1091. Hamo held Studland from the Count, Aelmer held it before 1066. It paid tax for three and a half hides and there was land for four ploughs. In lordship two ploughs, six slaves, five villagers, and 13 smallholders. There was pasture, one league long and as wide; woodland, two furlongs long and one furlong wide; 32 salterns which paid 40s. The value of this large manor was £8, and Studland was obviously no waste. However, there was no mention of the mill at Ulwell. *Ulewoll* is named in 1333, *Olewell* in 1412; 'Owl spring' is given as an alternative to 'Holy Well': there was a well at Bath, sacred to the goddess Sulis, whose totem was the owl.[8]

Until 1894 Ulwell managed to be in both Swanage and Studland, with a long tongue of Studland parish reaching down as far as Godlingston brickworks. Until the Sandbanks ferry and road was opened in 1926, Ulwell remained an old-world hamlet, and the mill had long been silent. It is worth quoting from C.E. Robinson's *Picturesque Rambles* (1882): 'In the valley bottom winds the road between Swanage and Studland … A clear spring

18 An idyllic scene, by Walter Field, showing Ulwell Mill in 1874. The mill house has gone, replaced with a busy road to the Sandbanks ferry.

bubbles up all the year round in sufficient volume to supply the brook which courses into the bay at the point where the Ulwell road leaves the beach.' Robinson describes the unique old water mill and its picturesque neglected state:

The wheel is on the east side of the small stone building, and must be approached from the meadow behind. Nothing ever more eloquent of torpor and decay, than this nevermoving piece of rustic mechanism, in its dark hollow under the pond. What a miracle of patching and mending in stone and wood is the cottage wall into which the axle is fixed: The ivy stems which tightly clasp it mingle too in a network as intricate as a woven fabric. So still! you hear the water-rats rustling among the ferns; you hear the dripping of a tiny leak from the pool on the broken mouldering boards of the wheel; and you hear nothing else – at least until a gruff human voice calls loudly from above; and looking up, you perceive the irate occupier of the adjoining cottage, purple with suppressed rage, under the impression that we are meditating a trespass among the apple trees in his back garden.

John Mowlem recorded in his diary (4 March 1846), 'We went to admire the beautiful spring water at Ulwell which had been flowing before my grandfather was born. It springs from the chalk and it drove the mill where my poor mother was brought up.' So it seems that the mill had fallen into disuse even before that memorable visit.

Whitecliff

The French knight, Serlo of Burcy, held Witeclive in Domesday. Alward held it before 1066. It paid tax for three hides and there was land for three ploughs. In lordship two ploughs, two slaves, two and a half hides. There was pasture, six furlongs in length and one furlong wide; there were 50 sheep. The value was, and remained at Domesday, 60s. There was a small area of 'Celtic' strip fields.

The present farmhouse is partly of Elizabethan date. The entrance is from the north, with two quaint 17th-century windows with rounded heads. It is said that King John used Whitecliff as his favourite hunting-box. Robinson tells the story of the King's landing at Studland, having changed his mind about going on a foreign expedition, but 'fined all his vassals a round sum for not aiding him with men and arms, when they knew nothing about it!'[9] Pondfield (Punfield) formed an inlet and freshwater pond below the cliff. Robinson thought that the enclosure was of Roman origin, perhaps to create a fishpond for the villa, not forgetting the discovery of ancient graves in the cliff. Others thought of it as a landing-place. It could hardly have been both at the same time. Brune Cockram, rector of Swanage, had Whitecliff during the 17th century (see illustration 19).

In 1829 John Cockram sold the property to William Morton Pitt. At the 1838 Chancery sale following Pitt's death, Lord Eldon purchased the estate. After the Second World War the National Trust acquired Studland Hill, the south face of Ballard Down and cliffs above Whitecliff, the first land in Swanage parish to have been protected in this way.

An interesting autobiography, *Reminiscences of English Country Life,* was privately printed in 1926 in America by Joseph White, then an old man, describing Whitecliff

19   Whitecliff Farm, the home of the Cockrams.

farm where his father was born and where he himself lived until he was 24 and then emigrated. It was held leasehold by his forbears for several generations. The author describes the house and outbuildings in some detail. He believed that there had been a stone courtyard, guarded by a moat and portcullis, the keystone of the arch bearing a rotund 'J'. In one corner was an ancient well, and on the farther side were the remains of a stone staircase and watchtower. Were Godlingston and Whitecliff similarly defended in olden days? The walled garden was laid out geometrically with walks, grapevines, and rows of fruit trees and bushes: pear, plum, medlar, fig and mulberry. There were all manner of vegetables, the best specimens kept for seed. The earliest potato was the 'Ashleaf'. The seaweed driven on shore made excellent fertiliser. This was brought up over the cliffs on the back of donkeys to the farmyard, later to be mixed with other material to fit it for different soils. The roots were always 'helled': heaped for store and covered with clean straw and packed earth to shed the rain. Thatching a roof was also called 'helling'.

The Ilminster Estate

We finally come back to Carrant's Court. It may be remembered that Humphrey Walrond had sold the house and some of his land to the Bonds in 1587. Denis Bond later gave his part of the manor to his fourth son Onesiphorus, who sold 19 acres of it to Thomas Chapman, marbler, in 1664; this was N & S Caldens on the west of 'Ulway' road, now called Northbrook Road. In 1609 Humphrey Walrond sold the remainder of the estate, about 124 acres, to the trustees of the Free School at Ilminster, Somerset. Courts Baron and Leet were held at Carrant's Court from early times. The transcripts of the few original rolls which had survived were translated by Marion K. Dale for the late J.E. Mowlem in 1935.[10]

The chief difficulty comes with the consideration of *A Survey of the Manor of Swanwich,* 1671, where George Mompesson appears as lord of the manor. References are made to copyholders of properties in Swanage Common Fields, Long Craft, Horsecrafts and Broadfurlong, and to Common Fields in Herston, Ilminster School, Exeter and Eightholds, and Mowlams lying under Godlingston. In the appendix, Hutchins (3rd edn) says, 'There is much reason to suppose that some confusion existed in the records of the 16th century between Moulham and the manor of Swanwych, as regards the tenure in which the latter was held.' As to Mrs Serrell's manor, described in the first edition, the continuator says:

'Be this, however, as it may, Mowlham and the lands thus called "the manor of Swanwych", in the 14th year of Queen Elizabeth were settled by Nicholas Perceye on his sister Thomasina, wife of Edward Mompesson of Maiden Bradley, Wilts, in case of failure of issue of his own body. He died without issue, whereupon this estate fell to the family of Mompesson, in which it continued till it was sold by Thomas Mompesson esq. on 10.2.1721 to Samuel Serrell, gent. Hence it descended to the late Sheffield Serrell esq. who left it to his wife Frances, daughter of the Revd Edward Bankes, rector of Corfe Castle, who now enjoys it.'

At least we are on firm ground with 'an accurate map and survey' of the Ilminster estate by Samuel Donne in 1762, by which time the trustees owned 361 acres. The principal tenants included:

Aaron Bower, 52 acres. The present recreation ground is marked as his cowleaze, with house and garden north of the Brook, and beach.

The Revd Mr Chapman, 66 acres, including his new house and meadow alongside 'Mr Chapman's lane', east of Northbrook Road on the site of the later Grammar School playingfields.

Robert Chinchin, 32 acres, including meadows at Ulway and Wild Meadow.

John Gannet (cf. the modern Gannetts Park), 57 acres, including his cowleaze, beach, and closes next to New barn (evidently Cauldon Barn, now named Cauldron Barn Farm).

Hester Pushman, 27 acres, including a cowleaze.

Elizabeth Searrale's 'Whitelands (late Cockeram's), 7 acres'.

Widow Elizabeth Tedbury, 103 acres, including eweleaze and mead at Ulway, and an item 'In Road where the Pound antiently stood'. It is marked east of the Brook where it crosses the lane now called Court Road. Hill Pole meadow is also marked alongside the future Victoria Avenue; WMH said that the proper name was Eel Pond (cf. the 'lake' there).

Samuel Donne's map shows the High Street, parish church and the *Swan Inn*, but only diagrammatically. The two road bridges are indicated, but no shore road as such. The present Ulwell Road began at Blacklin, Blacklands or Baglam Gate (Battlemill on the Tithe map of 1839, cf. the modem Battlemead, but there was no battle). The gate was to prevent cattle straying on the beach.

The most decorative item on Donne's map, though not within the estate, is 'Peveral Point', with eight guns. 'A is the flagstaff of the Fort on which Colours are placed; B, the Pavement; C, the wall or Breastwork; D, a Nine-pounder on the Beach; n.b. the guns are Nine-pounders.'

On the estate map, small detached closes and cottages adjoin Poor House meadow on either side of Carrant's Court Hill. In one of these cottages John Mowlem, a poor quarry boy, was born in 1788. After making his fortune in London, he purchased between 1857 and 1861 the whole of the lands belonging to the trustees of the Ilminster Free School which was henceforth known as the de Moulham or Mowlem estate.

St Mary the Virgin, Swanage

And so back along the High Street and down Church Hill. Apart from the tower, the parish church was entirely rebuilt in 1859 and was greatly altered in the 17th and 18th centuries. However, fragments of Early English carved stones survive and it is thought that at least a chapel was established at an early date. But why no incumbent? Swanage was unlikely to have been any smaller a township than Worth or Langton. One possibility is that, because Swanage had become a collection of small farms, some belonging to alien manors without a lord, it did not lead to parochial establishment until a later date. Blackstone says that 'the boundaries of a parish were originally determined by those of a manor or manors. With the spread of Christianity the lords began to build churches upon their demesnes or wastes … and obliged all their tenants to appropriate their tithes to the

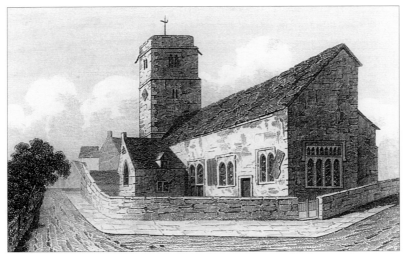

20 An engraving of St Mary's parish church, Swanage, from the southeast, from a drawing by W.A. Miles in 1826.

maintenance of the officiating minister.'

For whatever reason, the chapel of Swanage was under the wing of the rector of Worth, who seems to have had a curate, and one or the other would ride the four miles along the Priest's Way to celebrate mass there. But why the connection with Worth rather than Langton, which parish is between the two? It may have been because Worth had a curate and Langton did not. Then again, the ease of travel along the rough but level track, which can still be followed as a bridleway, would make the journey less arduous than by the hills, valleys and streams of Langton, which had no direct road to Swanage in early times (cf. Gully, Coombe, Steps – which really *were* steps – and Putlake: all in Langton parish). The Priest's Way probably followed the path below the great wall of Swanage to the chapel.

The list of priests begins with Henry Terry, 'Rector of Worth', 1297. Following Alexander Wendon, 1308, was Walter de Swanewich. Robert Iwayn or Sweyn, 1361, was 'Rector of Worth and Swanewich'. Later came William Talbot, 1408, to the 'Rector of Worth and Chapelry of Swanich'. But in addition to the rectors there were also 'vicars of Worth and Swanwich', from 1321 at any rate. The appointment of the vicar was in the hands of the rector for the time being, but by 1500 the relative positions of the churches changed (see pp.39-40).

The Worth Matravers registers date back to 1584. The oldest volume was lost to the church for a time but was found in a cottage at Swanage in 1824 and restored to the church by the Revd T.O. Bartlett who was both rector and vicar of Worth. The Swanage parish registers date from 1563, and those up to 1811 were printed and published. The more recent registers have also been deposited in the Dorset Record Office.

The Church Tower

It was Thomas Manwell, 'The Swanage philosopher', to whom John Hutchins referred as Thomas Manville in his introduction to the 2nd edition (1794) of his *History of Dorset*. Manwell had assisted him with information concerning Purbeck and, in particular, Swanage. Though a good stonemason and a knowledgeable student of science and history, his theories were accepted with some reserve. His opinion that the church tower was built before Corfe Castle, indeed before the birth of Christ, was unfortunately often repeated without much thought. WMH, in his book *Old Swanage*, 'knocked the bottom out of the old tradition' with some observations from his experience as a practical builder. But he spoilt his own record by stating that the cottage near the church 'bears a date 1018, which was, as we know, during the reign of Canute'. This was plainly as absurd as Hutchins on the age of the tower. There still remains a worked stone on the gable wall of the cottage suggesting the word GOD, but no figures can now be distinctly seen. Perhaps '1618'

21 Interior of the Church, which was demolished in 1857. This painting by Julia Colson shows the box pews, the triple-decker pulpit, the Gallery and the first organ (1829).

might have been acceptable, but even that date is early and it is unlikely for such a cottage to be dated at all.

There are two questions to be attempted: how old is the tower and for what purpose was it built? An official of the Royal Commission on Historical Monuments visited Swanage in 1943, somewhat surprisingly as local wartime bombing was at its height. He surveyed the parish church, and his notes are useful.[11] He judged it to be of early 13th-century origin, based on miscellaneous stone fragments (one an early 13th-century capital), broken shafting, and a reset moulded stone on the inner face of the south wall of the tower, though uncertain in date. The lower stages of the tower were thought to date from the 14th century, the upper stages from the 17th century. All is austere: the walls are coursed Purbeck rubble with ashlar quoins and dressings.

In 1824 the present vestry was formed on the ground floor, and the arch between the tower and nave was opened up, widened and heightened. A 15th-century window from elsewhere was inserted in place of the external 'ruinous doors', despite opposition by the rector, Mr Bartlett. It appears that a new floor was inserted above the vestry, but with seating over for the children.[12]

The Vestry Minutes, 21 October 1824, record that 'Mr Wallis present, engages on the part of Mr M. Pitt Esq. to erect a stable and sufficient floor, seating to be placed in the Tower at his private expence of the liberal offer of Mr Pitt, agree to erect a flight of steps on the outside north of the Tower and to make an entry through the Tower to the new erected floor.' So much for the story that this, the only door, was original and a ladder could be drawn up when all were safe inside and sheltering from the Danes, and that, to pass the time, swans could be shot from this vantage! There is a small opening in the east wall, now looking into the present nave high up: it is also said that this was originally used for shooting at sea-pirates!

Between the present vestry and bell-ringing chamber can be seen the outline of the east and west gable-ends of the original tower (cf. Studland church). In the north and south walls are corbelled stone wall plates which supported the low roof. The fourth stage contains the clock, and the fifth the bell chamber. WMH thought that the parapet stones were reused from the lower tower, and that the tower itself replaced an earlier building on account of the presence of Norman fragments used in the walls. The roof timbers appeared to have been 17th- or 18th-century work, with a raised centre, and early 18th-century lead, inscribed T. PUSHMAN R. TALBOT CH.WARD. 1713. What is puzzling is that externally the upper and lower stages match exactly, though the stone might have been redressed when the tower was raised, and there is no evidence of the junction between old and new work. As to the material, 'In comparing it with the ancient towers of Corfe Castle, it is composed of the same sort of stone, that has acquired a greater degree of nitrous incrustation and, like it, the mortar is almost petrified or turned to stone by length of time.'[13] However, WMH recorded that in 1840 the tower was pointed in blue lias lime mortar which sets very hard.

One other point: there are three rising external offsets, all similar in design. The first offset does not appear on the east wall, signifying that there was already a building against it on that side; there is also a straight joint between them. The chamfered plinths are evenly formed and the stones do not look ancient: in fact the whole tower, though plain, appears built in a very regular way (cf. Studland, which is much rougher). The small windows are of different date, some possibly reused with later surrounds to earlier openings. On the west and south elevations the small loops are obscured by the clock, above which are two-light windows to the bell chamber.

As Swanage was only a chapel-of-ease until the end of the 15th century, it is unlikely that this squat, immensely thick tower was built for ecclesiastical purposes (such as to contain bells). It is possible that it was a refuge or fortress, bearing in mind its proximity to the sea and the frequent raids carried out by the French in the 14th century. An intriguing suggestion is raised by the possibility of an external bulwark south of the tower. The land falls steeply from the south to the Brook or creek, where there was the only narrow crossing. The enclosures on the higher ground to the east of Church Hill, where the modem rectory now stands, was earlier called Paradise,[14] and the name derives from the French *parados*, 'a mound behind a fortified place to secure from reverse attack or fire'.

The Chapel-of-Ease

An interesting suggestion is made in Hutchins by his continuator:

> In this parish is an old building near the middle of the street, which was probably the chapel before the church was built here, and of course belonging to that at Worth, there being but few inhabitants at that time: it has one arched doorway on the north side, and is used as a carpenter's shop. On digging the saw-pit in a piece of ground adjoining, many human bones were found. Mr Hutchins seems never to have seen this building, otherwise he would have mentioned it in his history.

Unfortunately the archway disappeared long ago; the only clue to its position might come from the Chancery sale of 1823 where item no. 27 describes three tenements, carpenter's shop and garden, shown on the map as just east of the former *New Inn*. Another carpenter's shop and outbuilding, no. 23, is shown, also on the north side of the street, which appears to have been at or near the Independents' chapel (now the U.R.C.).

In any event, by the 13th century there is little doubt that the Swanage chapel was on the site of the present church. Sir Stephen Glynne visited the church in 1830 and his account is quoted in F.P. Pitfield's *Purbeck Parish Churches*,[15] who also gives comparative plans of the development of Swanage church and suggests that the tower was in line with the chapel. This seems to be confirmed by Thomas Manwell who contributed this paragraph to Hutchins (2nd edn) in 1796:

> From the foundation of a wall two feet and a half thick, lately discovered by digging a grave in it, it appears to have been only the same width of the tower originally, but has since been enlarged by removing the North wall farther from the centre. Its length remains the same as at first. That this edifice is of a much later date than the tower is evident from its having no wall on the west, except the segment that was built when it was widened, as before mentioned; the East wall of the tower serving for this purpose.

So there are still differences of opinion, and Swanage church remains a puzzle.

5

The Marblers; The Reformation; The Civil War

We need to retrace our steps to the age of Purbeck marble. We have noted that the Romans used it to some extent, but during the Dark Ages it was forgotten. The Saxons built mostly in wood, but in stone for some churches such as Lady St Mary, Wareham, which was demolished in 1840.

When the Normans began to build Romanesque churches and castles on a large scale, the style resulted from the construction of massive walls and piers with round arches and small windows, as can be seen in the churches of Studland and Worth Matravers. It was not until the pointed arch developed in the 12th century that 'Gothic' got into its stride, with the possibility of using slender pillars, larger windows, stone vaults and substantial buttresses to transmit the weight. The taste for polychrome decoration grew, and the use of white Caen stone and dark Purbeck marble made an impressive contrast. But more than this: the marble, when not affected by the weather, was hard and strong, and could support a tower or stone vault. The demand for it increased rapidly during the foundation or rebuilding of many of the cathedrals and churches in the 'Early English' style, as at Salisbury, Lincoln and Westminster Abbey, to name only a few.

The Temple Church

The earliest use of detached Purbeck shafts was at Canterbury in the new choir, built by the Frenchman, William of Sens, and completed by William the Englishman in 1184. Moreover the powerful and wealthy Knights Templar were building their new Round Church in London, begun before 1170 and consecrated in 1185, probably in the presence of Henry II.[1] The six main piers in the nave provide perhaps the earliest example of Purbeck marble used structurally on a large scale. They were replaced in 1842 with marble from Woodyhyde, in the parish of Worth Matravers, and again, after war damage in 1941, from Lynch, south of Corfe Castle. The provenance of the original marble is unknown, but the almost contemporary shafts at Canterbury show, in the texture of the stone, a similarity to the marble recovered from Peveril, including a large block from the seashore when alterations were recently made to the Swanage lifeboat slipway.

This raises the question of whether marble was excavated at Peveril earlier than inland and, if so, whether the stone was shipped from Swanage rather than from Owre quay in Poole Harbour which was the traditional place. Evidence is wanting to prove that Swanage was a port of any importance in the Middle Ages but, even so, it seems unreasonable to transport stone from the seashore five miles inland and over the hill to

22 Temple Church, London. Originally built in 1185, it was constructed using columns of Purbeck marble.

the Harbour, unless the marble was to be worked centrally at Corfe Castle on the way. This operation was thought to have been proved by the observation of scars and broken pieces of marble, found below West Street and therefore the scene of local 'bankers'.[2] However, recent discoveries suggest that the marble, at least inland, was worked in some degree at the quarrs along the valley.[3]

The marble outcrop, in beds of various thickness and colour, followed the Swanage street from Peveril to Herston, where the present school playing-field is on the site of worked-out quarr riddings. A considerable amount of stone must have left this area. A little further west, on a rise opposite Benleaze, Walter Haysom dug a little marble to complete the restoration of the Temple Church in the 1950s, though most of it came from Lynch.

How many men from Swanage, Corfe and the Purbeck villages worked along the marble line; how many more fashioned it at bankers, transporting and loading stone at the quays for delivery to Salisbury, Exeter, London, Durham, and even to Ireland and France? The tonnage must have been enormous. The trade started in the 12th century and continued into the 15th century, but its heyday was in the 13th century when columns, caps, fonts and slabs were mass-produced, and there were flourishing workshops in both London and the cathedrals where the marblers were working on site.[4] The King's works were the most important, especially as Purbeck was a royal demesne with a royal castle.[5] Henry III, a great patron of the arts, was rebuilding Westminster Abbey in 1245 and decided to be buried there rather than in the Temple Church, his earlier choice, though he had been present at the consecration of its Choir in 1240. Here a magnificent marble effigy of a bishop escaped the 1941 fire. King John's tomb in Worcester Cathedral is another of the many fine examples throughout the land, and nearer at hand are the effigies in Lady St Mary, Wareham.

The Black Death

The Dorset Lay Subsidy Roll of 1332 gives clues about the more wealthy inhabitants of Purbeck. It contains a list of those people who were assessed, and the amount of taxes on their movables or personal property, in the time of Edward III. The highest assessment in Dorset was 40s, the lowest 7 ¼d. In the hundred of Rowbarrow, where 55 people were assessed, including one woman: the highest was 10s., the lowest 8d., and the total was £7.[6]

Doubtless the Black Death put a temporary stop to stone-working, but the marble era continued and the nave of Westminster Abbey was resumed in 1375 and completed in the original style. The massive marble piers of Exeter Cathedral also date from the 14th century. Eventually alabaster and wood overtook Purbeck marble in decorative art, being so much easier to work, and colour being used even to a greater degree.

The population of England reached perhaps four millions at the end of the 13th century.[7] There was not enough cultivated land to feed the peasants, and low living standards meant poverty, famine and disease. The Black Death first struck in 1348, the plague spreading from rat-infested ships at Melcombe Regis. It 'carried off almost all the inhabitants of the sea ports in Dorset' then moved inland, where neither Purbeck nor its clergy escaped. Worth Matravers 'appears to have suffered from the ravages of the Black Death in 1349, when it lost its Swanage vicar, and still more from the later pestilence in 1361, when both rector and vicar died'.[8] Plagues continued to recur until the end of the century, and by the mid-15th century the population had declined by almost half. Swanage had only one or two hundred people in the parish, and the lot of those who survived eased somewhat, as there was now a shortage of labour.

The Hundred Years War

The centre of the village had evolved around the parish pump and above the crossing of the Brook. It lay some way inland, as other maritime villages, being thus less exposed against surprise attack from the sea. The so-called Hundred Years' War with France (1337-1453) was intermittent, but Purbeck suffered continually from these raids. A disastrous attack occurred in 1338, and the men of Studland, Whitecliff, Swanage and Herston were discharged of certain liabilities in consideration of their injuries. It is possible that the Swanage tower was built at this time as a refuge, as previously discussed. But it was not always one-way: in 1429 two ships, the *James* of Studland and *Welfare* of Swanage, drove a foreign ship ashore and plundered her.[9]

The Reformation

At the end of the 15th century, Swanage finally became a 'proper' parish.

> In 1486 and again in 1504, the presentation of new Incumbents was to 'the rectory of Swanwich alias Worth'. And from 1506 onwards the relative positions of the churches changed, for Swanage became the mother church with its rector, and Worth became an independent vicarage in the gift of the rectors of Swanage.[10]

From this it would seem that the oldest southeast part of Swanage rectory was built at that time, and probably the tithe barn, too.

In 1506 Walter Hyndebere was styled 'Rector of Swanwych' and in 1521 Edward Higgons 'Doctor in Decrees, Rector of Swanwich'. When Thomas Griffiths succeeded him

23 A drawing of the ancient key found near the Church from the Purbeck Society Papers 1852-69.

as rector in 1537, Henry VIII's Reformation had already begun. The churches had to surrender their gold, silver and other precious items and Henry received some £75,000 from their sale. It is remarkable how much wealth and how many relics were found in even quite small churches. There may not have been much of worth in Swanage, but all possessions had to be valued by Thomas Cromwell in his *Valor Ecclesiasticus*, a survey which was completed in six months, the first major tax record since Domesday Book. An ornate key, of Henry VII's time, was found near Swanage church and might have been the chest key.[11]

The lesser monasteries were dissolved in 1536; the greater houses, such as Milton, Cerne and Abbotsbury, went two years later.

Henry VIII reorganised the cathedrals and founded five new dioceses, one being Bristol, to which Dorset was transferred from Salisbury, until its return in 1837.

> The dissolution of the monasteries meant that nearly half of the County of Dorset which had been in church hands suddenly came on the market and was bought up by the 'new gentry'. The century between that happening and the Civil War is peculiar in that the old medieval manor system of local land tenure was kept going ... But the new world was also coming in on a rising tide.[12]

In 1560 a Royal licence was issued to alienate the manor of Worth and the advowson of Swanage. In 1570 Thomas Cook was inducted 'to Swanage with Chapelry of Worth'. He was involved with piracy, which was rife at that time, and a leading pirate named Valentine presented him with a handsome bible from a trunk full of finery destined for the English Ambassador in Scotland but seized in the Channel. Another bible went to 'the minister of Purbeck', as Studland, which was the centre of activity, was sometimes called.

At length the Privy Council clamped down and several notorious pirates were taken prisoner. Following confessions, seven were hanged, including Valentine. In 1583, 19 conspirators were to be cross-examined at the High Court of Admiralty including Mr Cook, 'he who received the piratical Bible and much else beside.' He had ceased to be rector of Swanage after 1576. 'A procession of glum people rode from Purbeck to London that autumn, crossing the bridge at Wareham as though being chased out of Paradise.'[13]

The succeeding rector of Swanage was John Whitcomb, and he was followed by Edward Abbott of Worth (1586-1614). In 1612 Edward married Agnes, only daughter of Christopher Dolling of Dunshay Manor. There were two tenements in Worth village called Abbott's Living. When the rector died his wife remarried John Collins in 1620. In the will of John Dolling II (1663) it was stated, 'Item, he gave unto the poor of Sandwich, fourty shillings'. An Act of Parliament in 1601 directed the Overseers of the Poor to be appointed by the Vestry.[14]

The Armada

1588 brought the Spanish Armada and great excitement.[15] Invasion was a real possibility, and hurried preparations were made for defence. Among existing fortifications were

Brownsea Castle, guarding Poole Harbour, and Studland Castle at the Foreland close to Old Harry, both built in the time of Henry VIII. Beacons were lit along the hilltops warning of the approach of the Armada. On 24 July the cliffs were crowded as people watched the spectacular progress of the rival fleets along the Dorset coast past St Aldhelm's Head, Durlston and 'Sandwiche' Bay towards the Needles and the Isle of Wight. There had been an engagement off Portland and a skirmish off the Purbeck coast. There was still the expectation of landings, though the fleets had enough to do to keep abreast of one another. Small vessels left every harbour to reinforce the English ships. Eventually the fleets disappeared up the Channel to meet at the final Battle of Gravelines off Calais.

The fate of the galleons after the battle and their dispersal round the Scottish and Irish coasts, where so many were wrecked, is well documented. Only one fetched up in England, upon the Devon coast, where the Spanish were well-treated by the local people. Nevertheless there is folklore enough.

> There is a tradition current that one at least of the Spanish galleons was wrecked in Swanage Bay, and those saved from here who settled down and married are held to account for the Spanish colouring and type of features seen in some of the women and children amongst its inhabitants at the present day.[16]

More likely was the wreck of a Spanish ship off Swanage when there was an Enquiry held in 1421. The story may also have evolved from the sinking of the Spanish galleon *San Salvador* in Studland Bay. This Spanish flagship had mysteriously exploded in Lyme Bay on 21 July 1588, with 300 badly burnt or dying men. She was eventually towed into Weymouth. After 16 weeks, orders came that she should be taken to Portsmouth. Patched up and with tattered sails, she began to leak off Handfast Point, where she sank. Some of the crew were drowned, though 33 were rescued by the *Lyon*, a small boat from Studland. But these men were not Spanish, of course. Divers still try to locate the remains of the *San Salvador*.[17]

The Royal Warren

In the 31st year of Henry II's reign (1185), the serving men of Roger de Poles de Sandwich answered half a mark for wrongfully seizing a royal fish.[18]

How far the Isle of Purbeck remained subject to strict forest laws, it is difficult to tell. It seems that it was a popular hunting ground for Saxon and Norman kings, and particularly favoured by King John who, it is said, had three royal lodges: at Slepe on the heath, at Creech Barrow and at Swanage, either at Whitecliff or Windmill Hill, a short distance from Godlingston. In his introduction to his handsome book *A Royal Warren*, C.E. Robinson described Purbeck:

> Disafforested as far back as the reign of Henry III, it became thenceforward merely a 'Warren of Conies'; but the spirit of the antiquated forest laws remained, to hamper the cultivation and improvement of this beautiful district, long secluded from the outer world.

There must have been plenty of deer as well as conies, both on the heath and in the valley, as there are still. 'Though James I in 1615 was the last English king who hunted in Purbeck, game was still abundant, and in 1618 and 1625 courts were commanded to be held in connection with game laws.'

Stone and Quarrs

Although marble had been all but forgotten, the less spectacular limestone had not. Demand for it was steady, but few records exist describing quarrying in Purbeck in

24   A very fine example of quarrying in progress. It shows the pony at ease having just hauled the large slab of stone on the far right, still chained to the quarr cart, up from underground, using the capstan and braced by the crabstones (near left). The pole, or spack, is still harnessed to the pony.

medieval times, apart from the rise and fall of marble. But much building stone was used in the county, and stone bridges had been built across the rivers at Wareham, which enabled the transport of building material inland.

Menaced by Spain and the Pope, Henry VIII built a series of coastal defences along the Channel. A castle was erected at the eastern end of Brownsea Island to defend Poole Harbour. This block-house was built of Purbeck stone, the original walls being six feet thick in the tower and nine feet in the barbican. Stone was ferried across in small boats, landed at the jetty and incorporated into the fort.[19] All signs of Studland Castle at Handfast Point have vanished, but it is shown on contemporary maps. The earliest known map of Poole Bay and Purbeck (c.1539) comes from the Cotton MSS in the British Library. It is drawn 'upside down' and includes a bird's-eye view of Peveril Point, Swanage, Godlingston, Studland, Brownsea and Poole.[20]

After the dissolution of the monasteries new farms and manor houses, such as those at Godlingston and Whitecliff, appeared in Dorset, with mullioned windows, elaborate doors and gables of Purbeck stone, built by the new and wealthy owners.

An interesting illustration of a stone windlass or whim is described in a classic 1556 book on mining by Agricola, *De re Metallica*. It appears to be of the same type as those used in the Purbeck stone quarries and survived virtually unchanged for nearly 300 years, which reflects on the small scale of individual operations and the relatively straightforward geological conditions of shallow-depth mining as seen in Purbeck. Curiously enough,

Agricola's real name was George Bauer, pronounced here as 'George Bower': a well-known Purbeck name.[21]

With the publication of Agricola's book, prominent Elizabethan miners invited German engineers to England. Daniel Heckstetter arrived in 1563, searching the whole country for metallic ores. Two joint stock companies were then formed, each being granted a Royal Charter in 1568. They were the Governor and Company of Mines Royal, and the Governor and Company of Mineral and Battery Works. It was not until the following century, after the religious wars in Germany (1618-48), that refugee artisan miners began to arrive in England in some numbers. At this time a primitive copy of *German Mining Technology* appeared in Purbeck and spurred on the development of the stone trade.

As we have seen, marble outcropped narrowly through the vale while the older limestone lay higher on the plateau. Durlston Bay was one of the earliest sites from which stone was excavated. The cliff stone at Anvil Point was there too, of course, but it was standing sheer above the waves and impossible to work without platforms, cranes and boats, to say nothing of calm sea. So this use came later in the 17th century, and especially in Napoleonic times, with the demand for fortifications, which the cliff stone was most suitable for.

Inland, the Purbeck building stone was overlaid with useless shale and marl, and at first 'ridding' was resorted to. This was early 'opencast', with the use of horse and cart, pick and shovel, crowbar and hammer, mallet and chisel: before the days of the bulldozer. The deeper the stone, the more overburden had to be removed, and this led to underground working. There was no organised quarrying by the landowners, but one or two men, often members of one family, obtained permission from a farmer to establish a quarr by a 'fine'. After clearing the site digging began, and unsuitable stone was used to build a perimeter wall with two or three open sheds in which the quarriers could work, sheltered against the weather. There was also a lock-up shed for the gear and pony or donkey. Having dug down a short way, a stone archway was built at the entrance, and an inclined slide formed to enable a laden quarr-cart to be brought to the surface with the aid of the donkey who would walk in a circle, pulling the long 'spack' or ash pole attached to the capstan, round which the chain descended underground. Two large 'crab' stones supported the elm capstan post. By now, many quarries were dotted about the landscape, and the stone men had became a race apart.

The Purbeck Stone Quarry Preservation Group was formed by local Swanage men interested in Industrial Archaeology. John Burry of New Milton purchased 162 acres when Townsend Farm was sold in 1964. Failing to get planning permission for development, he engaged the PSQPG to do an underground survey of the old quarry workings, this being the first time any such undertaking had been tried, as over the years no records of underground workings had been kept. The survey was carried out by the four founder members of the group: Dennis Smale, his brother Fred, Brian Bugler and Charlie Turner. Their reward for this mammoth undertaking was the saving of all adits and their underground tunnels or galleries. More local members joined the group and through all their hard work the quarries of Townsend were saved for posterity. Subsequently 32 acres of the estate were acquired by the Trust and now form the Townsend Nature Reserve. This attractive rough quarry land is open to the public, who can enjoy the many butterflies, wild flowers, grasses and grasshoppers there. To the north of the reserve was an area of more abandoned quarries, some of the deepest in Swanage, until their disappearance.

Through Miss Brotherton, of the Dorset Naturalist Trust, the conservation of rare bats in the quarries was also achieved.[22]

The Marblers

It is uncertain when the 'Ancient Order of Marblers and Stonecutters' was established. Some thought that the Charter dated 1651 was a copy of an original of 1551, but this is doubtful. Formerly there were two stone-wardens: one for Swanage and the other for Corfe Castle. The minute books only date from 1837 when Robert Burt, as warden, kept the records which had been dispersed from Corfe, but in them there is little beyond the lists of admission.[23]

The regulations for the working of the quarries were kept exclusively within the hands of the Freemen of the Isle of Purbeck. To be able to take up the freedom one had to be the legitimate son (or grandson if the line was through a female) of a Freeman and 21 years of age, up to which time the wages belonged to the parents. Each year, on Shrove Tuesday, the Marblers still meet in the tiny Town Hall at Corfe Castle and, after transacting business, such as the issue of apprenticeship certificates, arbitrations between quarriers and the election of officers, they set out with the customary football and pound of pepper along the old road to Ower in order to preserve their right of way.[24]

> At some remote period a charter was given to the quarriers, authorising any member of the Company, after obtaining permission from the landlord or agent, to dig a shaft and put up a capstan where he chose. This once done, the shaft belonged to the quarryman as long as he worked it and paid stone dues, not as freehold but as a sort of perpetual leasehold.

If he ceased working for more than a year and a day, he lost the possession. Agents often gave permission without the knowledge of the landlords, and disagreements arose. In 1903 a quarryman was imprisoned for contempt of court but not because he had not a right to work his quarry.

Ida Woodward, in her attractive book, *In and around the Isle of Purbeck* (1908), described her visit to the Wareham lawyer who had acted for the quarryman in the lawsuit. There she saw the papers of the Company of Marblers, consisting of:

> 1. The original articles of agreement of the Company of Marblers, dated March 3, 1551 [1651?] and signed by a large number of quarrymen, those who could not write making strange hieroglyphics as their mark. The little pieces of parchment still form a fringe at the bottom of the deed, but the seals are gone.
>
> 2. A copy of the same, unsigned, and dated March 3, 1651.
>
> 3. An enlarged edition of the articles, having more signatures appended than the earlier one, and the seal of the Company of Marblers. This has an heraldic device, on 'a pale three roses slipped proper'.
>
> 4. An original agreement of the Company of Marblers to Object to the payment for the examination of stone required by London buyers.
>
> 5. A copy of the charter grant granted by Charles II to the Borough of Corfe.

This seemed to conclude the evidence of the quarrymen's rights.

Cockram and the Parish Church

Brune Cockram DD became rector of Swanage in 1614 and remained the incumbent until 1667 throughout the many upheavals: the beheading of Charles I, the Interregnum and the Restoration of Charles II. Perhaps he was related to the vicar of Bray! Swanage was an out-of-the-way place, and possibly this helped to keep him out of the limelight.

The Cockrams were landed gentry and Brune was evidently not short of money. He did not live in the rectory but at Whitecliff where he no doubt farmed in addition to tending his human flock. WMH says that Dr Cockram had the church 'all pulled down

25   The same quarry (see illustration 24) shows the skilled marblers and stone cutters at work in all aspects of masonry. The quarr stone sheds (far right) are for working stone at the bankers during inclement weather. The stack of finished stone (near right) is awaiting transportation.

with the exception of the south transept' and then rebuilt it. But Hutchins (1st edn 1774) described the church then as

> a large ancient building, and consists of a chancel, body, a narrow north isle, almost equal with the chancel, a small south isle, a pretty high tower, in which are four bells and a clock. The body is covered with lead, the rest with tile. The chancel is large, and is one-third the length of the whole fabric.

It is clear that Cockram more than doubled the height of the tower. Four bells[25] were listed in Edward's inventory of 1552. John Wallis of Salisbury recast three of them in 1621. The fourth, in 1594, read 'Think on God'. This bell and one of the others still survive. It seems that Cockram opened up the east wall of the tower into the nave as the large arch, the upper part of which can still be seen in the tower, is not medieval or pointed but appears to be of 17th-century origin. This archway was apparently walled up in the 18th century, because in 1824 it was resolved 'that the Arch (now filled up) separating the body of the Church from the Belfry be thrown open and that the Belfry be white-washed and the old holes in the Tower be filled up'. However, the arch visible in Julia Colson's drawing (c.1850) does not appear to be as large as the Cockram arch and is possibly also pointed: all very puzzling, as is the whole tower.[26]

Turning to the nave and chancel, F.P. Pitfield[27] suggests that the removal of the chancel arch took place in the 17th century, probably in Cockram's time, but this did not happen until 1792 when a faculty was granted that 'the party wall which separates the church from the chancel be taken down and the side walls of the north aisle and of the Chancel now covering the same be made one in regular form with the body of the Church'. The galleries and pews were also to be taken down and new ones built. The agreement between the churchwardens, James Chinchen and John Harden, and the contractors, Joseph Ellis and William White, included taking down the old roof on the north side of the church, 'also the strikes and walls, and to rise the side and end walls to the same height as the body of the church'. There was to be a new tiled roof and the aisles were to be paved with stone. Mention is made of new floors to the seats, framing, doors and galleries, vestry room, plastering, whitewashing and a new chandelier. The payment to Ellis and White was to be £455 17s. 0d.

On completion there was now one common, double-pitched roof, which externally gave a lopsided appearance from the east. The drawing by W.A. Miles in 1826 (illustration 20) shows this clearly. There remained a large two-storey south transept-cum-porch, which incorporated the baptistry and vestry. The church remained substantially the same until its total rebuilding (except for the tower) in 1859.

The Civil War

England drifted into war due to the duplicity and stubbornness of Charles I and the development of puritanism. There were few set battles and many changed sides, with much confusion. The majority of large landowners were royalist in sympathy, including the Catholic Weld family of Lulworth.

> Most of the inhabitants of Sherborne, Blandford, Corfe, Portland, Weymouth and Bridport supported the King, while Dorchester, Poole, Wareham, Lyme Regis and Melcombe Regis were Parliamentarian … The passing and repassing of armies caused a great deal of damage, plundering, requisition of goods and the dislocation of ordinary life, apart from the destruction caused by actual fighting.[28]

By 1645 most people were heartily sick of war, which led to the rising of the Dorset 'Clubmen', who claimed to be neutral and were only concerned to protect themselves and their property. They were drawn from yeomen, farmers and tradesmen, and some clergy who were opposed to the religious changes.

Sherborne Castle was taken by the Parliamentary forces on 15 August 1645. This marked the beginning of the end of the royalist resistance in Dorset. In February 1646 Corfe Castle fell to the Roundheads, after a very long resistance by Lady Bankes, and then only through treachery. Parliament then ordered the 'sleighting' of the castle. An enormous amount of gunpowder, following undermining, failed to topple the keep completely. The entrance tower to the inner bailey split, half of it sliding down the hill yet still erect, where it remains to this day. One can imagine the local people watching the destruction from the hillsides and wondering about their future as the thunderous explosions rent the air.

In 1649 the king was beheaded. The Anglican Church and the Prayer Book were abolished, yet the old services and feasts continued to be quietly practised,[29] possibly also by Brune Cockram. Many of the royalist clergy of Dorset were ejected from their livings, but with the Restoration the Puritan clergy lost theirs in turn. Oliver Cromwell, a man of great charisma, died in 1658. 'With his death, the republic collapsed.' Charles II was recalled in 1660 and the old order returned: though not exactly as it had been.

6

The Restoration and the Stone Bankers

What was the effect of the Civil War on Swanage? Probably little until the destruction of Corfe Castle. The supply of fish and farm merchandise from the Purbeck parishes for the Bankes household must have dried up, and the employment of labour for the castle ceased. But Corfe villagers took advantage of the ruins by plundering the ancient stones to build themselves better cottages, while Sir William Erle of Charborough Park and Colonel Bingham, Governor of Poole, helped themselves to stone, timber, tapestries and other treasures confiscated by Parliament, though some items were later restored to the Bankes family.[1]

With the Restoration in 1660, Charles II ratified Elizabeth's Corfe Castle charter and added a rider declaring that he wished it to be no way prejudicial to the heirs and assigns of Sir John Bankes, who had died at Oxford in 1644. Lady Bankes lived on to see the restoration of the Crown but not of the castle: that was beyond repair. The overbearing castle was no more; time had to pass before it could be seen as a picturesque ruin in the 18th and 19th centuries, and an ancient monument in the 20th, with a charge for the privilege of standing amid the shattered walls.

The great key given back to Lady Bankes following her brave stand and surrender still hangs at Kingston Lacy, the mansion built by her son, Sir Ralph Bankes, and designed by Roger Pratt in 1663 as a replacement for the castle, now that the family was back in favour. Their Corfe Castle land remained safeguarded but their Godlingston estate was not to be acquired for another century. The Welles family who held the property sold it in 1687 to John Frampton, whose descendant sold it in turn to John Bankes in 1765.

The Dissenters

Although most Englishmen were scared of Popery, the Puritans were nevertheless now under pressure from the re-established Church, and the Act of Uniformity of 1662 required all parish clergy to declare publicly their use of the Prayer Book. Many dissented, and these 'non-conformists' were ejected from their livings, among them the parsons of Wareham, Wimborne, Bere Regis and Lytchett Matravers. John Bond LL.D., a member of the well-known Purbeck family, who had been educated under the influential Revd John White of Dorchester, was deprived of his preferment at the Restoration; he retired to Swanage where he died in 1676.[2]

The introduction of Nonconformity to Swanage is largely due to the efforts of William Clarke, Minister of Wareham from 1670 to 1722. Mr Clarke used to walk to Swanage on a weekday and preach in

26 & 27   Two studio pictures taken by William Powell of two worthy Swanage gentlemen in 1906: on the left is Nathan Chinchen White, Stone Merchant; on the right, in his Lifeboat suit and cork life jacket, is David Hibbs.

a private house to the marblers, quarrymen and other Christian friends, who were informed of his arrival by a prearranged signal, as the Meetings had to kept secret. It is said that on one occasion he was pursued by his persecutors and escaped by hiding in one of the quarries.

Another tradition says that some Swanage dissenters started early on the Sabbath, drove in a covered waggon to Ower and crossed by boat to Poole to join their brethren there.

More happily Celia Fiennes, the nonconformist daughter of a Cromwellian colonel, came to Purbeck about this time on horseback and visited 'Sondige'. She remarked in her journal that she had enjoyed lobsters, crabs and shrimps, and pronounced them 'very good'.

Rectors and Landlords

Brune Cockram, rector of Swanage, was by 1662 an old man and unlikely to have resisted the Act of Uniformity even had he wished to. One adornment to the parish church at this time was the hexagonal Purbeck stone font presented by Dr Cockram. The double panel on one side of the bowl bears the date and initials of the churchwardens, another side the initials of Lewis Cockram, baptised 16 April 1663. When St Mary's was rebuilt in 1860 and a new Purbeck marble font took its place, the font was removed to St Mark's church, Herston. Brune Cockram was buried in the family vault which was in the south transept, as was the font. WMH remembered working at the vault as a boy when the last of the Cockrams was interred in 1847. He added:

> The Cockram's coat of arms and escutcheons have disappeared, and where they and other relics are now is a mystery. If old Vandal's knapsack was searched, some of the missing treasures would probably be discovered. The old gable finials belonging to the Early English transept is [sic] now fixed over the rectory front door.

The Dorset Hearth Tax Returns of 1662-4 list 38 names in the 'Swanidge Tithinge'. Cockram's eight hearths possibly refer to both Whitecliff, his home, and the rectory; there was one house with six hearths, two with five, two with four and three with three, the rest only one or two.

Swanage settled down again – if, that is, there had been any social change – to its customary life of fishing, farming and quarrying. A new rector after 53 years must have brought some new shoots, but William Rose was another landed gentleman who was installed to the living in 1667. As Dr Cockram had lived at Whitecliff, it seems that the rectory was in poor condition. Rose repaired it, and the date 1667 is over the main door. Rector Rose purchased Carrant's Court house and farm from Onesiphorus Bond in 1676 and the 'New House' (later called 'Magnolia') from the marbler Anthony Serrell in 1681. A year later he bought Rempstone, which then passed to his eldest son, William.[3] 'The latter conveyed it by fine, in his father's time (1689) to Thomas Rose his brother, who resides there.' Thomas died in 1709 and left Rempstone to his son, William, who sold it to John Calcraft in 1757.

The Fire of London

What *did* affect Swanage was the Great Fire of 1666. George Manwell wrote in a letter to his son dated 2 March 1814:[4]

> After London was burnt some years and the city began to rebuild and flourishing, there was an uncommon call for Purbeck stone, and paving was sold at so high a price as 30s. per cwt. This of course attracted the notice of the neighbourhood round; and numbers of boys from different parishes, at the distance of 20 miles, were apprenticed here to the stone trade and premiums given.

Contemporary family records suggest that five Haysom brothers, whose father had died as a younger son of a family with a little property in north Dorset, came to Swanage at this time and entered the stone trade; by 1800 one in 20 of the population of about 1,000 was named Haysom! The quarries rang with the sound of chisel and hammer; the stoneboats and ketches were busy with loading paving, steps, kerbs and gutter-soles for London.

Daniel Defoe, describing Purbeck in 1724, wrote:[5]

> This part of the County is eminent for Vast Quarreys of Stone, which is cut out Flat, and us'd in London in great quantities for Paving Court-Yards, Alleys, Avenues to Houses, Kitchins, Foot-ways on the Sides of the High Streets, and the like; and is profitable to the Place, as also is the Number of Shipping employ'd in bringing it to London. There are also several Rocks of very good Marble, only that the Veins in the Stone are not Black and White, as the Italian, but Grey, Red and other Colours.

The Bloody Assize

On the death of Charles II in 1685, his brother and heir, the catholic Duke of York, succeeded to the throne as James II. The protestant Duke of Monmouth, eldest illegitimate child of Charles II, had gone into exile in Holland, but now he landed at Lyme Regis, proclaimed himself king and raised for rebellion a motley army in the West Country which was sympathetic to him. 'Many peaceable Nonconformists had been suddenly torn from their homes and thrown into prison; others had been reduced to poverty and distress by huge fines and confiscations of their goods.'[6] The uprising was short-lived and Monmouth was defeated at the battle of Sedgemoor. He fled and made for Poole in the hope of escape, but he was discovered in disguise on Horton Heath near Wimborne, taken to London and condemned to be hanged, drawn and quartered. It was said that he showed great courage on the scaffold. 'I die a Protestant of the Church of England.'

The infamous Bloody Assize at Dorchester followed when Judge Jeffreys dealt with those who had taken up arms against the king. These wretches were tried for treason: some were transported to the West Indies with hideous results, some of the better-off were fined if they could find the money, but as many were hanged. Sir Charles Robinson of Newton Manor told the story[7] that Newton Cottage was haunted, following the hanging of three men nearby after the Assize. No one was in fact hanged in Swanage,[8] but the mortised Gallows Stone, which formerly stood in the pavement on the south side of the high road, supported the post on which were displayed portions of the quarters of the five victims executed at Wareham on 22 September 1685. Eighty-six were executed in Dorset towns (Lyme, Bridport, Weymouth, Dorchester, Sherborne, Poole and Wareham) and some of the heads were displayed 'with ghastly barbarity' in various prominent places in the county including Swanage.

The Gallows Stone was removed early this century in the course of repairing the pavement but was preserved by J.E. Mowlem in his yard at Northbrook. The late William Powell, the local photographer, noticed it when the old cottages were being demolished and it is now displayed in the forecourt of the Tithe Barn Museum.

A romantic tale by Mary E. Palgrave, 'Under the Blue Flag: A Story of Monmouth's Rebellion', refers to several Purbeck locations, more particularly to 'the Thorndykes of Godlingston'. She describes the old house, also Whitecliff, and 'Mr Jonathan Marshfield, the Rector of Swanford', who was thought more likely to be a typical dissenter than the real Swanage rector, William Rose.

> Swanford was a long, narrow village, consisting of one street of rough, little stone houses, inhabited by quarriers and fishermen … A fine group of elms cast a pleasant shade over some rough wooden benches that were much resorted to in the summer evenings, and the rustling of their leaves mingled with the splash of the waves … A beautiful stream of clear, cold water, that welled out from among some large stones meandered away among the beach pebbles to the sea. It filled with a generous abundance the pitchers and jugs of nearly all Swanford.

In contrast another scene at 'the grim name of Gallows Gore, on the high road between Langton Matravers and Kingston', describes the hanging there of three Puritans involved with the plot. It is only an adventure story: in truth the spot was called Callas in the 18th century and Gore means a triangular piece of land; there was never such a gallows there. But it is a good yarn all the same and brings out the anguish between members of the same family divided by loyalties to a King and the Church, or to his rival and Nonconformity.

The Old Meetin'

But the Catholic James II was replaced by the protestant William III and Mary II in 1689 so the pressure eased and, not long after the passing of the Toleration Act, a company of Dissenters met together in Swanage and decided to erect a chapel there. The opening ceremony took place on 15 August 1705, and the records say that the chapel was filled to overflowing, with the minstrels perched high above the congregation in their own gallery. The first minister in 'the Old Meetin'' was Jonathan Wheeler; the second was Richard Darracott in 1709. The chapel, or meeting house, of the Independents or Presbyterians, as they were variously called, was erected on a part of the garden of John Stevens who conveyed the land to trustees. Under the Act, the new chapel was certified by, among others, Samuel Serrell, Anthony Serrell and John Pushman.[9] No burial registers remain, but there are records of a few people who were interred within the Meeting House near the door, including the Revd John Morrison (d.1787) and his wife Elizabeth, and also the Revd William Sedcole (d.1821), his wife and, with her, a stillborn infant. Two early baptism registers survive, covering the years 1794-1837.[10]

By 1774 the chapel was in a sorry state and the Methodists were in the ascendant. However, with the pastorate of John Collins and Robert Chamberlain the congregation increased greatly and a larger chapel was built on the old site.[11] George Gallop of Poole drew the plans, and Mr Smedmore and Mr Spencer were the builders. It was dedicated for worship on 10 January 1838, and the charming 'listed' building remains as the hall of the later church built in 1907 which took its place. It appears that Mr Smedmore of

28 Peveril Point and the Downs from the main beach, *c.*1830, showing Preventive Station, Alpha Cottage, Marine Villa, *Manor House Hotel*, the quay and part of the stone bankers. This is the earliest known illustration of stone being transported from the bankers on shore to the small barges lying off shore by two-wheeled horse-drawn carts, which then delivered the cargo to the mother ship, ready for export.

Upabout Lane gave a piece of land for the Dissenters' burial place, and some of the tombstones may be seen against a wall adjacent to Queen's Mead.

The Bankers

Hutchins (1st edn), regarding Ower (Ore), the medieval port on Poole Harbour, records that 'This was formerly the chief if not the only key for exporting stone, which has been neglected since 1710 and that branch of business removed to Sandwich.' Whether this precise date has any significance or not, it is probable that the use of the foreshore south-eastwards from the mouth of Swanage brook began when, due to the rebuilding of London, demand for stone increased so rapidly. Large stocks of stone in a variety of forms were now piled up along the shore as 'bankers' by the merchants who bought the stone from the quarriers, to be sold and shipped away as required.

Hutchins wrote:

> Of the pier there is no remains; and the stone lodged on the banks is carried in carts to the boats, and by them to larger vessels. Round the bay, the bankers or stone merchants, who form a society governed by some rules or statutes, have their several places to lodge their stone for exportation.

There is some confusion regarding the word 'banker'. Hutchins says 'the bankers or stone merchants', and when we come to the subject of the Truck system it will be seen that the merchants *were* bankers, when using stone rather than money in their financial transactions. However, the bank or banker was the stone bench on which the stone was worked, or the place in which it was stacked.

An old MS, formerly in the hands of Mr Thomas Bartlett of Wareham,[12] gave an account of the procedure:

> About 60 years ago ... the stone was conveyed from the quarries to the bankers on the men's backs.[13] No acknowledgements were paid before these banks were raised, from which time acknowledgments of 2d. a hundred were received by the different proprietors of them; and if the stones were carried immediately to the boats, they claimed the privilege of conveying them in carts kept for the purpose, and their accustomed demand was 1s. a hundred, and no acknowledgement was paid for lodging the stone on the banker.

Centry and the Great House

This raised the problem of the ownership of the banker land. The length of foreshore used by the merchants was the northern end of 'Centry'. Sir William Phippard (1650-1723) bought the estate in 1700. He was M.P. for Poole five times and traded with the West Indies during the early years of Poole's 'Golden Age' (based on cod). He reported in 1699 that his ship *William & Elizabeth,* laden with a cargo of tobacco bound for London, had been captured off Newfoundland by a French pirate.[14]

There is no evidence of a manor house on the site when Phippard bought Centry. WMH followed Hutchins in stating incorrectly that Thomas Chapman built 'a very pleasant house and large malt-house' here in 1664.[15] There is no doubt[16] that the Great House, later the imposing central section of the *Royal Victoria Hotel,* was built by his son, John Chapman (1681-1735), stone merchant, soon he purchased the estate from Phippard in 1721,[17] pursuant to a Chancery decree for the sale; Sir William had been in financial difficulty following litigation.

Hutchins continues:

> The land lying on the bay (at least on the south and south-west) is supposed to have belonged to Sir William Phippard as waste ground of his manor of Swanwich; shortly after Mr Chapman's purchase in 1721 he instituted a suit for the recovery *of* the several bankers erected on the shore or waste of this manor, but in consequence of the length of adverse possession in the then proprietors, the suit was discontinued.

'Steinschmatzer' explained it all in his letter of 12 February 1849 to the editor of the *Poole & Dorset Herald*:

> About the year of 1550 there were at Swanage eight cottages and gardens facing the bay, and extending from the present Hotel to the *Ship Inn* ... in the reign of Richard II they were held of H.M. in free soccage, as a parcel of the dissolved College of St Stephen at Westminster, and the marblers and mariners dwelt in these cottages. About the beginning of the last century, Mr John Chapman claimed the manor of Swanage, of which the eight cottages were held by copies of Court Roll, or at least Chapman said so, and as he became lord over the quarries and the wastes, wrecks on the coast, felons' goods and other privileges, he grew very uneasy about the encroachment whereon the bankers were built, in short he wanted the bankers. He made a complaint to the Lord High Chancellor that Thomas Pushman and others had combined to defraud him of the bankers, and the Chancellor sealed them up in Chancery wax. Pushman and the rest wrote in answer saying that Chapman was in error and hoped the Chancellor would let them and their bankers alone. Not only them but others had time out of mind set up the bankers and sold them whenever they liked by taking a receipt only, just as the quarriers of Portland did ... Mr Chapman thought it best not to reply to the marblers' answer, so the Chancery seal was broken, and they continue to deposit their stone to them unto this day.

But 'Steinschmatzer' thought that the bankers were unfortunately doomed and foresaw a beautiful esplanade in the future.

Stone Merchants

The Chapman family, already settled in Swanage when John Chapman married Elizabeth Gover in 1605, was now prospering in stone. Their son Thomas (1610-96), Swanage surveyor, was a marbler. Thomas Chapman Jnr (1649-1711) was one of the elected managers of the short-lived Joint-Stock Company of Marblers, established in 1697,[18] and was surveyor of Swanage highways in 1672, as was his son John in 1721. Besides Centry, Chapman bought a great deal of acreage from the Rose family. This included Gilbert Mead, House Close, 'the Hood and Half of the Wath' (20 acres west of Anvil Point), 'the other half whereof formerly belonged to Thomas Cockram', five pieces of arable (four acres) in Sandwich North and South Fields, and several houses and gardens including 'all that garden and plott of ground called pardis alias paradice' and the yearly rent of 20s. for the Mill wheel.[19]

The mill house itself bears the legend 'Ben Barlow, Mill Wright of Southampton fecit 1754'. Whether he formed the mill pond as well as rebuilding, or altering, the house is uncertain, but it is clear from the sale that the mill wheel was already there. Indeed

29 An early photograph of the Mill House and Pond. The old cottage on the right no longer exists.

there are indications in the present house of medieval work, and there was a mill here centuries earlier. The corn mill ceased working in 1928.

There are two Chapman monuments in the parish church, one to Thomas Chapman, who died in 1711 aged 63 and his wife Joan, who was 80 when she died in 1727; the other to John Chapman, Merchant, who died in London in 1735 and was buried in St Olave's, Hart Street. Also inscribed are Mary, his daughter, who died at Silton in 1749, and Susanna, his youngest daughter, who died in 1774.

Another name of considerable standing in the stone trade was that of the Serrell family (alias Searle, among many variations of the name). Anthony Serrell, who died in 1627, had been a Swanage churchwarden, mentioned in 1614 and 1624; his son Henry Serrell (1621-82) was an elected manager, with Thomas Chapman, to the Joint-Stock Company of Marblers. Henry's son, Anthony Serrell (1669-1742), was also a stonemason and married Thomas Chapman's daughter Elizabeth. Their eldest son Thomas was a stone merchant, his son Thomas a stonemason, and in turn his son John Serrell, also a stonemason, was the only surviving son and heir. He brought an action for recovery of lands as an heir also of the last Chapman in 1781, but lost the case.

John Chapman and his Will

The Revd John Chapman, MA (1708-81) was the only son of the John Chapman who had built the Great House. He was at first paid curate at Langton Matravers between 1735 and 1738, then became rector of Silton, a village at the northern tip of Dorset, from 1740 for the rest of his life. One wonders how often he made the long journey from Swanage. No doubt he had a curate at Silton but then he is described in his will as 'of Silton'. On the other hand he also had a house and land on 'Ulway' lane, Swanage; being a bachelor he may not have lived in the Great House, but in any event he was a wealthy man. Without issue, John Chapman made his will shortly before his death:

> As to my funeral I desire it may be private as possible without any unnecessary expense or attendance but that the Body being rolled up in Lead as soon as cold and inclosed in a decent Coffin, be carried at nine o'clock in the morning by six poor men to be paid five shillings a piece to the Grave in the Church yard … And that a heavy stone of the most durable kind and a Coffin form be provided to lay upon it without any inscription but of the Name Rank and Date.

John Chapman left to Lewis Cockram of Newton a moiety of his lands called Carrant's Court and Ware's lands unless he should choose to accept £800 in lieu, which he clearly

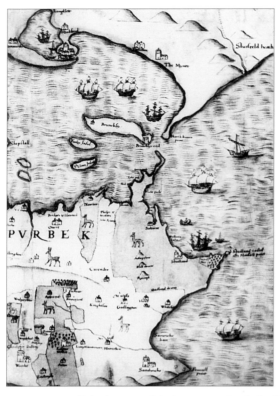

30 (left)   Part of the Isle of Purbeck, drawn by the cartographer Ralph Treswell in 1586.

31   First edition Ordnance Survey map of 1811. Note the
absence of the Valley Road (A351), which was made in 1862.
The hatched area shows the old Swanage Parish before 1894.

did. Among his bequests he left £500 to the widow of Thomas Mist Serrell in trust for
their children; he gave £60 and 'all my Upper Garments to my servant James Bradden';
to his servant Rosanna Read he bestowed 'my linen Cotton and Silk Garments and in
consideration of her extraordinary care and attention an annuity of £12'. He recommended
her 'in particular manner to the care and kindness of John Dampier, his wife and family'.
He also left £20 each to the poor of Sandwich and Silton.

Following smaller bequests he left all his estates, rents, household goods, plate, linen,
china and books to his executor, John Dampier of Wareham, Mercer, and his wife Mary,
in trust for the use of their children. The relationship between John Chapman and the
Dampiers is not known, but in a later chapter the far-reaching result of their wills will
be seen: this, the first, in 1781, the second, John Dampier's, in 1810.

Maps and Turnpikes

John Chapman's long cross-country journeys to Silton may have improved after the
development of the Turnpike Trusts when many existing roads were improved and a few
new ones were opened. The road from Swanage through Langton Matravers, Kingston and
Corfe Castle to Wareham was 'turnpiked' in 1766, with a tollgate at Herston. Similar roads
continued on to Blandford, Shaftesbury and Gillingham where Silton was hard by.

Maps were beginning to be more accurate, following such decorative Dorset maps
by Saxton (1575) and Speed (1610), where 'Sandwich' is shown. The fine Purbeck plans
were made by Ralph Treswell in 1586 for Sir Christopher Hatton of Corfe Castle. But it
was Isaac Taylor's large-scale map of Dorset (1796) that gave so much accurate detail,
approaching the standard of the future Ordnance Survey one-inch maps just after the
turn of the century.

7

The Sea; Boney's Threat

Imagine that it is October 1788. Across the Channel come the distant rumblings of revolution, but we are about our lawful occasions. We are aboard the market boat from the port of Poole bound for Swanwich in the Isle of Purbeck; a fair breeze fills the sails and speeds us across Studland bay close to the bastions of Handfast Point. There stands Old Harry and his wife, and other pillars of chalk that following centuries will erode. The waves batter ceaselessly at the base of the cliffs; white foam breaks in the resounding cavern of Parson's Barn and other caves, which will later fall in and be transformed into yawning gaps between the chalk stacks. It is not so difficult to believe that these foreland cliffs in prehistoric times joined those of the Isle of Wight, and that Old Harry and the Needles were then as one.

We sail on towards our destination. Wrecks of many centuries lie not far beneath us. The foam at the base of the cliff is 'in the shape of heads, shoulders and arms of snowy whiteness, apparently struggling to rise from the deeps, and ever sinking back to their old levels again, reminding an observer of a drowning scene in a picture of the Deluge'.[1]

With a shudder we remember that it is only three winters since, on 6 January 1786, the *Halsewell*, East Indiaman, bound from London to Bengal, encountered a storm off the Isle of Wight; becoming unmanageable, she struck the Purbeck coast near Seacombe and was dashed to pieces on the treacherous rocks with the loss of 168 lives.

But it is not long before we enter the calmer waters of Swanwich bay and, looking astern, see the familiar face of the Bollard, 'the cliff rounding off at the top in vegetation like a forehead with low-grown hair'.[2] The bay discloses the softer prospect of green fields above an amphitheatre of low red and yellow cliffs with (unlike in later centuries) no sea wall, no beach huts, no hotels or villas, and few people. One or two isolated grey stone cottages crouch near the strand and, to the north, on the slopes below Ballard Down, nestles the ancient farmhouse of Whitecliff. Further inland we may just discern the old manor house of Godlingston, half hidden in the trees. Nearer at hand, a stream runs down to the beach from the mill pond at idyllic Ulwell, the sleepy hamlet lying on the road through the hills to Studland.

Swanwich lies 'snug between two headlands as between a finger and thumb'.[3] The thumb of the Bollard we have passed; the finger of Peveril Point lies on our port bow with its cruel ledges of tumbled marble and rag, like a jagged nail, stretching out beyond the bay eager to catch the unwary mariner on the ebb tide. An old battery ready to receive the Spanish Armada has been washed away by the sea, but now there are new fortifications in case of trouble with France. The hillside above us is 'quarried, like some gigantic rabbit burrow, with the stone workings of seven hundred years'.[4]

We tie up at the quay, built a few years since by the parish at a cost of some £300, the quarriers giving the stone and a day's work each.[5] As we make our way from the quay into the town we first pass the old stone farmhouse called White Hall, with its nearby dairy, pond and Tap alehouse.[6] Next we come to the imposing Great House facing the bay, built by the stone merchant John Chapman some sixty years ago.

Stone, fish and ale

This stretch of the shore is banked up with tons of stone, ready for shipment. But Swanwich is still also very much a 'fisher town',[7] and this month of October is the height of the herring season. The enlightened Mr William Morton Pitt of Encombe, M.P. for Dorset, has this year established the industry here, with the help of several reputable merchants. Buildings have been erected for smoking and curing the herring, and the quality of the dried fish is considered equal to any in the market. They are in part disposed for Portsmouth, London and elsewhere. In addition Mr Pitt, 'animated by a desire to draw off the demoralization of smuggling, and to develop the natural resources of the place, established at considerable loss to himself a factory at Kingston for the manufacture of flax and hemp to twine, cordage, dowlas, sail-cloth and rope'.[8] At this time he employs more than two hundred people.

Resuming our progress we come, a short way beyond the mansion, to the cliff which not long since stood above the beach by a dozen feet or so, but from which the sea has been in retreat. Here stands the *White Hart*, built and occupied by the Haysom family fishermen and members of the Ancient Order of Marblers. Bearing inland, the mile-long High Street begins, comprising virtually all this town-aspiring village. Nearly all the cottages have stone-tiled roofs and walls of rubble, many of them whitewashed, and much of the timber in them won from wrecks. Only one or two of the larger houses are built of ashlar (fully-dressed stone). We pass, or perhaps pause at, several plentiful inns and alehouses, the *Ship*, the *White Swan* and *Red Lion* on our left, the *Anchor* (the posting inn) on the right. Just beyond the inn is the smithy, with a stone-pitched crossing opposite. The street is an unpaved highway of deep ruts made by the spanned wheels of the heavy stone-carts, a quagmire in winter and choking with dust in summer. Ship Lane, East Drove and Bullhouse Lane, which drop down to join the High Street on the left, form the droves from the farms and quarries on the south hillside.

John Wesley

The street mounts the hill in a series of minor switchbacks or 'knaps' passing, on the left, old Purbeck House and, on the right, at the foot of a flight of steps, a row of cottages; in one of them John Wesley stayed in 1774 during his first mission to Swanwich, whither he had been brought by Mary Burt, wife of Robert Burt, a local stonemason.[9] Wesley came through Corfe Castle where he

> preached in a meadow near the town to a deeply attentive congregation gathered from all parts of the island. I afterwards met the society, artless and teachable and full of good desires ... In the evening I preached in a meadow near Swanwich to a still larger congregation ... few of the Society (between 30 and 40 in number) appeared to be convinced of sin. I fear that the preachers have been more studious to please than to waken.

In 1787 Wesley had returned to the town, having been driven by adverse weather to shelter in the bay for a few days. When he came ashore he went to the low-ceilinged, upstairs room used by his followers, opposite the *New Inn*, and saw that it was not big enough for his meeting. He was offered the use of the Independents' chapel by the minister, William Sedcole,[10] who was 'married with many children' and by a mutual arrangement lived at the Rectory, while the rector, Richard Williams MA, a young bachelor, lived in a glebe cottage in the High Street. Wesley wrote in his diary, 'Swanage, 1787, Monday August 13th. In the evening I preached in the Presbyterian Meeting House, not often I believe so well filled, and afterwards passed half-an-hour very agreeably with the Minister in the Parsonage house which he rents, a neat retired house with a delightful garden.'

Parish pump and church

Continuing up the High Street and over Spring Hill knap, we pass on our right the *New Inn* which, like most inns of that name, is very old-established.[11] After negotiating the Narrows, where the width of the street between the houses is hardly wide enough for one cart, we come on the right to Belmont and the Independents' chapel where Wesley preached. Just beyond this point is the centre of Swanwich where Upabout (Hopabout) Lane ascends to the south, and Church Hill falls steeply to the north from its junction with the Street: here stands the town pump on a circle of steps. Lower down is the mill pond with its antique cottages and, at the far end, the mill house. The church tower nearby is plain and unembattled and has the appearance more of a fortress than a religious building. Attached to it is a nave and chancel of varied antiquity, with some hoary headstones in the churchyard. We pause to

32 A sketch by Alfred Dawson, *c.*1882, of the Brook (La Trenchye) below Purbeck House and the *New Inn*. The door shown in the 'great wall of Swanage' was one of several which gave access to the 'creek'.

admire a more recent one, beautifully carved, to the memory of Katherine Henrietta, daughter of Timothy and Mary Chinchen,[12] who died 3 March 1781 aged one year and three months, with the following bitter-sweet verse:

Behold sweet infancy from Earth is fled, Nipt in the bud, to mingle with the dead;
Permitted by an all prevailing pow'r To bloom, to wither, as the tender flow'r;
Yet mourn not friends, for know the lovely clay Is snatched from evil, to eternal day;
'Tis vanish'd hence, but only to unite With saints in endless mansions of delight.

33   A Walter Pouncy photograph showing haymaking above Newton Manor near the Priest's Way, *c.*1890.

The lane winds down Paradise Hill, round the east end of the church and past some cottages on the left by the brook, where the Manwell family live, and on the right the 'neat retired' rectory with its old tithe barn and 'delightful garden' of which Wesley wrote. We now come to the ancient ford and narrow bridge where there is a watering place, and where cattle graze in the oft-flooded water meadows. On the other side the leafy lane leads up the hill to Northbrook farm, thence to Ulwell and Studland, but for the present we retrace our steps to Church Hill and regain the High Street. Here we turn right past the *Black Swan* with its decorative wrought ironwork, and come to a fork in the road at another smithy. The left-hand cart road is the Priest's Way, leading across the fields and along the hill for four miles to Worth Matravers.

34   The Narrows in the High Street, *c.*1900. On the extreme left is the house which was used as the first hospital in Swanage. The cottages beyond have been restored, but all the buildings on the right were demolished after bombing during the Second World War.

The Quarries

The quarry tracks run from south to north into the Priest's Way, the main artery for the stone waggons from the Herston and Langton quarries. It avoids the steep hills on the main road at Coombe, Steps and Langton Matravers. The quarry droves on the hill form a peculiar pattern, each having tributary tracks.

35 Upper High Street, 1906, with the *Black Swan* on the right and, in the distance, the spire of the Methodist church. Note Cleall's horse and cart from Corfe village.

This is because the hillside has been divided into farms, each separated from its neighbour by a continuous straight wall without break or gateway. The payment of a royalty allows way-leave only on the one farm, so that all the quarry tracks on that piece of land run into the main drove and so down into the high street.[13]

From its junction with the Priest's Way, the highway continues by the lower right-hand fork and is here at some height above the valley. This is (Carrant's) Court Hill, and we see amid the elms the high road falling and rising again in the distance, over Newton knap towards the hamlet of Herston and the turnpike gate at the western end of the parish. But now, at a triangular open space, we turn down a steep road branching to the right where there is a pond and spring. Above the farm are two rows of humble cottages; one of the upper dwellings is occupied by John Mowlem, a worthy marbler, and his wife Hannah. They already have two daughters but it is 12 October 1788, and today has been born to them their first son: to be named after his father, John Mowlem, and destined to become a Swanage man of renown.

On this note, the reverie fades.

Mowlems and Burts

John Mowlem senior had married Hannah Froom in 1782. She had been brought up at Ulwell mill 'whence she rode daily to Corfe to school to one Mr Burt who was a first-rate schoolmaster'. She no doubt helped to teach her own children, the boys being John, Joseph, Robert and James. Her husband John may have attended the dame school at Church Hill[14] but in any case he would have been at work in the quarries at a tender age. There seems to be no record of a Mowlem family quarry, but his friend Robert Burt had his in the Common Fields. It is also said that both families worked at Tilly Whim.[15] John Mowlem (junior) recorded in his diary,[16] 22 February 1847, 'Walked to my brother's quarry. There was room for thankfulness. It was where my forefathers worked, but though the selfsame woodbine is still there, alas, where are those who toiled there when I was a boy?' 'My brother' meant his brother-in-law, Robert Burt. His own brother, Robert Mowlem, was the only one of the family who remained in Swanage, but it seems that both the Burts and the Mowlems worked in the same quarry. If it was not Tilly Whim, then the only clue comes from the Swanage tithe map returns, which indicate that Robert Burt was occupying plots on the North and South Common Fields.[17] Robert Burt senior had established himself as a stone merchant, and in 1803 opened a stone, coal and bakery business in a quaint cottage in the lower High Street, which survived until 1908.[18] John Mowlem senior kept a general goods shop in the west wing of a

36   John Mowlem (1788-1868), in an 1823 portrait by Ramsay Richard Reinagle, R.A.

'picturesque old-time residence with a grand old balcony supported on round stone pillars and caps'. This was on the site of Albion Place in the 'Square'. The portico appears to have been enclosed at some time to form a shop.[19]

The stone trade

A contemporary account of the trade given by John Claridge[20] in 1793 states that

> upwards of 400 people are employed in digging and tooling the stone which is raised here from pits, some 20 others 40 feet deep; they are not open at the top, but are underminded and underbuilt; it is excellent stone for walling, floors, steps, and in particular for foot pavement for towns, for tombstones, troughs, and feet and caps for rick staddles. Another sort of stone is here found and used for pitching streets, and some of the thin stones on the tops of these quarries are used for covering of buildings: about 50,000 tons are annually shipped at Swanage.

But this figure does not tally with Hutchins' 14,000 tons a year for 1764-71, nor with G.A. Cooke's report[21] that

> Mr Chinchen of Swanage estimates the exports of Purbeck stone at 38,750 tons in the five years preceding 1801. The sort is mostly flag stones for paving, and the great part are sent to London; the quantity carried inland is about 150 tons a year. The men employed in stone work earn about 20s. per week, and including boys amount to 300.

Claridge reported that quarrymen earned about 2s. 6d. per day in summer and 2s. in winter. The price of best cliff stone delivered in the vessels was 12s. per ton; paving stone was 24s. per 100 square feet at Swanage. Freightage to London cost 6s. 6d. per ton, but this rose to 8s. 6d. during war. Pitching stone for streets was priced 5s. per ton at the pit; 200 stones to the ton would pave 100 square feet. Tiling stone was 8s. per ton at Swanage: 'this stone is sometimes burnt into lime, which is said to be of the best quality and preferred to any other in the kingdom, and is sold at 7d. per bushel or 14d. per cwt.' A ground rent average of about 6d. per ton was paid to the landowner for all stone raised.

The Tilly Whim quarries adjacent to Howcombe were still in production as young John Mowlem was growing up and learning the stone trade. In the cliff quarries gunpowder was employed, and it was possibly at Tilly Whim that he first learnt the use of it.[22]

France declared war on England in 1793. At the outbreak, economic conditions in Swanage were basically good. Hutchins (2nd edn) said:

> There is an appearance of affluence, especially on Sundays, in the inhabitants of this town. They earn great wages, and lay out a greater proportion of their pay in the articles of food and clothing that is practised in neighbouring places; yet the people are improvident, and spend all they get, and when any accident happens in the quarries to the father of a family, or he falls ill, causing only a short suspension of work, they instantly apply to the parish for relief. The rates have increased surprisingly of late years. The only disadvantages at Swanwich to counterbalance very material advantages are, scarcity of fuel for the poor, and the presence of masters not paying their workmen in ready money, but compelling them to take goods from the shops. Most of the poor women and children are employed in spinning flax for the Kingston manufactory, and are assiduous and industrious.

The Fencibles

But now Napoleon threatened invasion, and in 1798 William Morton Pitt of Encombe drew up a report on the Coast of Dorsetshire.[23] On the prospect of invasion he wrote:

> Swanage Bay lies between Peveril Point and Handfast Point. There is a regular Battery of seven Nine-Pounders at Peveral[24] which protects the Town and Road, with a Watch-House and Magazine, but there is no Gunner there, nor ammunition, and Privateers have frequently made prizes within the range of the Battery. Swanage Bay can hardly be considered as a probable place for the Enemy to land in force, though very likely to be insulted by a Privateer. They could have no object which would not be better answered by disembarking in Weymouth Bay … On Handfast Point there is a Signal Post, with a Battery of two NinePounders on top of the Cliff. They are quite unserviceable, and have no carriages, nor is there any Platform or Breastwork. No Watch House or Magazine would be wanted here, on account of the vicinity of the Signal Post.

Five years later all the talk was still of 'Boney' and where he would land. The Government had drawn up a plan of defence in case of invasion, under which the county was divided into ten, and each division into hundreds, towns and tythings. Nathan Chinchen, stone merchant, of Swanage, was appointed Captain of the hundred of Rowbarrow, and among his duties he had to make a classified census of the inhabitants on official forms

> shewing the Number of Males, how engaged, and capable of being engaged. Also Aliens, Quakers, and Females of all Ages; distinguishing the Number who, from Age, Infancy, Infirmity, or otherwise, are incapable of active Service, or of removing themselves in case of Invasion.

The returns are dated 14 October 1803. There are 71 sheets, 28 of which apply to Swanage and 11 to Herston and Langton Matravers.[25]

There are 38 categories enumerating, among others, clergymen, justices, constables, volunteers aged 17-55 already engaged as cavalry, artillery, infantry, riflemen and 'sea fencibles', and those men of similar age capable of bearing arms, including a column for 'Pioneers or Artificers'. Then come men of all ages chosen to act as guides, waggon conductors and drivers, and to take charge of live and dead stock. The list continues with millers, bakers, aliens, Quakers, seamen or seafaring men, males under 17 or over 55, and those incapable of active service or of removing themselves. All persons are numbered, and we duly find John Mowlem (a Pioneer), his wife Hannah, daughter Sarah (the second daughter had died), and their four boys: John (b.1788), Joseph (1791),

37   An aerial photograph of Swanage and Durlston Bay, showing Ballard Cliff, Peveril Point and Durlston Head. In the foreground are George Burt's Durlston Park, Castle and Great Globe and, on the left, Tilly Whim caves and the boundary with Eightholds.

Robert (1793) and James (1797), all under seventeen. Sarah Mowlem later married George Manwell III. In the Census we also find the Manwell and Burt families, who later play a prominent part in our story.

In the event of imminent invasion, the inhabitants of each division within 15 miles of the coast were to agree upon a place of rendezvous.[26] Everything likely to be of use to the enemy which could not be removed was to be destroyed in order to deprive him of means of subsistence: a sort of scorched-earth policy. A government officer was sent to consult Chinchen about the best position for a signal station for giving the alarm of an enemy landing. He suggested Round Down, west of Tilly Whim, where were duly provided a flagstaff for a signal by day, and a rick of wood faggots for a fire at night. The station is clearly shown on the first edition of the O.S. one-inch map of the district (published in 1811), and the Royal Commission on Historical Monuments has recorded the remains of foundations of five or six small buildings, now within the Durlston Country Park. There were further signal posts on Ballard Down and St Aldhelm's Head. Chinchen was granted letters of marque by the government, and had a small yacht to cruise around the coast.

WMH relates that on 1 June 1794 an engagement took place in the Channel between the British and French fleets. Ten of the enemy's ships were dismasted and seven were taken. Lord Howe had the glory of towing into Portsmouth six ships of the line: a superb sight visible from Peveril Point, and calculated to stir the spectators with immense pride and rejoicing. 'I well remember when a youth hearing this old inhabitant, Mrs Hixson, telling the story and singing a song which was composed to commemorate the battle.'

There were now some hundred volunteer 'sea-fencibles' – a sort of 'Dad's Army – ready to guard the coast. Their duty was to use boarding-pikes when the enemy was landing. On Sunday morning the fencibles, the infantry and their officers marched to church and packed their pikes and muskets in the tower. After service they all marched to the Fort where they drilled for an hour, watched by the town, and then went home to dinner. WMH tells us that this is how Marshall Row, behind the Hotel, got its name. These were patriotic days for Swanage, but in 1805 came the victory of Trafalgar, so the sea-fencibles were no longer needed and in due course were disbanded.

The Press Gang

But if the threat of invasion had receded, the arrival of the Press Gang was still to be feared. Young John Mowlem, when 13, hid in a house at Knitson, a farm below North Hill, to avoid being taken for the navy.

The only way for eligible men to avoid being impressed, short of hiding, was to provide themselves with a Protection Certificate. Francis Haysom of Swanage, who was aged 19 and five feet five inches tall, with a fair complexion, brown hair, and light eyes, was issued with one because he was master of the fishing-smack *Hart*, of the burthen of two tons.[27] The exemption was issued under an Act of Parliament 'for the better supplying the Cities of London and Westminster with fish and to reduce the present exorbitant Price thereof and to protect and encourage Fishermen'. The Haysom family still possesses a handsome rifle with a brass plate on the butt engraved: 'Presented to Francis Haysom by Nathan Chinchen'. According to the Census form of 1803, there were 58 persons living in Swanage with the name of Haysom. This was out of a total population of 1,173.[28]

Tilly Whim

While 'Boney' threatened, demand for stone continued strongly: particularly cliff stone for fortifications. Around 1808 there arose an interesting dispute regarding the quarries, including Tilly Whim in Eightholds, and the legal opinion of Mr John Dampier was sought[29] by the absentee Lord of the Manor, W.L.P. Taunton Esq. Unfortunately the learned lawyer's reply is not to hand. It was recited that

> great quantities of stone are dug in numerous quarries in Swanage parish by persons pretending to hold their quarries by a Peculiar Tenure, viz. by a parol grant licence to dig paying certain antient prices or sums for the stone they raise according to the quality ... being abut 1/30th part of the value of the stone when wrought. They say that their interest is not determinable by Notice, is descendable to the next of kin, alienable, and only determined by entirely omitting to work for a year and a day. There are now 13 or 14 of these quarries on Mr Taunton's manor ... It is not known how long these quarries have been opened but probably they are not all of the same antiquity. From enquiries made at Swanage ... nothing definite could be learnt but that most of them had been open longer than any living in the parish can remember.

Mr Taunton considered that several trespassers had opened quarries without licence, and in 1805

> caused notices to quit to be served on such of the quarrymen as the attorney could catch outside of their Holes, and soon after commenced an Ejectment and obtained a conditional judgement against about 8 of them, since which he has done no act to recognize the tenancy of any of the persons served with notice. Thinking that, under the grant of a manor, the Lord *pro tempore* was entitled to work or lease these quarries.

Mr Taunton leased to Henry Gillingham the elder, Samuel Marsh, Peter Marsh and Thomas Randell, stone merchants,

> All those two several ancient pieces of land immemorially used as stone quarries called or known by the name of Tilly Whim quarries, for 16 years ... to dig out hew win and work the stone ... paying each quarter for every ton of stone 6d. (3d. per ton for pitchers, 2s. per 100 sq. ft. for pavings, 4s. for steps, 2d. per pair of staddle stones, 1s. 6d. per ton for cylindrical stones for rollers, columns etc.).

38   A unique engraving by T. Webster in 1816 showing Tilly Whim quarry with hauling gear still in place for lowering stone into barges for export.

Mention is made of the stone being shipped, and the lessees were to 'remove and throw over the cliff into the sea all useless stone earth clay and rubbish'.

Mr Taunton had recently obtained a new lease of Eightholds from the Dean and Chapter of Exeter, ground landlords, for 21 years from 1808, but on 2 March the Chapter Clerk wrote that he had omitted to inform him that the Chapter had made a rule in all future leases to reserve the rights to timber and minerals. Mr Taunton appeared to be hoisted with his own petard, and was anxiously asking his lawyer 'in what manner would you advise me to meet the announced intention of the Dean and Chapter of reserving minerals?'

Soon after the cessation of the war the Tilly Whim quarries were closed;[30] indeed half-finished blocks still stand in the caves. As to the inland 'quarry holes', perhaps Mr Taunton took no further action in view of the edict from Exeter adverse to himself.

Hard Times

Opportunities in Swanage were not so good now.

> A set of old farm accounts show that in 1813 the poor rates in Swanage were 13s. 4d. in the pound! This was at the end of the great war with France, when the demand for stone for fortifications suddenly ceased, and the most bitter want was caused among the quarriers. In these farm accounts a guinea is charged for every day's ploughing, with three horses. The rent of land seems to have been about the same as what it is now, but wages were very low.[31]

The underground quarries were less affected by the fall in demand for stone than those at the cliff. Although the Tilly Whim quarries were closed, they continued to be used for more nefarious operations.

There were other ideas beginning to be expressed. Charles Robinson of Newton wrote in 1881:[32]

> In turning over some old papers as far back as 13 April 1812, a letter addressed by the gentleman who was then owner of Eightholds Farm to his agent shows remarkable foresight: 'While you are at Swanage, if the weather permits, have the goodness to go up into the fields on the ascent of the hill, just at the south of the street, and you will see what a very pretty situation for building, and how convenient for the carriage of materials (viz. stone and lime down hill from the quarries, and slate and timber from the sea, and sand and mortar from the shore) this place affords … if you know any persons from Poole or elsewhere who would like a marine retirement and have money to spend on building, be so good as to improve the opportunity and recommend the place.'

But it was to be 70 years before any houses were built upon this estate.

8

Andrew Bell, Rector

The celebrated Revd Andrew Bell DD was appointed Rector of Swanage in 1801.[1] Backed by influential friends he had gone to India in 1787 to lecture and teach, and there he was appointed superintendent of the new Madras Asylum for male orphans, founded by the East India Company for the education of sons of military men. There he hit on the idea of self-help; seeing children fingering the alphabet in sand on the seashore, he brought sand-trays into the classroom and introduced a 'do-it-yourself' system, whereby the pupils largely taught each other.

With a fortune of £25,000 from judicious investment, Dr Bell returned to England in 1796 and published a Report on his 'Madras System' which, he said, 'was alike fitted to reduce the expense of tuition, to abridge the labour of the master, and to expedite the progress of the scholar': surely admirable aims! The new system was introduced at St Botolph's charity school, Aldgate, in 1798. Child education was now his passion.

Andrew Bell sought a resting-place and found it in Swanage. The living was then worth £600 p.a. plus about £200 for Worth Matravers. He preached his first sermon on Christmas Day 1801. The Rector evidently found that the inhabitants of Swanage were 'orderly and well-disposed, and from their insulated position preserved much of primitive simplicity and hospitality'. But it was clear that one section of the population was not so responsible.[2]

The Blind House

As usual, things were not what they were in the good old days, and social conditions in Swanage at the turn of the century gave cause for concern. The rougher element was getting out of hand. There was much rowdyism and horseplay in the street, and general bad behaviour to such an extent that at a Vestry on 25 November 1802 it was decided to build a House of Correction for offenders, and it was agreed:

> That the House of Confinement be built on the north side of the Church Tower, 5½ feet by 7 feet in the clear; Secondly: that the said house be built by voluntary subscription; Thirdly: that a number of the Parishioners form themselves into a Committee for the purpose of enforcing good conduct and regular behaviour, consisting of the churchwardens and overseers for the time being.

The Blind House, as it was called, no doubt because of its lack of windows, has been moved at least twice from its original site. WMH recalled that it subsequently stood in the south-west corner of the churchyard from which it was reached down a long flight of steps. It had thick walls and a stout, nail-studded door, over which was 'perhaps the

39 The Blind House, photographed in 1943 by the Royal Commission on Historical Monuments. Note the signs of bomb damage behind the building, and wartime notices. On the right is the pump at Frogwell erected by George Burt.

most canting inscription that the wit of man could devise'. It read: 'Erected for the Prevention of Vice and Immorality by the Friends of Religion and Good Order, AD 1803'. Perhaps the rector chose the wording.

> The proper way to gain access to this place was to get drunk and lie down in the street, whereupon the constable would drag you down Church Hill, down the steps and place you inside, where you could make your own bed with a little dirty straw on the cold stones. The constable would lock the door and leave the prisoner to the tender mercies of the quarry boys who would bombard the oak door with stones for the benefit of the poor wretch inside.[5]

Nevertheless the door has survived to the present day.

In 1805 there were further complaints of disorderly conduct by the young people particularly on Sunday evenings, 'as to disturb and annoy Peaceable and well-disposed part of the inhabitants'. It was proposed that James Allen and Thomas Carter be sworn Constables or Watchmen to attend in the streets every night (if necessary) until 12 o'clock. They were to be paid 3s. 6d. per week each by general rate, and were to be empowered to take up all disorderly persons and confine them till morning and then, if necessary, take them before the magistrates.

The Swanage philosopher

Dr Bell soon met an extraordinary character, Thomas Manwell, who lived at the foot of Church Hill, opposite the Rectory. His wife told the rector that her husband spent all his spare money on books and all his leisure in their perusal, though he had been a quarryman. In 1814 Thomas's brother, George Manwell II, gave some details of the family history to his son Henry: Joseph Manwell had come to Swanage from Winterborne Stickland early in the 18th century as a carpenter. His son George Manwell I was only one year old when his father died in 1723 and, at the age of 11, without much education, he was apprenticed to a quarryman. 'Father was a man of uncommon strong memory, could easily have learned anything, but had no chance for improvement and scarcely or never wrote his name till after he was working about Westminster Bridge.'[4]

George Manwell had an excellent ear and learnt the art of singing from a visiting music teacher who gave similar lessons to other young men, 'and a foundation was thus laid for the musical knowledge which has since been much cultivated in Swanage'. The second son, Joseph, learnt the rudiments from his father and was subsequently celebrated for his knowledge of music. 'He frequently composed tunes while at work in the quarries, and kept humming them till it was time to go home, when he would make all possible haste to write them out while they were fresh in his memory.' He selected poetry and set it to music, played the 'cello and was much given to the composition of sacred pieces'. But John Mowlem wrote of him:

> He, poor man, had an idea he could compose music and passed a great deal of time in arranging in score. His sons were his band. He sang as well as he could, then found fault, then sang again, then altered a few notes until some of the quick passages looked as black as a thundercloud. He did his best and all his arts were moral, but he was *not* a master of music.[5]

Of Thomas Manwell, the eldest son, often called the Swanage philosopher, it is said that he never attended any school after he was eight years old, when he was taken to the quarries to learn the stonecutting trade.

> He was of a delicate constitution, and his father, perceiving this and his great love for reading, kindly supplied him with a few books. By the time he was 14 he had instructed himself fully in the theory of navigation, and before he was 17 he had constructed a sundial, and afterwards made one for the church.[6] He continued his trade until the French Revolution when from the excellent character he bore and from his scientific knowledge he was appointed midshipman under the lieutenant of the signalpost at Round Down, which appointment he held, except during the ten months peace of Amiens. The solitude of this place was well suited to his habits and feelings, and gave him an opportunity of following his favourite studies.[7]

The 2nd edition of Hutchins' *History of Dorset* (1794) acknowledged the assistance rendered by Thomas Manwell.

The three brothers Thomas, Joseph and George, were 'men of no ordinary powers of mind'. They spent hours in conversing on philosophy, astronomy, history, the arts and sciences. An old lady said that

> Thomas was always talking about thunder and lightning, earthquakes, mountains, eclipses (which he calculated with great exactness) and other matters which we could not understand. Had he received a liberal education he would doubtless have distinguished himself in scientific pursuits; he does not, however, seem to have possessed much ambition, or indeed ever wished to quit his native place.

Dr Bell often visited him or invited him to the rectory for conversation on philosophic and scientific subjects.

When Thomas Manwell died in 1822 at the age of 70, Bell composed the epitaph on his tombstone. Unfortunately very little of the lettering is still decipherable:

> Near this stone lie the earthly remains of Mr Thomas Manwell who (unassisted by education) by the strength of a superior genius, and Nature for his guide, broke thro' the barrier to literature, and acquired a degree of knowledge which might have rank'd him with the first Philosophers of the Age; but being a child of solitude, his retired meditations were far dearer to him than the requirement of Fame, and if Charity, Humility, and Meekness, with Faith in a Redeemer, be Christianity, he was a perfect Christian.

Straw-plait

One of the rector's favourite walks was through Swanage Field, where many quarrymen worked, to Round Down. At the signal-post he would find his old friend Thomas Manwell 'whom the Rector treated more as a brother than as an ordinary acquaintance'.[8] When returning home one day he was grieved to see two young women at a quarry doing the work of a donkey, pushing round the spack of the capstan to wind the quarr cart to the surface with its burden of stone, up to their ankles in mud and clay, because their old father had no one else to help him. This, together with the sights he saw when he looked in at the doors of the poor cottages, determined the rector to do what he could to alleviate the suffering of this parish.

Dr Bell had in mind the straw-plaiting industry which had been introduced into Christchurch in 1803 and also at Wyke near Weymouth. Meanwhile two daughters of Mr Cole, a Swanage stone merchant, tried making bonnets for themselves with common threshed straw; they then obtained suitable straw from London and a machine for splitting it. Dr Bell was delighted and showed their work to Mrs Bell. Mr Cole proposed to have his daughters properly instructed if the committee would place the parish children with them at 6d. per week. The proposal was accepted and the Cole girls went to Wyke for instruction, soon returning to open a school in their father's house. They started with 12 children, and Dr Bell at once introduced his Madras system, visiting the school almost daily. Monitors were appointed to each class and the pupils soon numbered thirty. The first part of the day was devoted to reading and writing, and the remainder to straw-plaiting. One of the sisters soon died, but the other continued. The rector suggested that Miss Cole might instruct the children without charge on condition she could sell their work. This was agreed to, and now there were nearly 90 children.

Dr Bell was still organising everything. He brought back from London patterns for the use of the school. He was the first person in the parish to set the fashion of wearing a straw hat, which at first excited much notice but was soon followed by others. Miss Cole gave up the school from ill health but married James Stickland, a stonemason. He had to travel widely and she extended the sale of the school's products to surrounding towns.[9] It was said that over 4,000 bonnets were sold annually, and plait sufficient for 8,000 more.

Previous to the introduction of this manufacture, knitting had been the chief female employment and had been mentioned by Defoe in 1724. There were schools where knitting was taught, and numbers of stockings were annually disposed of. But straw-plait annihilated knitting and was much more profitable, finding its way into almost every house in the town. For many years the industry flourished and it was a common sight to see cottagers seated at their doors working on the fine straw-plait which was made into hats and baskets. It gained a great reputation and women set off for distant shops with their produce. Communication was mostly by sea, and passengers were carried by 'hoys' to the Isle of Wight, Portsmouth and further afield. Dates of sailing and return were uncertain, and many were the adventures of these early female commercial travellers. The trade could be said to be worldwide, as bonnets were exported to Newfoundland, the Cape, Madras and Calcutta.

Straw-plait benefited Swanage except for the barter system, which meant women were often paid in clothing instead of money. Their health was injured by the sedentary nature of their employment; as the hands of the plaiter must not be hardened, domestic concerns also tended to get neglected. When other occupations were thrown open to women, straw-plaiting declined, but new life was infused into the craft when a Frenchman took over the business, bringing new ideas and patterns from the Continent. The family had great success, and in 1910 plaiting was still being carried on at Mrs Colleau's in Station Road and at the Straw Basket Shop in the lower High Street.[10]

The dreaded Smallpox

An epidemic in 1761-2 had resulted in 53 deaths from smallpox in Swanage, as shown in the burial register. Dr Bell was something of a social reformer as well as an educationist, and it was said that he introduced vaccination in Swanage about 1803 'when he brought some vaccine matter from Edinburgh after a visit there', though people were as afraid of that as they were of smallpox. It may be noted, however, that an entry in the Vestry minute book for 17 April 1796 (before Bell's arrival) reads: 'Benefit of inoculation to be offered to the poor for 5/- a 6d. per week.' It seems that no action was taken, for a further minute of 25 November 1802 reads: 'That the Vaccine Inoculation be introduced and recommended in the Parish', and is signed 'A. Bell, Rector' (his first signature in the book). He asked Mr Gover, the schoolmaster, to enquire whether any parents would have their children vaccinated. Mrs Webber agreed, and the same day Dr Bell vaccinated the boy and Mrs Bell the girl at the Rectory, with favourable results. That spring they carried out over 200 vaccinations and visited the people afterwards to mark their progress. A later rector checked and found that not a single individual vaccinated by Bell contracted the disease.

Bell became acquainted with Benjamin Jesty of Downshay Farm, Worth Matravers, and championed his claim to the original discovery of vaccination, rather than that of Edward Jenner. Bell drew up a paper, dated 1 August 1803, in support of Jesty's claim. Jesty had inoculated his wife and two babies in 1774 at Yetminster. In 1805 he went to London in his country rig with his son Robert, at the invitation of the Jennerian Society, when his portrait was painted and he was presented with some gold-mounted lancets.[11]

On Sunday 15 July 1806 Dr Bell preached the same sermon twice 'On the subject of inoculation, in support of Benjamin Jesty of Downshay, whose discovery of the efficacy of the cowpock against smallpox is so often forgotten by those who have heard of Dr Jenner'. Soon Bell had vaccinated 658 people of all ages between one and 78; Thomas Stickland was the oldest 'patient' who had a horror of smallpox. Bell set schoolmistresses and others vaccinating in the neighbouring parishes.

The Educationists

Dr Bell found little in the way of education when he arrived in Swanage. Child labour on the farms and in the quarries was universal. The new rector naturally interested himself in the Sunday schools which had been established, chiefly through the efforts of William Morton Pitt, the philanthropic M.P. for Dorset, and Mr T. Everett who was secretary to the Purbeck District Committee of the Sunday School Society; the movement had been launched in 1780 by Robert Raikes. The master of one of the two schools was John Stickland whose father, Thomas Stickland, was the most skilful stonecutter in Swanage, his work commanding a higher price than any other. He had three sons and all were musical, especially as singers. Subscribers to the school fell off, so the curate, Mr Gent, established a regular subscription but this worked little better. Mr and Mrs Gent also helped personally with the school and Stickland persisted, providing books and giving instruction in sacred music. 'He was a thoughtful man, and the children were much attached to him.'

Dr Bell did not find it easy to establish his system. 'He hammered it into them,' John Stickland would say, 'like a blacksmith on an anvil.' He was not afraid to speak his mind: finding the rector's perambulations up and down the room and his beetle-browed countenance affecting the attention of the children, he had recourse to request him 'to be pleased to pitch himself'.[12]

Stickland's successor was also a quarryman, Warren by name. He was better educated than Stickland and not so prejudiced in favour of old ways. He continued in charge until 1809, when he was appointed to a more important post by Dr Bell. The children were again put under the care of their old master until his death in 1813. He was succeeded by his son Thomas whose name appears in the books as master until 1828.

Bell found the going slow, but in 1806 things were improving. An annual examination was held at the Rectory when parents and the gentry met there and the children were given tea on the lawn. Dr Bell's 'love for children never left him'. There were 193 scholars for examination in 1808: more than an eighth of the population. This was Dr Bell's last anniversary there. In 1807 there were no less than 13 day schools in the parish in addition to the three Sunday schools, 'so that it certainly could not be said that Swanage was deficient in the opportunities of education'. One of these schools was kept by Mr Gover, who was also clerk and postmaster, manager of the benefit club, attorney, collector and accountant. He had 45 scholars, but, being busy elsewhere, he entrusted the school to a mere boy, and it got into a disorderly state. In 1806 Dr Bell succeeded in introducing

40   The Revd Andrew Bell D.D., Rector of Swanage from 1801-9.

his system into Gover's school and was delighted at the rapid improvement: 'In a word, the school astonished me and, in breaking up this day, I had many reward-books to give for desert'.

The Benefactor

Dr Bell also interested himself in the Friendly Society established in Swanage before his arrival. In 1806 it had 306 members and funds amounting to £3,000. He was a conscientious and zealous parish priest and a constant attender on the sick. He had 'friendly intercourse with all his parishioners, was bountiful in his charities and supplied the poor with a liberal hand'. An old man of 84 spoke of Bell in 1838: 'He was irritable and passionate in his temper and had plenty of fire, but the blaze was soon over and he had a better and warmer heart than most.' Another woman parishioner said of him after his death: 'the inhabitants, especially among the working class, are indebted for much of their present prosperity to his unwearying exertions in establishing the straw-plait manufactory.' However, he would not tolerate idleness in anyone, rich or poor. Although hospitable, he himself was frugal and remarkably abstemious. Perhaps the most marked feature in Bell's character was his love of money.[13] Concerning his marriage in 1800 to Agnes Barclay, daughter of a Scottish doctor, 'there is little information', but evidently Bell and his wife became estranged in 1806 following 'some unhappy dissensions', and a deed of separation was finally drawn up in 1815. De Quincy, in his Essay on *Coleridge*, gives an account of the persecution to which Bell was subjected by his wife. But Bell, vain, imperious and with tendency to miserliness, was more than half to blame.[14]

In the absence of much national enthusiasm for his 'Madras System', he continued to interest himself in parish work, stocked his garden with choice trees and made presents of their fruit. Some of the apathy was due to the rival 'Monitorial System' of Joseph Lancaster, a Quaker, which was projected with much greater drive and influence. Lancaster operated on a large scale and set up schools of hundreds of children. Although a nonconformist, he was called to audience with George III at Weymouth, who awarded him an annuity of £100 so that 'all children in my Realm might be able to write and read the Bible[15]'. Lancaster had stayed at Swanage for a few days and met Bell who regarded him with some amusement 'from the height of academic honours and experience'. Bell was not unduly worried at the rivalry, but Mrs Sarah Trimmer, a pamphleteer on religious and educational subjects, certainly was. It was said that 'she was trying to woo Dr Bell'.[16] She saw in him a means of preventing the undermining of the Church's authority by Lancaster and his supporters, and persuaded the Rector to come to London in 1807 to organise a campaign. 'It was in fact in great measure owing to her that Dr Bell was induced to leave his retirement in Swanage.'

A charity school was opened in Whitechapel, and Lewis Warren, a boy of 13 who had been one of his assistants in the Swanage Sunday school, was sent up to London to help. Dr Bell went up later, taking with him Mr Gover, whom he put in charge. In May 1807 Bell was licensed to leave his parish for two years, 'upon keeping a curate daily resident'. At this point the connection between Bell, Gover, the Manwells, and the Mowlem and Burt families becomes apparent. As children, they had all come under the influence of the rector and thus received a considerable amount of education.

The London connection

Henry Manwell, son of George Manwell II and nephew of Thomas the philosopher, was educated at Gover's school, as no doubt were his brother George III and sisters Laetitia, Susannah and Anne. At the age of 17 in 1804, Henry went to Portsmouth as a stonecutter on government works, then to Calshot Castle and on to London. From there he wrote a long and interesting letter to his sisters at Swanage which was shown to Dr Bell who expressed himself greatly pleased with it and observed: 'It is a pity this young man should have to work with his hands. He ought to have a better situation, and I shall do what I can to procure him one'. Just then Bell received a request from Dr Andrews, Bishop of London, to find 'a Lewis Warren (or, if it could be, one looking more *like a master)*' for the Offertory School, St James's. Dr Bell got the salary increased from £50 to £80, introduced Henry Manwell to the Bishop as a candidate, and he was duly appointed. He left his stonemasonry work at the R.N. School, Greenwich and Woolwich Arsenal[17] and took a course, visiting the schools in London which had adopted the Madras system, and soon becoming Bell's chief agent. 'He is an excellent youth, deserving of notice … See him and his school. You will see there a school in order, in all its parts, and a man to your mind.'

Manwell continued to give the greatest satisfaction, and it was not long before he obtained a better situation. In the summer of 1809 the master of the charity school, Marylebone, was appointed collector of the parish rates, and resigned. Manwell was advised of the vacancy and got the job. We hear little more of him in Southey's *Life of Bell*, but his story is picked up, curiously enough, by Frank Baines[18] who discovered, after much searching of directories and rate books, that Henry Manwell was by 1824 himself rate collector of St Marylebone, thus following in the footsteps of his predecessor at the charity school.

The 'System' in the New World

The story of Lewis Warren, the 13-year-old Swanage boy, is so extraordinary that it cannot be omitted. He was such a success with Dr Bell that he was sent to help schools in the Midlands, but he longed to see his home again. The Madras system was certainly spreading far and wide, and the Bishop of London now sought to introduce it to 'the Governors, Legislators and Proprietors of Plantations in the British West Indies'. The system was considered 'very suitable for educating Negro children (1) because one master suffices for each school, however numerous, and (2) because *Sunday alone* will suffice': i.e. school would not interfere with work in the plantations! Dr Bell was asked to recommend someone. Despite his father's reluctance, Lewis accepted the situation and received further instruction from Henry Manwell, as well as being confirmed by the bishop, who treated him with great kindness and supplied him with money and all necessaries for his voyage. Lewis Warren left in October, just before his 15th birthday. The bishop wrote to Bell:

> I pray God to prosper his voyage and mission; if he succeeds he will be the greatest blessing that ever was imported into the Islands. He will be ranked among the greatest benefactors to mankind, and (though it is a bold thing to say) he will be doing as much good in the Atlantic Ocean as Bonaparte is doing mischief on the Continent of Europe!

These extravagant expectations were not realised, but the bishop did not live to witness the result. Dr Bell was later asked to recommend other young men to follow in Warren's footsteps, but there were no developments, and nor is there much information about Warren's subsequent career. Soon after his arrival he seems to have made a good start, but no important results followed. This is not surprising in view of the opposition which any scheme for improving the moral and intellectual condition of the Negroes met with from the majority of planters. The sympathetic Mr Holder, who had looked with favour on the Madras system, sold his estates in 1815, and his successor was 'a gentleman of the island who paid no attention to education'. And there, far from his native Swanage, we must leave Lewis Warren, ignorant as we are of his eventual fate.

Swanage Rectory

Before his two years' leave of absence was up, Dr Bell realised that he must give up the Swanage living altogether, as the demands on his time and presence were increasing. He eventually secured the mastership of Sherburn Hospital, Durham, which enabled him to give undivided attention to his educational pursuits.

Bell's successor at Swanage in 1809 was the Revd Samuel Gale MA, a nominee of the Bishop of Durham.[19] He was 64 and does not appear to have been well-fitted to succeed so active a man as Bell. The change was regretted by not only the inhabitants of Swanage, but also by Mr Gale himself. In a letter to Dr Bell soon after his arrival in Swanage from Yorkshire, he wrote:

> You begin yours by saying you hope I am in love with Swanage ... In winter, as you too well know, you are up to the neck in puddle and mire, and in summer you are smothered with the dust ... I am in a sad mess. Since I have been here, the carpenters and bricklayers have never been from the house, outside and in ... Most of the frames of the windows are so rotten that they must have new ones ... I have told the bishop that instead of doing me a service the expense of this place will be the ruin of me; and I am most truly sorry that I was so great a fool as to come to it without having seen it, and well for me had it been at the bottom of the sea before I ever arrived at it ... I have had some passing invitations from some truly respectable persons to Lulworth etc., so that I shall get out of this place probably for the whole of the summer ... The bad roads, and having to send a dozen miles for a common hack chaise, make this a most sad place for an old man. I cannot see to make a pen, and this is one of Mr Gover's which I never can write with. I have no news of Swanage, as I never come into the town, having not even exchanged a dish of tea.

Mr Gale's curate, Mr Sanders, had been recommended by the bishop of Durham and was 'a man of ability and an active and exemplary clergyman'. He was 'very cordially

41   A photograph of the Rectory, *c.*1910, taken from the Tithe Barn. The south-east section, nearest to the camera, is the oldest part, probably built in the 16th century. The centre section dates from the 18th century, and the extension on the right from the 19th century. The Rectory became a private house in the 1920s.

received' but did not remain long in Swanage. Southey quotes from a letter addressed to Mr F. Warren (Lewis's father) by George Manwell:

> Dr Bell's loss is, I fear, irreparable ... We have now no more books given away, no encouragement for learning, no sympathising discourse. The schools are in rapid decline ... The Revd Mr Sanders had a manner of life and preaching truly evangelical, and had he continued here the church could not have contained the people that would have attended; and since the weather was getting fine, it was no uncommon thing for people to come near 20 miles on a Sunday to hear him preach.

In a letter to Sir Thomas Acland regarding the need for a schoolmaster, Dr Bell wrote, 'While I was at Swanage, I was often able to dig youths out of the stone quarries there, but since I resigned the living I have often been most grievously disappointed in my attempts to obtain fitting and qualified men.' One appointment, however, he did help to arrange, when the Madras system was introduced into Ireland. The bishop of Meath wrote to the Primate regarding the Mastership of Wilson's Hospital, then vacant. Dr Bell was asked to make a recommendation, and the situation was offered to, and accepted by, James Wilmot, another of his protégés. 'He was the natural son of a man of property at Swanage and, from a child, had been noted for his steadiness and good conduct. He had been well educated, and had kept a small school at Swanage, where he had given much satisfaction. The chief objection to him was his youth; but this was waived in consideration of his high character.' Wilmot was a great success in Ireland, and the Bishop wrote to Bell for another like him, but nobody suitable was found.

42 The 16th-century Tithe Barn, viewed from the Rectory. It is now the Swanage Museum.

Bell's last years

The rivalry between Bell and Lancaster continued, and they were lampooned in the press as 'Bel and the Dragon'. But the 'Society for the Education of the Poor in principles of the Established Church' and the 'Royal Lancastrian Institution' (which in 1814 became the 'British & Foreign School Society') outgrew their respective founders. Lancaster was involved in a bankruptcy, and in 1818 was quickly packed off to America by Quaker friends 'to perpetuate his blunders'. Dr Bell, given less and less attention by his Society, due to his fiery temper and domineering manner, obtained authority to travel as an inspector of the schools, but again antagonised nearly all he met. After travelling extensively on the Continent, he retired to Cheltenham. He died in 1832 and was buried in Westminster Abbey of which he had been made a Prebendary; the funeral was attended by the archbishop of Canterbury and the bishop of London, and his bier was followed by a throng of distinguished mourners.[20] On his tombstone, by his own request, was inscribed: 'The Author of the Madras System of Education'. A memorial tablet in the south choir aisle depicts Andrew Bell seated aside, while a group of children teach themselves![21]

Bell was much troubled about the disposal of his large fortune. In 1831 he transferred £120,000 to trustees, half to go to the University of St Andrews, the other half to be divided between Scottish schools and the R.N. School in Greenwich. Bell left £20 to his gardener, Peter Notley; he had wanted Notley to go with him when he left Swanage, but Mr Gale requested his services. Bell also left £20 to Sarah Manwell, one of his maidservants, but both her name and Notley's were omitted in his last will, 'probably through misadventure'.

To sum up: in the opinion of many, Bell's achievements were less than supposed. After his death the schools of the Society were examined by government inspectors. The teachers were found inefficient and ignorant; the use of monitors meant that instruction was almost entirely by rote, leading, on the moral side, to favouritism and petty corruption; 'the schools were generally in a deplorable state in every part of England'.[22] Bell was in favour of doing away with corporal punishment, but towards schoolmasters under him he was a despot, threatening to diminish their salaries if they should deviate from his own methods.[23] The system depended too much on youthful and immature agents and diminished the cost of teaching, leading to the later pupil-teacher system of 1846. Bell 'may be said to have as much retarded education in one way as he forwarded it in others'.

Actually in 1612 John Brinsley, schoolmaster, in his *Ludus Literarius* had set out the monitorial system very clearly for all who wished to use it.[24]

9

Swanage in Chancery: The Dawn of Development

The Revd Thomas Oldfeld Bartlett, Rector of Swanage 1817-41, was a very different person from his immediate predecessor, and he was also young, He was ordained deacon by the bishop of Bristol, and priest by the bishop of Bath and Wells in 1816, and in the following year, at the age of 29, was instituted and inducted to the living of Swanage. He had just married Elizabeth Leach, whom he first met at the dancing classes at Sherborne School. Their first son was born in August 1818, and the bells were rung morning and evening. Thomas Bartlett also became rector of Sutton Montis, Somerset, from 1820 until 1825, and vicar of Worth Matravers in 1822, but resigned from the latter the same year in favour of his brother, William.[1] There was a curate for each parish and, when serving away from Swanage, the rector sometimes went by horseback. On 18 June 1824 he 'bought a horse of Hatchard of Langton – £15.15.0.' TOB kept a diary which throws many shafts of light upon contemporary Swanage.[2]

Perils of the Sea

Unlike Mr Gale, TOB loved Swanage and was a dutiful parson, considering the plurality normal in those times. His diary shows his sympathy when recording the all too frequent tragedies, though he feels 'God's will be done' and also 'thanks be to God!' In December 1819 the smack *Hope* was totally wrecked upon Peveril Ledge 'not more than a gunshot from the Fort'. The crew of six perished, including the owner and master William Dearling and his two sons. After the inquest he buried the bodies, which had been thrown up on the shore one by one. In November 1823 the brig *Globe* – 'a beautiful vessel new built', and laden with 300 tons of coal - also struck the Ledge. 'We all witnessed her demolition by the waves. It was a grand but awful sight. Providentially the crew of 10 were all saved.' But in 1837 the schooner *Sister* of Exeter capsized off Peveril with the loss of seven lives. A stone-boat with three men aboard sank in Durlston Bay in August 1836; Harden and Norman clung to the mast and were rescued by the coastguards but 'poor young Norman, who was to be married next day, sank and was no more'. With heavy easterly gales it was common to see vessels in difficulty in the Bay. A violent storm in 1825 drove both market-boats (Swanage and Poole) on to shore but they were freed without damage.

Swanage has suffered continually from floods. On 28 December 1821

the water at Wareham was as high as the rails on the causeway and washed down three houses at Stoborough. At Swanage the tide was so high as to wash into the chamber windows of Mr Pushman's

43 A panoramic view of Swanage Bay in the Victorian age, painted by Leonard Patten in 1892. The fishing fraternity at Peveril Point can be seen and a Customs Cutter is to the right of the picture. A stone-carrying brigantine and a pleasure steamer are departing from and arriving at the old Pier.

house. Mr Festing, my curate who also lodged there as well as the rest of the domestics were obliged to wade out middle high, so rapid was the influx of the tide.

In October 1823 the Rectory garden was under water and the kitchen flooded 'upwards of a foot high in less than a quarter of an hour'.

But the greatest devastation in Dorset occurred on 22-23 November 1824. As the tremendous gale came from the south-west, Swanage suffered less than some other places, but it was bad enough; two stone-boats were driven out of the bay and lost, and all perished. A Dutch vessel and crew were lost on Dancing Ledge. 'The Revd Richman of Dorchester and his wife were killed in their bed by the chimney falling in upon them. The Esplanade at Weymouth was totally destroyed.' TOB later went to Weymouth and Fleet to see the havoc wrought by the hurricane. 'The church was quite demolished.' This happened when the sea came right over the Chesil bank, bringing a vessel with it.

Disasters and Providence

The rector continued to record the many baptisms, marriages and burials of his flock, and other more memorable events. The quarrymen were a stalwart race: digging in the bowels of the earth and some not coming up alive. He buried Matthew Benfield in 1823, George Haysom in 1830, Samuel Norman in 1831 and John Harden in 1832. All were killed by 'founders': the falling in of the roof of their quarries. Quite often men worked alone or with only one other mate. In August 1829 a stone fell on a man 200 ft down who managed to extricate himself in darkness. Later a limb was amputated by Dr Delamotte[3] and the man recovered.

There were many other sad deaths. The Revd George Taylor, curate of Langton Matravers, died following a gunshot wound, and similarly Francis Fane White, aged 29, 'who went with young Carruthers to shoot gulls at Tilly Whim. In loading his gun it

accidentally went off, when the ball and part of the ramrod passed thro' his head … the whole town in gloom'. He was buried in the vault with his uncle Mr Nat Chinchen, the stone merchant. Elizabeth Bishop, aged one year, was killed by a waggon when the wheel ran over her head. Thomas White, aged five, was suffocated in a stable, having fallen headfirst into a deep pile of straw in the morning and not been found until evening. A macabre note seemed not unusual: in May 1830 Captain Cockram died suddenly after a good dinner. TOB 'touched the corpse' on the next day: 'I only shook hands with him last Wednesday.' He buried him in a vault under seat numbers six and seven. A great number of people were present. In March 1833 the revered minister of Swanage, John Collins, died, and TOB wrote a hymn for the occasion. 'N.B. I looked upon the Corpse some time before it was screwed down – it was very pleasant.'

To cap the woeful stories in the diary with hope, the rector was christening Susan Haysom after service, when the ceiling of the long gallery fell onto the seats beneath with a great crash. 'What a providence is here evident. If it had happened eight minutes before, lives might have been lost, the seats underneath being full. Blessed be God for all His mercies!'

There were more cheerful recordings in TOB's diary. The end of slavery in the British colonies was celebrated in the church and chapels. All the children gathered at the Fort where each was given a bun. The united Sunday School Jubilee in 1831 was a great occasion when TOB addressed the children; the space adjoining the Methodist chapel was christened 'Jubilee Square'. It is now the forecourt of the later church. Once again, all the children and their teachers walked out to the Fort and back, and tea was provided for all. Perhaps TOB's greatest achievement was his creation of the new school. The Swanage Bazaar, lasting for three days in August 1835, brought sales of £85. 'Object: To erect a school for Sunday Church children and to be used as infant school on weekdays.'

Mr Calcraft laid the foundation stone in September, and in December 1836 there was a public opening of the new School Room. 'The teachers sang an Acrostic which I wrote for them.' After singing the 100th Psalm, each child was given a three-halfpenny plumb [*sic*] bun and an apple. Twenty-four teachers came to the rectory for supper with 'a large round of beef with plenty of potatoes, bread and cheese, beer, raisin wine, apples, raw and baked'. They departed at 10.15 p.m. Quite an evening!

Royalty

There is much on this subject in the diary. On the death (6 November 1817) of 'our much beloved and amiable Princess Charlotte of Wales, daughter of the Prince Regent',[4] the rector gave orders for the whole day to be observed with solemnity, and the great bell to be tolled all day. There were more than a thousand people in church. Twelve months later Queen Charlotte, consort of George III, died, and so did 'our dog Dapper – believed poisoned'. No such muffled bell was mentioned for either.

On 29 January 1820 the poor, mad King George III expired aged 81, having reigned for 59 years. On Ash Wednesday, the day of the interment, there was a cessation of all business, and again the great bell tolled all day. In church, the pulpit, gallery and communion table were hung with black cloth, and a transparency was put in the east window: 'G.R.III – MY KINGDOM IS NOT OF THIS WORLD'. All was done at the rector's expense, as 'the churchwardens to their disgrace refused to comply with my request to pay the cost by a rate'. But he was pleased that 'Mr Collins[5] with his congregation attended and shewed his usual respect'. On Sunday 12 March the rector 'read the first Proclamation of King George IV for the encouragement of Piety and Virtue and for the preventing and punishment of vice, profaneness and immorality'. Did the notorious former Prince Regent ponder on it himself?

In November news arrived of the dismissal of the Bill of Pains and Penalties against Queen Caroline. George IV had wished to divorce his wife on the grounds of adultery, but such was his unpopularity that the public were wholeheartedly behind the Queen, and there was great rejoicing in Wareham and Swanage, with bell-ringing and bonfires, on account of her victory. Beef, mutton and plum pudding were given to 500 children. 'An effigy of Majocchi [was] carried through the town in a donkey cart, preceded by a band of music, and afterwards burnt.' Theodore Majocchi had been a witness against Caroline in her trial. In August 1821 the king, on the royal yacht bound for Ireland, came into Swanage Bay, attended by many warships, 'a great sight, and remained overnight'.

The Chancery Sale of 1823

The Revd John Chapman, Rector of Silton, had died in 1781, the last of the line. He devised his extensive estate to John Dampier, a wealthy Wareham mercer, in trust for his children, Edward, John and Mary. Edward Dampier was described as 'of the Excise Office, London, Gentleman'; the Revd John Dampier (junior) became Rector of Langton Matravers[6] in 1808 where he acquired Leeson, a small country seat in the parish; Mary Dampier had married the Revd Thomas Morton Colson of Dorchester in 1790. By his will, John Dampier senior left to his wife Mary his mansion, called the Great House, at Swanage and all his lands, houses, bankers and stone wharfs. After her death the estate was to be divided among the three children, except that certain parts of it appear to have been left individually. For example the Carrant's Court property of 134 acres went to Edward, the Peveril leasehold to John and the banker ground at Swanage and £6,000 stock in annuities to Mary; provision was also made for the education of her children. His wife was appointed sole executrix.

John Dampier died on 15 August 1811 but his wife renounced the probate and never proved the same; it seems that she had lost her reason. Edward (a declared bankrupt) and his brother John procured letters of administration, and this led to the Chancery case in 1817,[7] in which the plaintiffs were the Revd T.M. Colson, Mary his wife, their son the Revd J.M. Colson and their three daughters. No doubt Mrs Colson and family were trying to secure their rightful share of the inheritance. Eventually, by decree of the Court of Chancery dated 11 February 1820, it was directed that all the property should be sold and the monies paid into court. Presumably the Colsons received their due share of the proceeds when the slow wheels of the Law finished turning.

The sale particulars number more than a hundred properties on the plan and are listed in 19 Lots;[8] the names of the tenants and occupiers are also given. We have a good idea of Swanage at this time, seeing that half of the town and its environs was sold. The sale was by auction and took place on 8 and 9 September 1823 at the *Ship Inn*. All the Lots were freehold except number XI: the Peveril lands attached to the ancient manor of Kingston.

Lot I comprised the Carrant's Court estate, including Court Farm, the ancient barn, and the extensive meadows together with the cowleaze, fields and quarries to the south, terminating at the sea-cliff where stood the old signal station at Round Down. There was also a small detached parcel known as 'The Nooks' adjoining 'Froghole', land on the south of Swanage Brook where it meandered to the east of the Rectory; it has since been straightened and put partly underground in King's Road.

Lot II comprised Long Caldon, South Caldon and Blacklin Mill Gate. The first two were long fields bounding the west side of New House Lane (now Northbrook Road), and the name has since been sometimes written 'Cauldron'; there are now in Swanage both Cauldon Road and Cauldron Barn; Blacklin Mill Gate was a field, now known as Battle Mead.

Lot III consisted of a 'substantially-built messuage or dwelling-house commanding views, with a garden and orchard in the occupation of the widow of the Revd William Taylor'. It was known as the New House, later as 'Magnolia' and still stands on the south side of the High Street up the hill: a fine bay-windowed house and garden facing east.

Lot IV comprised various properties including Clarence Cottage at the top of Derrick Lane (now Chapel Lane), occupied by Joseph Smedmore, a member of a well-known nonconformist family.

Lot V listed cottages and gardens near the Church including Weare's House, adjoining the churchyard and occupied by the parish officers, 'Late Hurlock's [cottage] called the Old Kitchen, near the mill pond'[9], a 'tenement adjoining the last, with detached garden and plot of ground in Paradise, in which a Brewhouse has recently been erected'[10]. It is evident that the area was just south of the church, across Church Hill (also known as Paradise Hill). Included in this Lot was the house nearest the brook, still occupied by the widow of Thomas Manwell, the 'Swanage philosopher', who had died in the previous year.

Lot VI takes us back to the High Street and included the blacksmith's shop at the junction with Priest's Way, and the vineyard owned by William Cole, aged 67, probably the former Captain of the famous Fencibles.

Lot VII was at Wareham.

The Mansion House

Lot VIII comprised 'the Manor, or reputed Manor[11], of Swanage with the Rights, Royalties, Liberties, Privileges, and Appurtenances belonging thereto', and included:

a capital substantially-built Mansion or Dwelling-house, late the residence of John Dampier Esq., containing Entrance Hall, Dining, Drawing and Breakfast rooms, numerous Bed and Dressing rooms, excellent Offices, replete with Conveniences, good Cellaring, large Brewhouse, Malthouse, Stables, Coach-house, Yards and Garden. The House is pleasantly situated commanding a view of Swanage Bay and the opposite cliffs of Studland. The Sea Bathing is excellent.

Perhaps this was the earliest mention of public bathing here.

Lot IX included, west of the Mansion, a cluster of old buildings including the stone, coal and bakery business carried on by Robert Burt from 1803 until 1836 when he moved to Victoria Terrace.

Lot X listed Lower, Middle and Upper Sentry. 'These Lands form the Bay, called Durlestone Bay and Point, and possess numerous and valuable Stone Quarries, in full work, yielding considerable Profit, in the Occupation of Mr Thomas Randell, as Tenant at the yearly Rent of £40.'

Lot XI was the leasehold estate 'called Peverell', including Whitehall House and dairy, boathouses, summerhouse and pleasure ground (later The Grove), 'Peverell Racing Ground', Peveril Point, house and garden, and stone quarries at Durlston Bay.

Other Lots included the *New Inn*, the *White Hart* and the *Ship Inn* in the High Street, eight stone bankers on the shore, 36 pieces of arable and pasture in the North and South Swanage Fields, and 'Shad's Croft with a stone quarry thereon in the occupation of Nathaniel and James Chinchen'.

Thus was a great part of Swanage sold by auction and was in due course released from the bonds of Chancery. The principal purchasers were a wealthy farmer Samuel Beaton for the Carrant's Court estate, the Wareham lawyer Freeland Filliter for Sentry (Durlston), and William Morton Pitt for the Mansion and Peveril.

Pitt and his Development

44 William Morton Pitt (1754-1836), of Kingston Maurward, was MP for Dorset and a local benefactor.

Swanage was on the brink of something new: its awakening rôle as a watering place for visitors; and what better situation or climate could be found for such a development? Small though it was at first, it was assured of a good start by the fact that its instigator was the M.P. for Dorset, William Morton Pitt of Kingston Maurward near Dorchester. In 1807 Pitt had sold Encombe and the Kingston (Purbeck) estate to John Scott, the first Earl of Eldon and Chancellor of England, but reserved to himself the land at Peveril which had always been a parcel of the manor of Kingston, anciently held by the Abbess of Shaftesbury. Lot XI had been held on lease by John Dampier, but Pitt acquired the remainder of the lease and thus became the owner not only of the Mansion but also of the whole of the Downs and Peveril Point to the east of it.

Although Pitt was not the first to have ideas for building houses for 'marine retirement', he was perhaps the first to envisage Swanage as a 'watering place'. He certainly wanted to visit the town with his family in the summer season and thought that other people of 'quality' would like to do the same. The problem was that there were no amenities or proper accommodation for visitors, unlike at Weymouth, Southsea or Lyme Regis. This he proceeded to remedy.

Pitt's first operation was to turn the mansion into a first class hotel and to clear away the old White Hall farmhouse and buildings, making a more genteel prospect towards Peveril. Dampier had been a great planter of trees here, and Pitt continued likewise up the hill, soon to be called Seymer Road.[12] The last of the row of elms was cut down in 1898.

It has been stated[13] that, in converting the mansion into a hotel, Pitt added the two projecting wings, but the sale plan of 1823 clearly shows that they already existed. What he did do was to fill in the recessed areas at the rear by adding rooms to both storeys; this can be observed from the garden, where the south elevation shows earlier windows and a string course to the centre block, which are lacking where the infillings were made. On the front elevation the Ionic pilasters below the pediment, part of the original Chapman mansion, were unobstructed until the verandah was glazed in much later, when the sash windows were brought forward to form the enclosure. Only recently have the heavy glazing-bars been removed; the original windows, however, remain on the upper floor. The house of the 1720s was ashlar faced, but Pitt's alterations and additions were finished in the fashionable Regency stucco, as were Marine Villa, the Rookery and his later Seymer Terrace, something new to Swanage.

A watering-place

A local newspaper reported that

> the town of Swanage is likely ere long to become a much-frequented watering-place. The worthy Member for the County, W.M. Pitt Esq., is expending large sums of money for the improvement of the place. A splendid hotel is rapidly building, beautifully situated close to the bay, and land is marked out for crescents … A new line of road from Corfe Castle to Swanage is contemplated, and there is every prospect of its being speedily formed. This will be of great advantage to persons frequenting the place, as they will be enabled to approach the bay, hotel and crescents without the inconvenience of passing through the town, and over a much more pleasant road than the old one.

The first new building by Pitt, following the hotel additions, was the Rookery nearby, when on 5 October 1824 the foundation stone was laid 'in a most interesting manner by the twin children of Mr Pitt, a fine boy and girl only 3 years of age'. The rector, Mr Bartlett, 'had the pleasure of assisting Mrs Pitt with my arm to the spot and back afterwards. It was exceedingly dirty and slippery'. The newspaper report added: 'A great concourse of people were assembled upon this pleasing occasion, who testified their joy by loud huzzas – the bells at the same time ringing a merry peal'. Then the Pitts returned home to Dorchester with 'the regret of the inhabitants. The poor especially have experienced much kindness and charity from them – but it is their intention to frequently repeat their visits'. The Rookery has a pleasant door-case, and the building was originally used as part Customs-house, part shop and library.

Furthering his vision of Swanage as a seaside resort, Pitt proceeded to erect Marine Villa, with its charming trellis porches, close to the shore. It is dated 1825, and the architect was Mr Wallis of Dorchester. On 24 February the rector recorded, 'Our little daughter Mary[14] laid the foundation stone of the new Baths, Billiard and Coffee rooms to be built by Slippery Ledge. She did it very well. I gave the workmen a pint of beer each.' However, Pitt soon took over the Villa for his own seaside residence. There were dining and drawing rooms, six bedrooms, good cellars, a library, and all requisite offices.

The new road from Corfe Castle did not materialise, nor did the proposed crescents as such,[15] though Seymer Place terrace followed later. WMH says that Pitt made the new road along the shore from the 'County Bridge', which he seems to have reconstructed, to Battle Mead gate; the road to Studland was still by New House (Northbrook) Lane. Pitt also made a road from the Hotel to Peveril Point over Folly Knap. And that was not all: at the north-east corner of the Hotel he constructed a most welcome and useful amenity, 'a Private Pier or Quay, handsomely built and finished as a place of Embarkment and Landing, whilst it forms a marine Promenade for the visitors'. There had been a quay of sorts, but the new one projected into the sea and was a great asset for the steamboats which were now beginning to be seen more frequently in the Bay. The arrival of several gentlemen's yachts were reported in the DCC of 7 September 1826: 'This morning came in the *Briton*, schooner belonging to N. Powell Esq., and the *Black Dwarf* belonging to Joseph Garland Esq., R.N.' In July there was a sailing match, between the yacht of the Marquis of Anglesea and Mr Weld's yacht, from Cowes to Swanage and back, when many Revenue cutters and other vessels came into the Bay.

The Hotel

The actual date of the opening of the *Manor House Hotel* was not noted in the DCC, but it was probably early in 1825. WMH says that Pitt employed cabinet-makers and upholsterers, making most of the Spanish mahogany furniture on the spot to suit the rooms. There was a large ballroom, and the brick-vaulted cellars were converted into a Tap room, taking over the name and licence from the demolished *White Hall* tavern. In the 1828 rate-book it is referred to as *Pitt's Arms*.

The hotel got off to a good start. An account of 'this little town' was given in the DCC for 15 May 1828: 'The Manor House which is so well conducted by Miss Hardy and affords such excellent accommodation is rapidly filling; and there is every prospect of a most successful season.'[16] Already there had been a visit by the Duke of Gloucester from Lulworth Castle, the seat of the Weld family, who expressed his pleasure with the appearance of Swanage. The rector recorded that 'he arrived about ten minutes after we were in church in the afternoon and left just before we came out – he might have set a better example.'

At the hotel more than a hundred and fifty people attended to consider the establishment of a branch Bible Society and a Ladies' Association. Pitt was in the Chair and the proposal was carried unanimously. By 1828 'a neat library with the best assortment of books and an excellent billiard table' offered 'their separate sources of amusement'. Numerous improvements had been made and in place of the bankers, shown on the 1823 map, there was now a delightful green in front 'where a respectable band of musicians formed in this place meet every Tuesday and Friday evenings'.

An advertisement for the '*Manor House Hotel*, Swanwich (otherwise Swanage)' in October 1828 offered reductions in terms from 1 November to 1 May, but with the same service. 'Pains have been taken to produce warmth in the passages ... From the solidity of the walls, and that the whole House is built on arches, there is every possible security against cold or damp ... There are warm, cold, and shower Sea Baths in the Hotel itself, so that no weather can cause any interruption in bathing.' There was a grand display of fireworks 'under the direction of a few gentlemen of this place ... A large and respectable assemblage[17] of persons was attracted, who were highly gratified at the brilliance of the scene.' It will be noted that *respectability* was the keynote to the development of Swanage!

Smuggling

The Preventive or Coastguard Service had just been re-established to combat the very prevalent smuggling which had a hoary history. Pitt obliged in 1826 by completing another block of buildings, the Watch and Preventive Station near Peveril Point, which consisted of eight tenements, the end dwellings each rising in a pavilion with recessed arch on the seaward side. There is a garden on the south, surrounded by a wall built of water-worn stones from the shore. At the hotel there was also a part of the orchard garden 'in occupation of the boatmen of the Preventive Service as yearly tenants'.

45 Swanage Bay from the Downs, *c.*1830. Belvidere and The Rookery, on Seymer Road, are on the left of the picture, and Marine Villa is on the right. The stone quay can just be seen in the middle distance.

46 Swanage Bay from Peveril, *c.*1830. On the left is Alpha Cottage. The Grove was built in 1838 and the stone quay in 1823.

Many a battle of wits was fought between the customs men and the quarriers or fishermen.[18] Thus: 'Seized at Eastington by John Kingman, chief officer of Swanage, 42 casks of foreign spirits and a cart, which were brought to His Majesty's Warehouse at this port' (Poole).[19] Two years later, '102 tubs were picked up near Ballard Cliffs by Lt Holman and his men', and 58 casks of spirits off Durlston in 1830. Often the tubs were sunk at sea, to be recovered later with the help of cork 'lobster-pots'. The object was to take the goods across Poole Harbour inland and avoid Poole. Studland was a favourite route across the heath to Redhorn Quay on the harbour. Parson's Barn, a great cavern near the Pinnacles, was used for temporary storage, but in 1747 a large quantity of tea was seized by the Customs officers. At Swanage tubs were hauled up Ballard Cliff, then taken along the Down to Jenny Gould's gate. The cottage was notorious as a halfway house for smugglers, where contraband was stowed away in the cellar. WMH says that formerly it belonged to the Swanage Church Lands Trust, and 'probably shared the same fate as other Church property of Swanage did when it got into the hands of wicked and unprofitable stewards'. 'Another good landing place was near Battlemead Gate, from which the goods were carried across the fields to Calton Barn. This barn was another favourite hiding-place, and was the abode of one of the chief smugglers.' Durlston Bay cliff was honeycombed with quarries so it was very difficult to spot likely storage holes. Quarrymen found their large rush baskets for provender useful for taking back contraband goods. In the ancient cottages in Swanage there were secret places such as small trapdoors covered with a picture or wallpaper, removable floorboards beneath the bed or paving stones concealing cellars.

There were some ugly incidents. TOB recorded (20 September 1827), 'A severe fight took place between the Swanage Preventive men 11 in number and, it is supposed, more than 100 smugglers. All the Preventive men were more or less hurt. Lt Holman lost some teeth as well as bruised about the face.' Three years later,

> On Sunday evening an affray took place at St Alban's Head between some smugglers and the Preventive forces, when Bishop, a man from Dorchester, received a wound in the neck, and it is feared will prove fatal as he is unable to be moved from a small public house at Worth Matravers, where he was removed after receiving the injury; it appears that he fired a pistol in the air in coming into contact with the Preventive party, which one of the men immediately returned fire.[20]

47 Peveril Point and the Preventive Station, lifeboat houses and fishermen's huts. This early picture shows the *Peveril Point Hotel*, the first home of the Smale family, with its own stone slipway.

Church and Grave matters

The Vestry met concerning the necessity of a new burial ground, and the rector's brother, Charles Bartlett, came to prepare the conveyances for the piece of ground, purchased by the parish, which was to be in 'Paradise', south of the church. Swanage was still in the diocese of Bristol[21] and the bishop came to consecrate the graveyard on 12 August 1826. He, his wife and daughter spent a fortnight at the hotel, and the rector was invited there to dine with them. He found the bishop kind and unaffected: 'there is nothing of show or pomp about him'. He preached, and robed and unrobed, at the rectory where 'he admired the coins and was amused with the birds and petrifications' in TOB's 'museum'. He was pleased with the neatness of both rectory and the church, where a collection was taken for the Church Missionary Society – £19 12s. 2d. – with Mr Pitt at one door and Captain Cockram at the other. Special collections seem to have been well supported such as those for the Starving Irish (June 1822) and for the sufferers from the late fire at Wool whereby 27 houses were destroyed and 100 made homeless (July 1823). In the church the first organ was installed in 1829[22] but 'the singers' had been mentioned by TOB before: 'In the evening entertained the singers and quarriers 32 in number with beef and plumb [*sic*] pudding.' On 2 January 1824 he wrote, 'Entertained 13 quarriers who pay me stone dues, with beef and mutton pies and strong beer.' He usually mentioned Tithe day. He built 'a water-closet of my own invention in the passage upstairs'. He went coursing and 'killed 5 hares', saw the first swallow and for three nights listened to a nightingale on a pear tree in the garden.[23]

TOB was musical and twice mentioned 'a hymn of my own writing' though perhaps not the tune. 'The Revd Mr Bankes and wife Lady Frances, the Lord Chancellor's daughter, called – found me playing my violin to the children and completely in disabile ... They were very pleasant and admired the birds and the musical box.' In October 1825 TOB had begun alterations to the rectory by making new entrances into the music and dining rooms, and a year later inserted two French lights, fixing 'the organ in the recess and the birds in their places'. On his death in 1841[24] there was an important sale at the rectory of his 'very valuable collection of stuffed birds, rare fossils and antiquities'.

King George IV died in 1830 and the great bell was again tolled. The rector repeated the arrangement in church with black cloth and transparency. Nearly a thousand people were present for the service. William IV came to the throne. A month later ex-King Charles X of France stayed at Lulworth Castle, having landed at Poole. The Duchess d'Angoulême *en suite* visited Corfe Castle, Encombe, the seat of the Earl of Eldon, and afterwards Swanage.

That year James Chinchen, 'that venerable character and opulent stone merchant, died in his 88th year, a neighbour to all mankind'. John Cockram also died without issue. His Newton estate was sold to farmer Samuel Beaton, and the house then deteriorated after he and his wife died in 1843. Cockram had in 1829 sold Whitecliff to William Morton Pitt, who continued with his good works.

The Tontine Scheme

Pitt's latest enterprise in 1830 was to build several superior houses in Seymer Road facing the Downs, and under the Tontine principle.[25] This was a chancy undertaking, though the prospectus explained that 'when a Tontine is considered, it must be evident that the *end is* obtained at *little or no risk*'. The proposal here was that the number of shares be eight and the amount of subscription £100 each. As ground landlord Pitt was the Chairman, and the Clerk was Thomas Hardy,[26] resident at Bockhampton on Pitt's Dorchester estate.

The minute book has survived which gives interesting information concerning the tradesmen employed, costs and progress. The architect was again Charles Wallis and the solicitors Bartlett and Filliter. It was intended to build only three houses for the first season 'but in the expectation for additional subscribers, the whole of the intended plan of completing 13 houses may then be carried into effect'.

By August 1831 there were 22 subscribers and contracts were signed. By June the following year the three houses were completed and ready to be let unfurnished, the southernmost at 40 guineas, the other two at 30 guineas for three, five or seven years at option. At first it was not easy to let them at these rents, only Dr Delamotte taking no.1, so Pitt took the others for the time being. Mr Wallis reported that no. 4 was completed except for the iron fence, and in June the Swanage Tontine report was given. The committee was very satisfied, four houses having been completed and three of them let. Demand the previous year exceeded supply and larger houses would be an advantage for temporary residence 'for more elevated ranks in life and of larger fortune, as well as for numerous families. Perhaps 30 houses at 50 guineas each might appeal to the first characters in the County.' So far, so good. But there were clouds on the horizon, though meanwhile a sunny August day brought excitement.

Victoria: Princess and Queen

This year was a milestone for Swanage, for a visit from the Princess Victoria put the little town on the map. She and her mother, the Duchess of Kent, were on tour, and Victoria was being introduced to her future subjects in the counties and towns of the south of England. She was to sleep at the *Manor House Hotel* on 8 August 1833.[27]

The royal party was delayed on the journey from Torquay, Exeter and Dorchester, and could not remain long in Wareham or view Corfe Castle except in passing. The rector, churchwardens and an immense crowd gathered on Court Hill at 5 p.m. and waited for three hours. At last messengers on horseback announced the approach of the royal carriage, escorted by a regiment of yeomanry under Captain Bartlett. Cheers grew louder and the bells rang out. It being so late and the Duchess and Princess much fatigued, having travelled 105 miles, Sir John Conroy requested to proceed: the band, gentry, clubs etc. immediately closed in and followed the royal party down to the hotel where they were again received with most hearty cheers and the path up to their apartment was strewn with flowers by the young ladies. A large white banner had been suspended over the street with the motto 'Welcome, thrice welcome, Victoria.' The crowd began to chant 'We want the Princess!' and eventually she looked out of the casement window on the second floor under the pediment, remaining there for a few minutes before bidding them goodnight.

It was only known the day before that the princess was coming, and great anxiety was felt as to what to present to her. At last it was decided that, as straw-plait was the chief local industry, a bonnet of that material should be given to the future queen. Mrs Shorey, the owner of the principal bonnet shop, and her assistants sat up all night to make the bonnet, which was lined with white satin. At 10.30 a.m. the following day in the ballroom, thronged with ladies, the rector read his loyal address and the presentation followed. His daughter Mary Bartlett (aged 12) and the Princess (aged 14) seemed equally nervous, so the Duchess said in a low voice, 'Say thank you, Victoria.' The Princess did so, and her mother added 'Thank you, she will certainly wear it.' A few of the gentry had the honour of being introduced. H.R.H. commanded that Mrs Shorey, who had made the bonnet, use her name and arms in future, and that the hotel might henceforward be called *The Royal Victoria Hotel*. The royal party soon embarked

48 The *Royal Victoria Hotel*. The central section was the Great House, built by John Chapman about 1721. The wings were built about 1777. William Morton Pitt converted the building into the *Manor House Hotel* in 1823 and ten years later Princess Victoria stayed here on a visit to Swanage.

from the quay where Lt Col White, CB, had the honour to assist them into the barge, which was steered by Capt. Capel R.N. to the *Emerald,* the royal yacht. Amidst the acclamation of the multitude the band played the National Anthem. In the Bay were many vessels with their flags waving in the wind. *The Emerald* then left for Cowes, and among the crowd when the party landed was a Swanage sailor who said afterwards that the future Queen disembarked wearing her new bonnet. 'The weather was delightful and the scene altogether such as we have never witnessed before but heartily desire to see repeated.'

On 29 May 1837 to celebrate Victoria's majority there was 'a magnificent display of colours' at the Fort, Coastguard and Customs House as well as on the vessels in the Bay, when the church bells were rung. On 27 June the churchwardens proclaimed the new Queen, following the death of William IV. 'Great interest was excited from the circumstances of Her Gracious Majesty having once honoured this retired and beautiful watering-place with a visit.' Several hundred people formed a procession on Court Hill and marched down the High Street to the Coastguard Station where three volleys were fired, 'the children singing, joined by all the people, both the National Anthem and Rule Britannia ... A brilliant assemblage of ladies added greatly to the scene.'

The Fall of the House of Pitt

By December 1834 problems had arisen from the Tontine. Some subscribers had not paid up and other difficulties resulted from the high cost of the lawyers' bill and the 'novel' regulation for payment of fees to Counsel. Mr Pitt said, 'Interested as I am personally in the successful progress of the Tontine, I trust I may be permitted to take upon myself the payment of the Balance,' and enclosed a cheque. This was helpful, but a bombshell followed: Pitt was bankrupt.

There is a blank in the minutes for 1835, and in June it was reported in the DCC with regret that the hotel had closed. It was hoped that it would soon reopen and would be in the hands of someone as popular as Miss Hardy. In July arrangements had been made that it would remain open as a lodging house. 'As to provisions, company either make their own arrangement or be supplied by Mr Hatchard of the *Anchor Inn* on very reasonable terms.' In December the hotel could reopen as soon as an eligible tenant could be obtained.

Then the final blow fell: William Morton Pitt, of Kingston House, Dorchester, died on 28 February 1836 in his 82nd year. In July, his young wife, Grace, also died. The DCC said:

> the loss which the County has sustained by the death of this estimable man is no slight one. Essentially a public man, throughout a long and laborious life, he had the rare success of obtaining the good will of, and giving satisfaction to, all classes and parties ... his time and exertions were unremittingly devoted to the public good. Nor was his private life less worthy. Beloved by his family, esteemed by his friends and honoured by all, he passed through life distinguished by the possession of a diffusive philanthropy, and extensive practical benevolence.

In *The House of Pitt*, the author comments:

> How this talented, well-meaning man managed to dissipate the vast fortune left by his father, John Pitt of Encombe, must remain a mystery. All that is certain is that he was the ruin of his house; and after having sat in the House of Commons as member for Dorsetshire for close on half a century, he was compelled to part with Encombe which Chatham had so loved to visit in his hours of leisure. Kingston [Maurward], too, had later to be given up; and thus the wealthiest branch of the House of Pitt, once powerful and distinguished, sank into obscurity of a landless middle-class.[28]

The Chancery Sale of 1838

By June 1836 it was decided to try to dispose of the Tontine houses, and an advertisement was entered in the principal newspapers for the sale of house no.1 at £600 and £450 each for the others. But there were no bids, so it was hoped to let them furnished. However, by December 1839 the solicitors reported that, by permission of the Court of Chancery, the houses had been sold freehold at a reduced price. There are no further entries in the minute book.

Swanage was in Chancery again.[29] The sale took place on Thursday 16 August 1838 at the *Victoria Hotel*, and also on 18 August at the *Kings Arms Inn*, Dorchester, in 39 Lots. The plan was based on that which was attached to the 1823 particulars.[30] One copy is marked 'Thomas Phippard, Wareham' where the bids are inked in. The principal purchasers for the Swanage Lots were Lord Eldon (£4,800 for Whitecliff), Mr Coventry for Alpha Cottage (£670) and for the Shrubbery (£340, and later becoming The Grove), Taylor for the Rookery (£370), Foot for the Preventive Houses (£620). Marine Villa is marked 'no sale'. The hotel was not sold at the time, but it was reopened, and once more Swanage settled down on a more even keel.

Trouble at the Quay

Following the 1838 Chancery sale, the architect Daniel Alexander,[31] who had designed Maidstone and Dartmoor prisons, purchased the *Royal Victoria Hotel* in 1842. Believing that he also owned the stone quay, Pitt having built it, he fixed a stone kerb and iron railing across the road, so barring all traffic to the quay, despite warnings from the parish. An interesting document of the time, headed 'Evidence respecting the Quay roads and Spring and Centry field, Swanage', lists the statements given by Henry Hibbs (76), William Stickland (56), John Haysom (78), Thomas Rendell (77), and Robert Barnes (55), in evidence that the Quay belonged to the parish and people had always drawn water from the spring, called Boil Well, without objection. Moreover, that the former quay, part of which was below Pitt's extension, was built by the parish in the 18th century, the quarriers giving stone and a day's work each, and that it cost about £300. Incidentally, the 1823 Chancery map shows bankers in front of the Great House and indications of a quay wall. It was said that neither Dampier nor Pitt ever obstructed the landing of goods there, and both had stated that it belonged to the parish.

WMH tells the story that the obstruction was too much for Henry Gillingham, whose forebears had used the quay for generations. He ordered a cask of beer, assembled 200 quarrymen, and got Robert Stevens to strike the wall with a hammer, the men pulling the lot away with chains. Mr Alexander never attempted to stop the highway again. WMH adds that in 1880 the Local Board again fixed stone posts across the entrance to the quay. This was too much for Martin Cole Ellis, a strong 'character' mentioned earlier in John Mowlem's diary, who got a man with a large spawl hammer to beat them down level with the ground. WMH himself helped with the operation. The Board were going to punish the offenders but found that they were themselves in the wrong.

At the end of the Quay there is a notice in the wall reading, 'ELDON ESTATE – Tolls are due for embarking or landing goods or animals from or on this slip or the beach between the pier toll house and this slip'. But long since the recurring troubles, the quay is now only used as a promenade and for the occasional small pleasure boat.

The Tithe Returns of 1839

The general Redemption of Tithes (monetary tax assessment replacing kind by payment) produced a large-scale map for every parish, invaluable for the historian today. Every field or parcel was numbered, and the Returns list the name of the owner, occupier, field name and acreage. See page 21.

The total area of the parish of Swanage was 2,923 acres and the total rent charges approximately £400. As already mentioned, some land in Herston, north of the High Road, was part of the parish of Langton Matravers until 1933. There was also the large wedge of land west of Ulwell village in the parish of Studland until 1894, and similarly a large tract of heath over the hill was part of Swanage parish.

The Chancery sale of 1838 had just taken place, and of course the name of Pitt does not appear; one notes the new owners of his former estate, the Earl of Eldon,[32] Beaton, Filliter and Alexander. The largest ownerships in the parish are represented by the following: W.J. Bankes (Godlingston and Verney – 700 acres), Samuel Beaton (Carrant's Court, Newton and Caldens – 350), J.H. Calcraft (Rempstone – 317), the Earl of Eldon (Whitecliff – 234), the Trustees of Ilminster School (Northbrook and Ulway [sic] – 200), the Revd S. Serrell (Herston and Benleaze – 187), Capt. Joseph Garland (Greyseed – 128), the Revd Harry Farr Yeatman (California – 124), Joseph Willis (the Cliff and Ulwell – 121), George Filliter (Sentry – 100), Widow Jane Edmonds (Townsend and the Common Ware – 76), William Taunton (Eightholds – 70), John Spencer (Prospect Farm – 57), Daniel Alexander (Peveril – 34).

Among the occupiers, three stone merchants stand out as prosperous landholders: William Grove White (200 acres), Thomas Randell (123) and Robert Burt (73). It was not until 1857 that John Mowlem began to purchase the Ilminster estate. George Burt bought Sentry and Durlston in 1864 and Charles Robinson acquired Eightholds in 1875.

10

The Return of the Native: John Mowlem

We left John Mowlem, an aspiring stonemason, working with his friend Robert Burt in their quarry in the common fields. Things had not been easy at first for the family. In his Diary,[1] back in Swanage, the entry for 17 May 1847 reads, 'Trade here very brisk, but provisions very dear ... I was one of six children, we were two girls and four boys, a father with no one to help him in the shape of friends – no one that could give or lend a penny to hard times for us all. Thank God it is not so now; all a man wish for I have at my command.'

John and Robert had been courting the Manwell sisters, nieces of Thomas Manwell the philosopher. In 1812 Robert married Laetitia ('Letty') in Swanage parish church and raised a family of six,[2] George Burt (b.1816) being the eldest, 'Susy' (b.1829) the youngest. In the same year John Mowlem married Susannah Manwell at St George's, Hanover Square; sadly they had no children as his Susan soon became chronically ill. But long before the wedding John had left Swanage, probably from news of better prospects from her stonecutter brother Henry Manwell, already in London. The story that John asked a ship's captain for free passage to London is untrue; that he only had 'ninepence in his pocket' may be true, figuratively speaking, but he was on his way to the Isle of Wight for a job at Norris Castle, East Cowes. The architect was James Wyatt who in due course recommended him to Henry Westmacott, a well-known sculptor-mason in London, and soon John became foreman over all the works going on in the metropolis. 'I was put over men old enough to be my father. It is true I knew little, but I moved upwards, knowing that I could any day go back to the bankers in Swanage ... My wife had to work with myself. On we went and here we are!'

The Capitalist

In those days £100 capital was enough to start a business, and by 1823 JM had launched out on his own. He leased a wharf in Pimlico Basin, now the site of Victoria Station forecourt, where he imported Purbeck limestone, York sandstone and Aberdeen granite. Later he moved to offices and a yard at Paddington Basin off the Grand Union Canal, which remained his headquarters for the rest of his life. John Mowlem prospered by keen but honest application to secure contracts for the repaving and kerbing of London streets: the responsibility of the parish vestries. Their minutes are full of references to Purbeck 'squares' and 'pitchers', and paving was his life. His first really big job was the contract gained for repaving Blackfriars Bridge with Guernsey granite setts, as

49 Haymaking in Sentryfields with Belvidere and Tontine houses in Seymer Road in the background, *c.*1895. Note the circular water tower and water offices in the distance, dating from 1864.

recommended by James McAdam. Little did John think that one day his firm would rebuild London Bridge.

As soon as he had secured the Blackfriars contract he found difficulty in procuring the Guernsey granite, so he bought about an acre of land in the north of the Island, making sure of the supply. He stayed there supervising the quarrying until he had sent the last of the stone to London in June 1840.

Last but not least of the party from Swanage was George Burt. He came up to London in 1835 at the age of 19 at the behest of his uncle, who already appreciated his nephew's 'good business qualities, shrewdness, fine character and energy of nature' (WMH), and saw that he would be an asset to the firm. Moreover, like his uncle, young George had learnt to handle a stonemason's tools the hard way: in the Swanage quarries. Another experienced stonemason, Joseph Freeman, from Yorkshire had already joined the firm, and in 1839 he married George Burt's eldest sister Elizabeth. So while John Mowlem was in Guernsey he left the business in London in the care of 'my two young men'. On 1 January 1844 he took them into partnership, when the firm became Mowlem, Freeman & Burt, before reverting to John Mowlem & Company 50 years later.

Retirement

Although not quite 50, John Mowlem had retirement to Swanage in mind. As early as 1838 at the Chancery sale he made a bid of £260 for Belvidere no.1, a seven-bedroom house built by Pitt at the top of Seymer Road. Cleall's bid was £270, but in the event there was no sale for this lot.[3]

Meanwhile his friend Robert Burt was prospering in Swanage. A plot of land in 'Mrs Colson's garden' in the lower High Street was situated to the east of Cliff Place and between the *White Hart* (later the *Purbeck Hotel*) and the old house and shop next to the

50 An Edwardian scene in Lower High Street. The substantial building on the left became the famous Trocadero Restaurant. In the centre of the picture is Victoria Terrace, with John Mowlem's Observatory visible above the rooftops. On the right is the *Ship Inn*.

Victoria Hotel, occupied by Robert Burt senior since 1803. Burt and Hussey purchased the freehold and began to erect 'five Lodging houses' thereon. The east wall is inscribed 'Burt's Place 1835', and when the first house was completed Robert junior and his family moved into no.1, now the *White Horse Inn* and much altered. Soon there was a shop at each end of the terrace: Burt's grocery to the east and Hussey's drapery to the west. In 1837 the new row was named Victoria Terrace and it was intended to complete the three houses remaining between the shops. However, John Mowlem decided to buy no.2 as a double-fronted residence for his retirement, so in the event there was only one more house, no.3, which became Walker's the chemist and druggist. Hussey's was no.4. It will be observed that the first-floor balcony railings of no.2 are more elaborate. Above the roof is John Mowlem's 'observatory': a small attic with four windows.

In 1845 John Mowlem moved, with his wife, into no.2, and almost at once he began his Swanage diary, using an old copy-letter book. It is highly entertaining as well as full of interest, not least his journey to Germany for his ailing wife to take the waters and, in a later diary, his continental holiday in 1853 after his wife's death. Memorable dinner parties took place at no.1, and Susy Burt became a great favourite. At 13 she launched the *John Mowlem* at St Sampson's boatyard in Guernsey, and later JM gave her a grand piano. On the death of his wife in 1849 he hoped that Susy, then nearly 20, would look after him for the rest of his life, and possibly marry him and bear children for him at last. But to his great disappointment, indeed disapproval, she married James Arbon[4] and produced 13 children, dying in childbirth at the age of 41 to universal dismay; the last child, William, died at the age of ten. A brass to Susanna Arbon's memory is in the south transept of the parish church.

Improvements, and the Cholera scare

Retirement for John Mowlem did not mean the thought of the quiet evening of his life. Indeed he was as busy as ever, journeying by train, coach and ship to Scotland, Cornwall and France to evaluate granite for the firm, as well as spending days at Paddington Basin and sailing across to the Guernsey quarries. His diary gives exciting accounts of the dangers of storms at sea, familiar to all seafarers. In 1851 he visited the Great Exhibition in Hyde Park and saw the Duke of Wellington in the Crystal Palace.

However, he now had time for his Swanage home: constructing a W.C. in the garden and installing a bathroom, including a hot water supply and a copper bath. But 'I drink a tumbler of cold water every morning and wash my body with cold water though there be ice in it. I have been too busy through the whole of my life to indulge in this sort of cleanliness.' He soon plunged into Swanage life. He was appointed overseer in 1845, a constable in 1846 and waywarden in 1847. He at once commenced lowering Spring Hill knap in the High Street, improving Church Hill by removing the steps in the roadway, and clearing the pond or trough at Court. 'It is strange indeed that 60 years have gone by without a single improvement here, and God Almighty has spared my life to improve the place where I first drew breath.' The Vestry minutes record that during 1850-52 the unemployed were to be set to work on the roads.

There was a bad outbreak of cholera in 1849, not least in Guernsey while John Mowlem was there and thankful to have escaped. Swanage was spared 'from the awful ravages of the prevailing epidemic'. On 14 November, when the fear had passed, 'all business was suspended here, and shops closed'. The church was opened for divine service and was attended by large congregations. The rector addressed them in the evening with 'And be ye thankful' (Col. iii), and in the morning another preacher gave a sermon: 'There is a cause' (I Sam. xvii). The cause was in fact drinking contaminated water, but at that time everyone, including JM, thought it was caused by impure air.

Farewell, Coachman; Welcome, the Iron Horse

The 1840s brought the Railway Mania and a great change to the whole country. The first tentacle southwestwards from the Metropolis was the London and Southampton railway, opened from Nine Elms on 11 May 1840; the Waterloo terminus followed in 1848.

As soon as the railway opened, the *Rose* paddle-steamer, plying from Weymouth, advertised the possibility of arriving in London from Swanage 'in the unprecedented short time of 7 hours', with a call at Yarmouth, Isle of Wight, on the way to the new Southampton terminus. The prices in 1845 from Swanage, either to Southampton

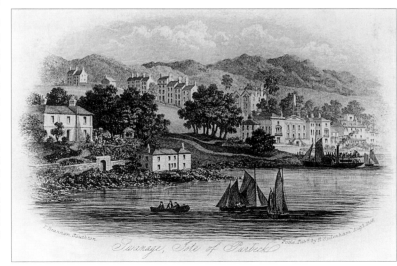

51 Swanage from an etching by Philip Brannon on 1 August 1856, showing a steamboat at the quay. The first pier was not built until 1859. From left to right are: The Grove, Marine Villa, Belvidere, Tontine Houses, Osborne House, The Rookery, *Royal Victoria Hotel* and Victoria Terrace, seen opposite the stone bankers.

or Weymouth, were 7s. for saloon and 3s. 6d. for forecabin. *Rose* was one of the first steamers to call at Swanage, and in the engraving by Philip Brannon (1856) a similar boat is shown berthed alongside the stone quay, the year before the first wooden pier was built. John Mowlem no doubt took advantage of this route when he first 'retired' to Swanage.

For Susy Burt's 16th birthday on 26 December 1845 there was a large dinner party at no.1 Victoria Terrace. 'George Burt came from London, Robert met him at Wareham with a gig. There was no coach from Southampton, therefore he posted it to Wareham with three others.' But soon they were able to travel down to Wareham by the 'Castleman Corkscrew' railway,[5] extended from Southampton to Dorchester in 1847. On 7 July, John Mowlem with the Freeman family left London at 12.30 p.m. and arrived at 5 p.m. 'by Express Train. We were all fatigued enough, for the rail road from Southampton is new and rough.'

Almost at once, when the first railways opened, the writing was on the wall for the coaches and their drivers. The *Poole & Dorset Herald* reported (3 June 1847):

> The opening of the line to Dorchester turned some of our friends, the stage coaches, off the road. The *Emerald,* Southampton and Weymouth, will in a few days be off the road altogether. The *Union,* Southampton and Poole, performed its last journey down on Tuesday night, and up on Wednesday morning, much to the regret of its worthy proprietor and driver Mr George Wiltshire.

Having driven the coach for nine years, a testimonial was presented to him. However, it was reported (2 December 1847) that a new omnibus, the *Enterprise,* had commenced running, Swanage-Kingston-Corfe Castle-Wareham, 'proprietors: J. Bailey & Son and J. Wignall (formerly well-known whip of the *Emerald* coach)'. The iron horse had brought London considerably nearer to Swanage.

Railway hope

The opening in 1847 of the railway to Dorchester and a station at Wareham stirred the forward-looking merchants and residents of Swanage to propose an extension for a branch line. A public meeting at the hotel in October was attended by some 40 prominent people, including Thomas Phippard 'who is, we believe, the originator of the scheme'. He was a Wareham solicitor and perhaps hoped to emulate Charles Castleman who had been largely responsible for launching the 'Corkscrew' line to Dorchester. Phippard gave details of the proposals: about 20,000 tons of stone was exported yearly and, in addition to a railway, a pier was necessary. Captain Moorsom, engineer of the Dorchester line, estimated the cost of the branch line, including the land, would be £85,000, and the landowners were generally in favour. The resolution 'That it is most desirable that a line of railway be formed from Wareham to Swanage with as little delay as possible' was proposed by John Mowlem. It was carried, and agreed that a committee be appointed to further the scheme. In November it was reported that Captain Moorsom had nearly completed his survey, and notices were being served on landowners. Mr Phippard thought that the Earl of Eldon was ready to subscribe to the extent of £30,000 for the work, and it was hoped that an application for an Act of Parliament could be made in the ensuing season.

Henry Gillingham Jnr, stone merchant, thought that stone must still be sent by sea as it was mainly used for docks and suchlike, but a pier and a tramway up to Langton Matravers, or even as far as St Aldhelm's Head to serve the many quarries, would be a great advantage. At the same time it would benefit both residents and the increasing visitors by abating the interminable clouds of dust in fine weather and the almost fathomless

52 Brown's Fishmonger Shop. The original 16th- or 17th-century building, the birthplace of both George Burt and William Masters Hardy, was demolished in 1908.

abyss of mud in winter. 'No longer must the din of the incessant mallet, from earliest dawn until evening, annoy the ears of invalids, nor the heavy shower of chips and scars flying around far and wide, endanger the lives of passengers by alarming horses unused to such salutations, to say nothing of blocks of stone invading the highways, or huge and unwieldy loading carts barring farther progress.' The proposed tramway could be constructed for £12,000 and would clear the banker land for building. He was not against the railway to Wareham, but he thought that, if there had been a good road through the valley, it would not have been so necessary.

Railway Mania was by now subsiding and the promise of financial support dwindled. No more was heard of a Purbeck railway until 1861.

The Truck System

A most informative article on 'Labour and the Poor' appeared in the *Morning Chronicle* from which extracts were given in the DCC in January 1850 entitled 'Swanage – its stone quarries and the Truck system'.

Condemned by many, it was the result of the dearth of money. Money value was put on everything, but the men were paid in stone; at 3s. a day he would get 18s. worth of stone at the end of the week, though sometimes instead he would be given an order upon the merchant with whom the quarrier was in credit.

There were two types of merchants, the first being an independent *dealer* who sold his goods for ready money – when he could get it – or for bread, which he could afterwards convert into money. The second was termed exclusively a *merchant* and who kept a general shop or store. He had his own bakehouse, the bread being the chief article which he exchanged for stone.

> His shop is thus, in one sense, a bank of issue; for he manufactures in it that which forms half the currency of the district – and its entire currency in the way of small change. Every quarrier must have his banker. To establish a credit with a merchant, the quarrier must deposit stone with him, and the extent of the credit is regulated by the quantity of stone deposited. The merchant has what he calls his *banker* which is neither more nor less than the spot of ground in which the stone left with him is deposited in it. An account is kept by both parties of the quality of stone deposited, as well as the goods taken by the quarrier or, on his order, from the shop. When he wants to know how he stands he takes an account, and the balance, in the shape of stone which remains to his credit on the banker, indicates the extent of his worldly means.

The merchants disposed of the stone as best they could, with Southampton being one of the most accessible markets. The truck system was a credit system, but many shops and inns that could not take stone in payment would take bread – which was a sub-currency. 'If the merchant does not stock say a pair of shoes, the quarrier must go to an independent dealer who will accept bread in payment. He therefore draws so much bread upon his merchant to pay the shoemaker.'

It was hard on the quarrier, the cost of living being 15-20 per cent higher than elsewhere in the neighbourhood.

> 5d. loaf in Poole cost 6½d. in Swanage to the quarrier. But when he takes it to the dealer he can only get 5½d. – he thus loses 1d. per loaf. A quarrier sent for some ale. His wife took with her a 6½d. loaf and brought back 5½d. worth of beer. The stranger would be utterly at a loss to account for the quantity of bread which he would see carried about in all directions. If a woman wants a piece of ribbon she must take a loaf with her to the shop … The quarrier loses all ways – commodities he buys are overcharged, the bread which he pays is undervalued. Another inconvenience is the length of time taken by merchants to balance the accounts with them. Sometimes years elapse without settlement, and begets reckless habits in the more thoughtless.

'An old Purbeck man' said that in almost every respect the statements were correct. The truck system was abominable, but 'altogether the stone trade of Swanage must be badly managed, for we never hear of the merchants amassing large fortunes.'

At the recent meeting regarding a branch railway, the Chairman had remarked that he wished to see quarrymen paid for their work in hard cash, the same as the men employed in the claypits, and not obliged to receive their wages in bread. The truck system had nothing but its antiquity to recommend it, and he hoped it would soon be abolished (hear, hear!). Several people spoke against the truck system and thought a railway would do away with it. But Henry Gillingham was a stone merchant: he did not defend it

> but every place possesses its own customs, the result of time and experience. Let it suffice that those who have so vehemently raised the cry against the merchants should exercise their eloquence against other parties. Let them appeal to the men, whom they represent as its victims; exhort them to throw off the burden by their own exertions … I am convinced we shall find that those who still continue to hug their chains will prove more censure than sympathy.

This was powerful stuff!

The working man

House and land rents were exacted in money. To enable the quarryman to meet these demands the merchants allowed a certain sum of money to be drawn each week. This also enabled him to buy a little fresh meat, which they did not often enjoy and for which they invariably had to pay money. So there were bitter complaints about the lack of money, and some would sooner have money at an even lower valuation of stone.

Even so, the quarriers were better off than the agricultural labourers. Their houses were superior and cleaner, and sometimes they might have four or five rooms, because of the abundance of material. Except for Upabout Lane, where the houses were inferior, the dwellings were spacious, clean and comfortable, with plenty of furniture and bedding. Rents averaged £4, rates about £1. Their diet was better than for the farm labourers, and though they seldom had fresh meat, bacon was more plentiful, though still insufficient for their occupation.

The working man was generally ignorant and almost entirely illiterate. If he attended school, he was sent to work too early to derive much benefit from it. Boys of nine became useful about the quarry and were sent below as soon as they were strong enough. On the whole they were considered 'an orderly and well-regulated set of men'. But John Mowlem commented (24 November 1845):

> There are large demands for stone from this place at the present time; but I see no improvements in the inhabitants, there is nothing like want with those that can work, but not one thinks of old age; public houses are in great request, the manners are more rude than they were 50 years ago, both men and women; this is to be much regretted by all who wish them well.

Herston House

Just beyond Newton Manor on the High Road stood Herston House. At the turn of the century it was occupied by Captain Martin Cole R.N. (1729-1803); his daughter Sarah (1775-1847) married her cousin, John Cockram (1770-1830) of Newton, late in life. The Manwell sisters, Letty and Susan, great-nieces of Captain Cole, were often at the house, and it was there in the adjoining paddock that young John Mowlem and his friend Robert Burt had whistled for their wives, as described in the Diary.

But on 1 January 1849 John Mowlem had bought the house for £185, Mrs Sarah Cockram having died, the last of the family. 'Little did I think the maid and the property would be mine in 1849.' Mr Smedmore came to build a new wing, as Mrs Mowlem (his wife) wished to live there, thinking a change of air would do her good. Alas, by November, Susan was very poorly, and on 12 January she died there, aged sixty-one. John's

53 The 18th-century Herston House, seat of the landed Cockram family, and later of Captain Cole RN. John Mowlem purchased this property in 1849 and added the crenellations. The house was demolished in 1967. The stone 'battlements' were preserved, forming a path to a house facing Swanage Shore.

54 John Ernest Mowlem was born at Herston House in 1868 and was the great-nephew of John Mowlem. He remained a bachelor and lived with his two sisters at De Moulham Villa in Victoria Avenue. He died in 1946.

diary is very touching; Miss Rendell, her companion, Susy Burt, the nurse and two maidservants were present besides himself. Her remains were taken to Kingston and the handsome oak coffin deposited in a vault in the churchyard; two years later granite blocks arrived from Guernsey in 85 packing cases, and John started to level the foundations and helped to build the unusual and impressive monument which he designed. In 1854 it was taken down and re-erected in the new Swanage cemetery where in 1868 John was himself interred with his wife. In the same year his brother Joseph's grandson, John Ernest Mowlem (1868-1946), the last of the Mowlems of Swanage, was born at Herston House.

John Mowlem completed the west wing after his wife's death and capped it with crenellations. 'It was a home that my poor wife was delighted with. It will be a nice home for children. It is a place I shall always reverence as long as I live.' He discovered the well, '18ft deep, full of very beautiful clear water'. He then formed a hall and bathroom 'which will be very convenient'. It was sad to see the whole place demolished in 1967 and redeveloped with indifferent dwellings. All that remains is a stone, set into the back of the High Street wall, bearing the initials 'J.M. 1850'. The crenellations were saved and can be seen in a garden on Shore Road.

Mr Jackson

Following T.O. Bartlett, the Revd J.L. Jackson MA became rector of Swanage (1841-54). John Mowlem was complaining in 1848 about the parish church 'which is frousty, dusty, dirty, and not ventilated scarcely once in a week. And this is the Rector who had been kind enough to go from house to house to caution people to be clean.' (Cholera was making its appearance in England.) JM was not too fond of the Rector; he heard him preach on, 'Can a mother forget her suckling child?' and commented 'I can say some in Swanage do.' As a treasurer for the regatta, he brought down from London £10 worth of fireworks, which was a considerable quantity. 'Mr Jackson, poor stupid man, had a fling at our fun. He thinks himself a god.' The rector was much against the regatta, probably because in the previous year it was reported that many fireworks were let off on banker land and in the street. 'The wild ones did not forget to kick about the dangerous fireballs very freely. These matters are, we think, carried too far and ought not to be allowed in the town.'

However, on his wife's death, JM wrote, 'I have called today on Mr Jackson to thank him for my poor wife, he was very kind in her last severe affliction. He was very polite and very gentlemanly to me - nothing about my having taken her to Kingston churchyard.' The reason was that Swanage churchyard and burial ground were cramped, and he wanted room for his proposed large memorial.

The Grove

Having bought for £340 the Shrubberies by the shore, in the sale of 1838, Mr Coventry began to build his house 'The Grove'. He had also purchased Alpha Cottage, just to the east, for £670. It had six bedrooms, a small lawn and gardens, 'lately occupied by Captain Meredith'[6]. 'The Grove' was illustrated by Philip Brannon in 1858 and by a later photograph (before the extensions which eventually became the *Grosvenor Hotel*. now demolished). A plan of the ground floor shows the hall, a drawing room 29ft by 20ft, dining room, library, conservatory, kitchen, offices and brew-house. The main entrance was from the west gates and pleasure grounds, surrounded by fine trees. There were coachman's and gardener's cottages, stables, coach-house, harness-room and conveniences, nearly three acres 'forming in its entirety one of the most complete marine residences in the kingdom'.

55   The Grove was built by Mr Coventry in 1838. After numerous extensions it became the *Grosvenor Hotel*, seen here in 1907. On the far right can be seen one of the Ionic columns from London, which were recently reset in Prince Albert's Gardens.

It appears that Frederick Coventry, descended from the Earl of Coventry, never lived at 'The Grove' but built it for his wife after their separation, the details of which were not given in her will. He himself lived at Henbury House and died in 1859. In the parish church there are memorial tablets[7] to Mrs Coventry, and to a son and two daughters who predeceased her. Two other sons and one other daughter survived her. We read in the DCC (5 July 1860):

> Coronation Day. The steamer *Ursa Major* brought us the Wimborne Rifle Corps, commanded by Capt. Coventry. The Volunteers are fortunate in having such a gallant man for their commander. They formed up on our pier, paraded the town and marched to the coastguard station, returning through the beautiful garden of their captain's highly respected mother, Mrs Coventry, to the court opposite the hotel.

After an excellent dinner, they departed in *Ursa Major*.

Mrs Coventry lived on, doing good works for Swanage. On her death in 1865, Thomas Docwra, a retired London contractor, bought The Grove at the auction in the following year.

Lord Eldon enters the scene

Sir John Scott, Lord Chancellor, had been created the first Earl of Eldon and purchased Encombe from William Morton Pitt in 1807. He died in 1838 in his 87th year and was succeeded by his grandson, Viscount Encombe. The body was brought back from London and nearly two thousand people watched the cortège leaving Encombe house for the lugubrious family catacomb hard by the earlier Kingston church, where he joined the Countess and their son. The second Earl, who died in 1854 and was also buried in the mausoleum, was intent on extending his Purbeck estate. We have seen that he bought Whitecliff in the sale of 1838. Daniel Alexander, who had acquired the hotel and Peveril, died in 1846, and two years later his son Philip sold the property to Lord Eldon. As a result, the DCC reported visions of good roads, docks and a canal, 'beautiful villas inhabited by the wealthy, cottages full of comfort for the labouring classes, and a new era commencing in the social and moral condition of the people'. Richard Row was the already well-known manager of the hotel which had recovered from the earlier financial disaster at the death of Morton Pitt, and was looking forward to more visitors and increased trade.

The Brewery

Another of Lord Eldon's enterprises was his purchase of the Swanage brewery. It stood near the later railway station and, amusingly, on the site of the modern Health Centre. The date of its establishment is uncertain but it was owned by the Edmonds family in the 18th century. Following the will (1794) of Joseph Edmonds, it was sold by his son in 1804 to Henry Gillingham for £800.[8] His son, Henry junior, sold the brewery to the Earl of Eldon in 1849 for £1,700. James Panton of Wareham was for many years the agent. The brewery was supplied with good water from a spring below the High Street, the nearby footway (now off King's Road, and named Spring Hill). Swanage Pale Ale was renowned.

WMH gives an account of the great brewery fire on 9 November 1854, reported briefly in the DCC. He says that the premises, except for the house, were entirely burnt out, only the walls left standing. The roof was covered with thatch, and in the cellar stood four enormous vats; when the roof fell in, the flames and sparks soared upwards to a height of 150 feet and next morning vessels in the bay were covered with black ash. When the vats collapsed, beer foamed and hissed everywhere. Some two hundred men helped to put out the flames and carry the sacks of barley and malt out into the meadow. The manager came from Wareham next morning and saw little left but sackcloth and ashes. There was no damage to the house, at that time occupied by Mr Brodie, a retired banker of Salisbury, and his family. Men came down from London to reconstruct the whole premises with new machinery.

For many years James Panton was manager of the Wareham and Swanage breweries, and was Mayor of Wareham in 1857. His wife, Mrs J.E. Panton, wrote an interesting and engaging autobiography, spanning the years 1858 to 1908, entitled *Fresh Leaves and Green Pastures*, published in 1909 but unfortunately withdrawn to avoid libel action.[9] The book contained descriptions of Swanage, particularly of the brewery.

> Every Friday for more than twelve years we used to drive through the valley or up across the hills on our way to the little seaport where we had then a small and most picturesque brewery. It had, moreover, an old house and garden attached, and in the latter most delicious asparagus grew, while on the house grapes used to ripen – the small sweet water-grapes that one never sees nowadays … The brewery opened out of the dining-room, and here the master was always at his post. Occasionally he would be washed out of it, or roused in the middle of the night because the little brook outside had risen suddenly; the office was afloat, the dining-room furniture making out to sea; while, worst of all, the maltings were in danger, and all hands had to be summoned to save the most important harvest of the year.

Mrs Panton recalled that in the gardens of some of their inns there grew masses of peaches.

> Our garden would not grow peaches, though it produced apricots and the most beautiful great golden plums that I have ever seen … The seaport in our day was most primitive, and appeared to go to sleep from about 1st October to 1st July … Some bold souls might come down about Easter, but visitors were rare enough to be objects of interest.

Christmas Eve

WMH gives an amusing account of carollers in the 1850s. There was a small band with two fiddles, cello, two clarinets and a trombone, and most of the singers were members of the church choir: no women of course. The group began with carols and refreshment at the *Globe*, Herston, and then visited Newton Cottage, Court Farm and the Rectory 'where Mr Jackson's butler rewarded the thirsty performers with the best of the cellar's contents'. There were more halts at the *Red Lion*, the *Anchor*, and the *White Swan*. John Mowlem at Victoria Terrace, Richard Row at the hotel, the Revd J.M. Colson at Belvidere, Captain McKenzie at Osborne House and Mrs Coventry at The Grove were all serenaded. The final refreshment was at the brewery. 'By this time, five o'clock in the morning, the waits were somewhat weary, retiring to their homes for a much needed rest until the bells, ringing for the afternoon service, called them to play and sing the hymns and carols from the gallery at the west end of the old church.' On Boxing Day the waits visited the farms at Whitecliff and Godlingston, finally returning once again to the brewery to quench their thirst where the collections were distributed among the singers and players.

Both WMH and JM give an account of the infamous 1851 Christmas Eve riot. In June JM wrote to Mr Jardine of Bow Street, a regular visitor, asking him to send a policeman for Swanage, and he would pay him for a year. 'The conduct of the boys here is so disgraceful and I am really ashamed not only for myself but for the stranger.' On 21 July 'our policeman, John Cripps, a fine fellow' arrived, and it was hoped that there would 'now be peace in our borders. The boys are rather frightened of our man.' But on 22 November, 'William Craft was put into the Blind House last night for striking our policeman – this Craft is a bad character.' Then on Christmas Eve

> our policeman was nearly killed. There was a mob of boys and men to the number of 100, and had it not been for Mrs Melmoth[10] I think the poor fellow must have lost his life. Yesterday I was at the Rectory with Dr Wilcox and Mr Serrell taking the depositions of sundry persons respecting the attack. I sincerely hope the guilty will be brought to justice and transported if possible. William Craft is the ringleader of the party and a worse man there cannot be, he is a bad husband and a drunkard to boot.

After Christmas 'the idle people about the street are rather more dull today, they fancy there is a rod in pickle for them, and unless something be done to protect the quiet inhabitants of this place, all that can move away from it will do so. I often regret I settled down here.' But on New Year's Eve he had the pleasure of giving 22 old men a good dinner. 'All that were there this twelve-months were alive to this day. I close the year with gratitude to God for all his mercies.' He continued to give this yearly dinner to the old men of Swanage for the rest of his life.

William Craft was evidently not transported, for in 1858 he was charged under the Aggravated Assault Act. On board the *Ursa Major* from Poole to Swanage was a clergyman with his daughter, and so was William Craft. He kept staring at her, and when they landed at the Quay, Craft 'pulled her down and kissed her'. She was unhurt. Craft said he had done no harm and would do it again. He was given six months hard labour, but a question was raised in the House of Commons to much laughter. It was said that the Act was being used for purposes never intended and the Home Secretary would look into the matter. Later 'Her Majesty has granted a reprieve to the man William Craft'. So that was that.

I I

A New Rector, Church and Pier

A new rector from 1854 to 1887, the Revd R. Duncan Travers MA, took the Chair in the Vestry on 16 November 1854 with the newly-elected Burial Board for the creation of a cemetery for the whole parish. The Board was 'composed of dissenters as well as churchmen, thus unity of action is the more praiseworthy'. Two acres of the Ilminster estate at Northbrook were purchased, and John Mowlem's offer to advance the loan, not exceeding £1,000 at five per cent, was accepted. The cemetery was enclosed with a stone wall.

The consecration by the Bishop of Salisbury took place on 23 August 1855. After an 'admirable sermon by the Prelate' the Procession followed 'over the new bridge to the cemetery at North Brook'. This tells us that Church Bridge was rebuilt at that time. The procession was headed by the contractor, Mr T. Farwell, followed by the members and clerk of the Board, the rector, a dozen other clergy, the registrar, Chancellor of the Diocese, the Bishop and his Chaplain. After the consecration the procession returned to the rectory.

The first burial (9 January 1856) was of Joseph Mowlem, aged 64, JM's eldest brother, 'contractor of the Real del Monte Company, Mexico'. He married Sarah Warren in 1815, and they and their family emigrated in 1827. 'Mexico Joe' returned in 1855 for health reasons and died at Herston House. His eldest son John died unmarried, killed by a fall from his horse in Mexico. Thus Joseph's only other son Thomas became John Mowlem's heir.[1]

The three Burial Registers, kept until the opening of Godlingston Cemetery in 1932, give much interesting information. John Gotobed, innkeeper, died in 1857. Alice Phippard's burial was cancelled and transferred to the Congregational ground, Upabout Lane. Giles Philips (1860) only survived 18 hours, 'the son of a Travelling Jew'. Who was Murdo Munro, professional singer (31 in 1902)? Among several 'Gentlemen' there appear William Bird Brodie (83 in 1863), George Filliter (84 in 1863), the Revd John Morton Colson (69 in 1866) and his wife Julia (70 in 1865), and in due course John Mowlem (1868). There were many stonemasons and quarriers; there were also two 'Idiots'. A steady population indicates little increase until the railway came: it was 2,139 in 1851; 2,004 in 1861; and 2,151 in 1871.

A new Church

The new rector found the church in a poor state, and in 1857 an Appeal was launched for its improvement. It started well with an offer of £500 from Mrs Coventry, on condition that an additional £1,000 was raised; £100 each was immediately offered by the Earl of

Eldon, the rector and friends, John Mowlem, and another resident. Another £50 each came from J.H. Calcraft M.P. and Thomas Randell, stone merchant and churchwarden. There was a suggestion that the balance from the regatta should be given to the Appeal, but there was opposition, and the committee 'had no power to donate money given for one object to anything else'.

In February it was decided not to rebuild the present church but that a choice of site for a new building offered by J. Mowlem Esq. be accepted with thanks. This was to be situated on the right of the bridge, presumably across the Brook from the rectory. Mr Wyatt was requested to prepare a plan adapted to the proposed site. But in October the scheme was rescinded owing to the probable expense. Instead the church was to be rebuilt, including raising the floor level. At first it was intended to take down only the defective parts, but in the end total rebuilding resulted.

In March 1859 it was announced that the parish church, with the exception of the tower, was about to be taken down and rebuilt 'to provide for the increasing wants of the parishioners and persons visiting this pleasant watering-place'. It would seat about seven hundred people. The DCC reported that 'the Diocesan architect, T.H. Wyatt Esq. has supplied the plans and Mr Mondey of Dorchester is the builder.' On 15 June the foundation stone was laid, and on 19 July 1860 the new building was consecrated by the Bishop of Salisbury. In addition to the original £500, Mrs Coventry gave another £200 for the east window, oak pulpit and the communion rails. There was a new Purbeck marble font.

The new south and east walls followed the old plan, but on the north there was an entirely new aisle and transept. The new building was in 13th-century idiom but incorporated three original Perpendicular windows including the unusual south-west one which was formerly a section of the old east window. There were galleries north and south, and space for a vestry in the tower was formed by raising the belfry. The final cost was about £3,000.

56   Bell Street, Herston, c.1895. On the left is the *Globe Inn*, and the Methodist Reading Room is on the right.

After the consecration service, luncheon was served in the old tithe barn when 70 sat down including all the principal inhabitants. Mr Calcraft proposed a toast to Mrs Coventry, who was present, and who had done so much: 'if it had not been for her kindness it was extremely doubtful whether they would have met to celebrate this event.' The rector proposed toasts to Mr Wyatt and Mr Mondey: 'the workmen have been for 15 months under my window and I never witnessed anything unbecoming.' The Revd Lester Lester entertained 300 children from Swanage and Herston to tea and cake, of which an incredible quantity disappeared. The rector provided tea and cake for 120 aged persons. The day closed with a supper in the barn, given for Mr Gerard, the foreman, and about fifty workmen.

After nearly a century a new clock from the factory of Mr Dent of London took the place of the old inaccurate one, which had done all its work with one hand. The parish was chiefly indebted to David Jardine, 'the eminent metropolitan magistrate' who paid £50, nearly half the cost. 'The joyous peal of bells which greeted Mr Jardine's arrival the day before the consecration, showed how highly the inhabitants appreciated his liberality.' On the actual day he was unwell; he returned home shortly after and died in September. He had erected the boundary stone on Ballard Down on the way to Studland ('Rest and be thankful'), and another large block of stone, placed as a seat on the Downs, is engraved 'J. D. 1852'.

Herston

This hamlet was largely a 'poor man's home, being almost entirely occupied by quarrymen's families'. The cottages were mostly poor, but the grouping of stone-tiled buildings, which included the ancient *Globe* inn at the foot of Bell Street, must even then have been quaintly attractive, at least to the visitor. Most of the old cottages have either disappeared or been vastly improved, and Bell Street is now termed a conservation area. Westwards from the turnpike gate at Herston Cross there was a straggle of more cottages on the south side of the high road, where there was another old inn, the *Royal Oak*, before the Greyseed quarries and the parish boundary with Langton Matravers.

When Duncan Travers became rector of Swanage in 1854 there was no school in Herston, though the population numbered some three hundred souls. This was his first concern, and in the following year an infants school was built in Bell Street on a site given by Mrs Serrell of Durnford, the stone having been given by local quarriers. It was a simple schoolroom with a porch and Welsh slate roof, and in 1865 it was extended, probably to accommodate older children who hitherto had walked a mile to school (if they were not already working at the quarries, or their parents could afford to pay the few pence). Further extensions with more classrooms were made in 1871 and 1888.[2]

It is not surprising that a methodist chapel was opened in Herston well before the C of E church, since the inhabitants were predominantly nonconformist. Both buildings are in Bell Street. The chapel was opened in 1861; it was followed by a simple reading room in 1864. St Mark's church,[3] just above the school, was begun in 1869 on a site again given by Mrs Serrell with an additional gift of £200. But, due to shortage of funds, though only costing £1,400, it was not consecrated by the Bishop until 25 April 1872. It was designed by John Hicks of Dorchester, but after his death it was completed by G. R. Crickmay of Weymouth. Before he retired as an architect in order to be a full-time novelist, Thomas Hardy was employed by Hicks as pupil and assistant, and subsequently by Crickmay to supervise or complete several church projects. It is probable that Hardy was involved with the design and construction of St Mark's and the framed unsigned plan on the church wall appears very like his other drawings, though expert examination gave a negative result.

57 Herston Cross, with the entrance to Bell Street on the left, Victoria Avenue on the right and Jobey Webber's thatched cottage beyond.

The church is again a simple building, with walls and roof in Purbeck stone, capped with a bell-cote. Internally there is a chancel arch and a north aisle containing the organ and former vestry: there is now a small extension. The 17th-century font was brought from St Mary's in 1869.

Pier and Tramway

In 1847 Henry Gillingham had put forward the proposal for a tramway to the quarries. The next mention of this project is given in the report of a public meeting held in the hotel on 9 September 1858 which was attended by many influential people of the area, including some from Wareham and Poole and with J.H. Calcraft M.P. presiding.

Captain Moorsom had visited Swanage again recently and was deeply impressed with the barbarous manner in which things were carried on. This was the opinion of others, and this meeting was arranged to hear his proposals for a tramway and pier. There was unlimited stone, he said, and it was a beautiful watering place, but the trade had fallen off and expense was the reason. He felt that he had been transported into a district where modern improvements were unknown. The town was crammed with visitors, there were inexhaustible quarries of excellent stone around them, and yet the people appeared to be fast asleep; unless they roused themselves he saw no reason why their trade should not entirely die out. He proposed a tram road falling at 1:50 from Langton Matravers to a pier at Swanage which could also be used for importing coal, saving triple or quadruple handling of that commodity as well as stone. The pier would not interfere with the beautiful spot known as the Park. A breakwater was needed to shelter from the 'east swells', but this was beyond the capital envisaged. The pier would be 630 ft long, costing £6,500. The tram road would be carried over the street[4] and continue for three miles. Stone could be stored along the line, doing away with the bankers, and the cost of bringing it down would be halved. Merchants would have their own waggons instead of farm carts. With the cost of the pier the total would be £14,600. After explaining the financial arrangements, Captain Moorsom hoped he had not been intrusive!

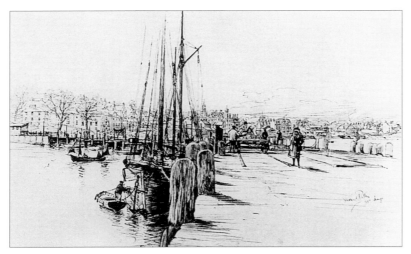

58 The first working pier in Swanage was built in 1859. It incorporated a standard gauge railway track which was intended, at some future date, to connect to a railway station, but, because of local opposition, this was never completed. The track was later reduced to narrow gauge, as only animal or manpower was allowed to use the track for transport. In this 1895 sketch the artist, Leonard Patten, depicts a typical scene: workers manually loading stone slabs into the boats.

Henry Gillingham gave some figures in support. Thomas Randell thought the trade in stone had been overstated, and the line would have to be longer to reach all the quarries. Mr W.J. Pike of Wareham thought the cost would be not less than £20,000 and that the traffic would not be remunerative; he was anxious to see a railway from Wareham to Swanage and questioned the smaller scheme. However, upon a show of hands, there was a unanimous vote in favour of the project. A committee would be set up to constitute a company when not less than £4,000 shares had been taken up.

In October another meeting was held in the National Schoolroom, where the scheme was explained to the quarrymen and who were invited to purchase shares, and a monthly payment of one shilling would be collected during the ensuing year. In November at the Black Bear, Wareham, Captain Moorsom produced plans and said that Mr John Walton of London would produce £12,000 if £4,000 was subscribed locally; £3,400 was already available. John Mowlem then proposed that the plans be approved, and that Messrs Phippard & Son form the company in order to obtain an Act of Parliament in the ensuing season. Henry Gillingham seconded, and the proposition was carried unanimously.

Success and Defeat

The Swanage Tramway and Pier Act received the Royal Assent on 8 August 1859 and the first stone was laid on 5 September by the Chairman of the company, John Mowlem. James Walton, the contractor, presented him with a silver trowel with ivory handle, suitably inscribed. JM proceeded to lay the stone using the trowel, mallet and level in a workmanlike manner, which brought hearty cheers from the gathering. The stone may still be seen (2004) in the sea wall near the pier entrance.

A dinner followed at the hotel, 'a truly excellent repast which did great credit to the culinary abilities of Mr and Mrs Row'. About seventy sat down, presided over by JM. The Revd G.V. Garland proposed a toast to the chairman and was quite convinced that they would not have arrived at the present stage had it not been for the willingness and readiness with which their worthy chairman had entered into the project; he was the third largest shareholder and he was the first who had come forward to give any effectual spur to the work. JM replied with an amusing speech. He saw that Weymouth was to be defended by 50 guns, while Swanage had only one which a Highlander could take under his arm to shoot grouse. He remembered when they had nine guns, but where had they gone? They had only half a gun to defend themselves!

J.S.W.S. Erle Drax M.P. replied to a toast to the House of Commons. When the pier was erected they would have steamers coming here continually, and it would be quite a favourite resort. Captain Moorsom hoped that there would be no obstacles in the way of the scheme, that there would be railways everywhere, particularly for ready access to the coast in case of any threatened invasion. He proposed a toast to Henry Gillingham who had brought this project forward, and a tablet to his honour was to be erected. Mr Brannon replied to the toast to the visitors. During the afternoon about two hundred people, including the workmen engaged on the pier, sat down to a 'bountiful dinner' in a large marquee near the foundation stone. Donkey racing and dancing made a gala day for Swanage.

In November several vessels came alongside the new pier bringing rails and timber, and in December the piles, ironwork, planking and cranes were in position. In February a 32-pounder gun weighing two tons was landed and sent on a truck along the railway, 'all done in half an hour'. Swanage was now defended! Captain Moorsom reported that the pier was practically complete, waggons were promised for March and 'you may then begin to earn revenue'. By September 1861 the pier was open to traffic; the toll was 1d. for each passenger and article of luggage landing from the pier.

But now there were problems. The tramway had been laid all the way through the banker land, but a few property owners were being 'obstructive to progress'. All the materials for the further extension inland were ready, and nothing but permission to enter on the land was needed to get the rails laid to Langton. 'Meanwhile the improvement of the most dangerous part of Swanage Street must be deferred and the quarriers would suffer by the delay.' In addition there was now difficulty in raising enough capital for the completion of the scheme. By 1862 the contractor had suspended all work and proposed to give up possession of the pier in exchange for £6,000 cash. The company was still short of £1,500 to purchase the site, and we read no more on the subject in the newspaper.

Philip Brannon

The range of this fascinating character was extraordinary. Artist, architect, civil engineer, inventor, engraver, writer, designer, surveyor, builder and contractor, Inspector of Nuisances, he was born in 1817 in Newport, Isle of Wight, but spent much of his life in Southampton.[5] He often attended meetings regarding the proposed Swanage pier and tramway, and lectured about his ideas for developing the Isle of Purbeck.

In 1858 there appeared, as he stated in his preface, the first illustrated guide to Swanage and the Isle of Purbeck, published by Sydenham of Poole. There was also another production, *Illustrations of the Geologic Scenery of Purbeck*, of the same date. The first edition of the guide was by far the most extensive and detailed account of the district, but his modified book continued as *Sydenham's Brannon Guide to Bournemouth and District* through 13 editions until 1877; the 19th edition, now without Brannon's name, was the last (1893).

There was a book of 32 *Views of Bournemouth and District engraved by John Newman and Philip Brannon Between 1855-77*. A few of his engravings were changed to bring the subjects up-to-date, such as the view of Swanage Bay when the new pier appeared in 1859. The drawings are highly romantic and his text poetic, if not flowery, but nevertheless they are attractive and informative. His inventive mind sometimes ran away with his enthusiasm; for instance, his proposal for Leviathan steamship liners to dock in Worbarrow Bay (there being eight fathoms close in shore), with a railway tunnel under the ridge to Wareham! He includes maps showing tramways along the cliffs to St Aldhelm's Head and across the heaths to Poole Harbour, with new docks. His plan for a new pier and harbour with fortifications at Swanage was 'similar to, but not the same as Mr Nicholls' '. For all his engineering proposals, he nevertheless enthuses on the scenery and splendid prospects for the visitor.

Brannon found time to design a church in Southampton, but the most astonishing projects were his first use of reinforced concrete in pile foundations at Walton-on-the-Naze, and his invention of the 'Arcustatic' airship or Navigable Balloon of 1870. These are but a few of his many inventions and proposals, but perhaps his business acumen was not so brilliant, as he was adjudged bankrupt twice. He died in 1890.

Rail and Road

Once again the prospect of the branch line railway seemed nearer in 1862. Now that there was a working pier and a short standard gauge railway John Mowlem, his nephew George Burt and the bankers were pressing for a connection to the main line, especially as others were trying to achieve a line to the Creech clay pits from Wareham. The Isle of Purbeck Railway Company was formed, with support of the South Western Railway, but opposition came this time from the townspeople of Wareham. The bill received the Royal Assent on 22 June 1863, but again with the lack of monetary support the powers lapsed in 1868. The promoters lost £1,000 in supporting the bill.

It will be remembered that Morton Pitt had proposed an improved valley road in 1824, which came to nothing. The turnpike road formed in 1766 had to pass through Langton and Kingston, but the corkscrew hill down to Corfe Castle was always difficult. The first O.S. one-inch map (1811) shows a lane striking east from Townsend in Corfe along the valley, but it appears to peter out north of Langton. Henry Gillingham was complaining in 1847 about the lack of a new road and the folly of the original route which he thought was made for private interest rather than public utility. 'The traveller, after ascending the toilsome steep Kingston Hill, finds himself actually further from Swanage than he had previously been at Corfe Castle.'

59 & 60 Views of Corfe Castle and the new railway stations of Corfe and Swanage, both built by Messrs Bull & Sons of Southampton. The engraving is from the *Illustrated London News*, 13 June 1885, announcing the opening of the new Wareham to Swanage line.

At last in 1862 it was proposed to abandon the existing turnpike road, that is, no longer to maintain it by the Trust, and substitute a new one between Townsend and Leeson Gate, the length being about 3¼ miles; the expense for making the road, including purchase of land, would be £2,020. (DCC 6 March 1862.) The Wareham Road Bill was read a third time and was passed by the Lords on 5 May. An advertisement for the *Royal Victoria Hotel* reads:

'a public omnibus leaves the hotel daily for the Wareham Station, awaiting the arrival of the 3.08 down train, reaching this place at 5 p.m.'.

Mrs J.E. Panton wrote:

> I do not think any place in the world ever grew such wild flowers. We drove through groves of golden gorse, crowding primroses, violets and cowslips. Later in the year the hedges were festooned with wild roses; foxgloves stood proudly among the ferns; several orchids could be found; and in the wide ditches, now desecrated by the presence of hideous red villas, the *Osmunda regalis* grew in profusion ... When we reached the shore I generally sat at the end of the rough wooden structure that was called the pier; where the occasional steamer called, and where coal and similar articles of commerce were unloaded. But the chief industry of the place was stone ... The eternal chip, chip, chip of the chisel mingled with the sound of the sea in a most weird manner.

There was still the disadvantage, after passing Herston gate, of ending up in the narrow High Street, choked with dust, mud and carts. In 1865 it was reported that a new road 30ft wide was being made by Mr Jesty, the contractor, leading to the shore from Herston, by way of Prospect farm and the cemetery. The length as far as Eel Pool (Hill Pole), the junction with Northbrook Lane, was named Eldon Road; the completely new road to the sea was called de Moulham Road. Later both sections became Victoria Avenue, de Moulham Road becoming a road parallel with the shore in recent times.

The Herston turnpike gate was removed in 1876. All the Dorset Trusts had ceased to operate by 1883.

Royalty again

The grand project of the formation of Portland Harbour was at last achieved and completed by the prisoners of the Verne citadel. The great stone-built breakwaters enclosed three square miles of sea. Albert, Prince Consort, opened the Harbour in 1849 and then left for the Isle of Wight. On the way the royal yacht anchored in Durlston Bay, a boat was lowered, and a party landed with the Prince. Accompanied by Captain Sir George Biddlecombe KCB, they walked across the headland and open downs to come upon the exquisite view of Swanage Bay, the scene of Victoria's visit as a young girl only 16 years earlier. The Prince was much impressed with the scenery and pure air. Sir George pointed out to him that the bay would make a first-rate harbour by building a breakwater from Peveril towards the Bollard. They then returned to the yacht.

The next royal visitor was Edward, Prince of Wales, who with two companions was on a walking tour, travelling incognito. They stayed the night at the *Royal Victoria Hotel* on 26 September 1856, and the story is told that the young gentleman had to sleep on a sofa, because the hotel was full. However, he said next morning that he had never passed a better night in his life.

A storm blew up with a heavy sea, and William Hixson's fishing boat was smashed, the only means of support for the family. 'H.R.H., witnessing the casualty, expressed his desire to aid in replacing it. With the consent of his royal parents, he contributed £13 to complete the necessary sum.'[16] Only then did the manager of the hotel realise that they had entertained the future king and were mortified about the lack of a proper bed for him.

Finally, in June 1880, there was a royal visit by H.R.H. the Duke of Edinburgh, Prince Alfred, second son of the Queen, who landed at 'Peveril slip'. He shook hands with Captain Mansel and inspected the coastguard station and men. 'His courteous manners gave a lesson which the young people of the place would do well to imitate. As William of Wykeham said some hundreds of years ago – "manners maketh man".'

The Albert Monument

The early death of the Prince Consort on 14 December 1861 brought widespread sorrow. His Royal Highness, his wife Victoria and his son Edward had all visited Swanage at different times, and a fitting memorial to 'Albert the Good' seemed more than desirable. George Burt wrote a letter from London to the rector, having read the account of the Lord Mayor's call for a national monument: 'Swanage should share in handing down to posterity the life of that great and virtuous Prince.' He could produce a design for an obelisk[7] and the cost should be shared by a wide subscription.

The site was chosen as the highest point on Court Hill where Victoria had paused on her way down to the hotel in 1833. The 'chaste and neat little monument' of Purbeck stone was completed by December 1862. John Mowlem gave the land, George Burt the railings, and John and James Haysom cut the inscription. Mr Farwell and Mr C. Burt erected the obelisk at the cost of £56 19s. od. The monument was to become parish property, and this led to problems: it was damaged in the blizzard of January 1881 but, after enquiry as to the ownership, was repaired by the Local Board. Between the Wars it again became unsafe and the top courses were removed to J.E. Mowlem's yard at Northbrook. By this time, too, the monument was surrounded by buildings and

61   The High Street, Court Hill, with horses being led down the hill to the stone depot. The Albert monument, in the distance, was erected in 1862 as a memorial to the Prince Consort, who had died in the previous year.

sheds. In 1971 developers inadvisedly demolished it on the disputed land, thereby causing an outcry (Mrs Haysom sat on top of it until the police arrived), since when the ghost of Albert has risen from time to time until its remains should be resurrected elsewhere.

The Alfred Monument

John Mowlem's next project was for a monument 'in commemoration of a great naval battle fought with the Danes in Swanage Bay by Alfred the Great, AD 877'. But it was first suggested by Philip Brannon during his visit in September 1859 in connection with his proposed breakwater scheme. The granite tuscan column was erected in 1862 adjacent to his new Mowlem Institute which followed. WMH explained the anachronism of the four iron cannonballs: at the end of the Crimea War the wooden battleships had just returned to Portsmouth, 'some of their hulls studded with unexploded Russian shells 13 inches in diameter. Mr Mowlem asked the local Captain of Coastguards to get him four to place on top of the column.' The balls were not originally intended, and they 'provoked a good deal of chaff'.

At the Crimean War Peace celebrations in June 1856 a dinner had been given at the Hotel to the coastguards who had lately returned from service in H.M.'s Fleet, together with their wives and children, about one hundred and ten in all, provided by liberality of the gentry, with Samuel Serrell Esq. in the Chair, and John Mowlem in the vice-Chair. There was an abundance of roast meats, puddings and pies. At the conclusion of the dinner and speeches the men were regaled with grog, the wives with negus. This continued till 4 o'clock when tea and plum cake were served. Quite a day, it seems!

The Alfred monument was undermined and collapsed in a severe storm in 1883, before the sea wall was built, but it was re-erected soon after. In 1965 it was moved some way northwards of its former site as it obstructed the approach to the new Mowlem Theatre. One councillor proposed that it should be sunk to the bottom of the bay. Fortunately wiser councils prevailed, and it still stands as one of the more endearing jokes of Swanage.

The Mowlem Institute

Efforts made to provide a reading room for Swanage met with little success, so a signed petition was made to John Mowlem to build such a room. The benefactor now possessed a suitable site and in due course

62 John Mowlem's granite monument of 1862, celebrating Alfred the Great's victory over the Danes in Swanage Bay in AD 877. Several drinking fountains along the front (note the young boy leaning against one) were provided by John Ernest Mowlem when the sea wall was built during 1904 and 1905.

the scheme came to fruition. The Mowlem Institute was built near the shore as a reading room 'for the benefit and mutual improvement of the working classes'.

The building, of local stone with a Bangor slate roof, was designed by G.R. Crickmay of Weymouth and the contractor was Mr Brooken of the same town. Details were given in the DCC (18 December 1862) of the new hall which 'will doubtless form a far more pleasing spectacle in contrast to the present small irregular tenements'. George Burt, deputising for John Mowlem, read out at a Vestry meeting the conditions for presentation of the room to the parish. It was 'to be used for lecturing, mechanical and scientific instructions, and intellectual improvement generally, not excluding occasional meetings on freemasonry'. In due course John Mowlem was appointed the first Master of the Masonic Lodge consecrated in the Institute. The conditions also stressed that, while religious principles were of paramount importance, the proceedings in the new room should be

> kept entirely distinct from sectarian influences, and the introduction of controversial topics, whether in religion or politics, shall in no case be allowed. Further, if the building were neglected despite the provision of a sum set aside for maintenance, it would revert to the donor's heirs-in-law. Trustees would be appointed, two of which would be perpetual, viz. the Rector and the people's churchwarden, who would keep the key. JM reserved to himself the appointment of five others for life, six further trustees would be elected by the ratepayers and eligible for re-election. The total number of trustees would be 13, five forming a quorum. Mr Charrington of the Brewery was appointed secretary.

At the opening, the rector 'passed a high eulogium of esteem and respect on John Mowlem Esq., noticing his career from earlier life till now, and the present high position of honour and influence he holds'. The bells rang merry peals during the day, and the National School had a half-holiday.

The last years

In January 1865, the anniversary of the Institute, a public tea and concert were held, the charge being 1s. 0d. Three hundred and sixty people crammed in to the Institute to hear, among other items, John Mowlem sing 'Lord Dundreary'. He was in the Chair at most meetings, including a lecture by given by the Revd J. Harper, Wesleyan minister, on 'Life in Swanage', with practical suggestions for the town's improvement. The Oddfellows fraternity was about eighteen months old in 1866 and had some sixty members. The Institute now had over a hundred members. Twelve newspapers and seven periodicals were supplied, and chess and draughts boards were provided, along with 'a famous bagatelle board'. There were about six hundred lending library books, and penny readings, lectures and music continued: the piano was well used.

As usual at Christmas JM entertained the men of the parish beyond a certain age, at his residence, to a 'thorough good dinner of good old English fare'. On 22 January 1868 the annual tea and concert took place at the Institute. Miss Haysom (a little girl) sang sweetly 'What is Home without a Mother?' George Burt presided in the absence of JM who was unwell. Then, sadly, the grand old man was no more. The DCC of 12 March 1868 wrote:

> We regret to report the death of this estimable gentleman, which melancholy event took place on Sunday morning at Purbeck House, where he had been staying for some time past. John Mowlem was the architect of his own fortune, and in him Swanage will lose a most generous benefactor and one who has done much to raise the character of this delightful watering place ... His disposition was peculiarly genial, and his chief delight appeared to be doing good to his fellow men ... his death will be the cause of universal sorrow and regret. His open and candid manner made him a great favourite with children as well as with those more advanced in age. He was as it were a child with children and a man with men.

His funeral was, as he expressedly wished, plain and simple. There were no pall, trappings, cloaks, scarves or long hatbands. 'The cushion and insignia of the "De Moulham" Lodge having been placed on the oak coffin, the service was beautifully read by the Rector, assisted by Dr Burrowes of Kimmeridge. Then the coffin was put in its last resting-place - the massive Guernsey granite tomb, built by himself, where in 1849 he had placed his beloved wife.'

John Mowlem's will was reported in June. He left a little less than £40,000: his residence, contents and the interest on £2,000 went to Mrs James Arbon (née Susy Burt); the freehold of his estate was given to his nephew Thomas; the residue of his real and personal estates were put in trust, one half for his grand-nephew, John Mowlem (son of his nephew Henry Hibbs Mowlem), and the other for Mrs Arbon's children.

After fulfilling the founder's intentions for more than a century, the Mowlem Institute was demolished and replaced in 1966 by the Mowlem Theatre, restaurant and shops, with mixed feelings. A bust of John Mowlem and the original inscriptions from the Institute are preserved in the entrance.

The Mowlem Estate

John Mowlem felt in his bones that he was a direct descendant from Durandus who built King William's wooden Corfe Castle in Domesday times and who was given the Moulham land as a reward. If he bought the Ilminster estate he would feel almost that it would 'come full circle'. Unfortunately the field called Moleham now belonged to another estate,[8] but nevertheless he purchased large areas of Swanage land between 1857 and 1861. Eventually his Mowlem estate stretched from Swanage brook northwards to Ulwell and from the bay westwards to Cauldron Barn. It remained virtually undeveloped in his day, but his brother's grandson, John Ernest Mowlem (1868-1946) who inherited it, set out new roads and sold many building plots in more recent times. Fortunately the later recreation ground and sandpit field facing the sea became the property of the local council, remaining open to the public; very little of the Mowlem Estate remains the property of a family descendant.

12

King of Swanage: George Burt

63 George Burt, (1816-1894). The motto 'Know thyself' was taken by Burt from an ancient Greek motto found at the Temple of Apollo in Delphi. The sculptor was C.H. Mabey, 1889.

George Burt: the name conjures a down-to-earth, no-nonsense person. Hard and go-ahead he may have been, but honest he surely was, and it was said that 'he was one who, underneath a brusque exterior, concealed a warm and sympathetic heart.' Inevitably some admired him while others disliked him as an upstart. But he certainly brought many improvements which were to change the face of Swanage. His motto was 'Know thyself': and perhaps he did.

The firm continued to prosper by improving London's streets, and George Burt, now a partner, was fast becoming wealthy like his uncle. He had married in 1841, and at the age of 40 had a family of six children. In 1850 he bought a substantial house in Paddington, but Swanage beckoned, and he wanted another home by the sea, though retirement was a distant prospect. His father, Robert, had died in 1847 but his mother continued to live at 1 Victoria Terrace, and his younger brother Charles now ran the shop: 'Burt, Grocer and Confectioner'. Although flourishing, 'trade' was looked down on by the upper classes, and GB was certainly on an upper rung of the ladder and still climbing.[1] Thus the family branches gradually widened after the death of their mother Letty Burt in 1861.

Frank Burt, another younger brother of GB, founded the local firm of 'Burt & Burt' with Henry Weeks Burt;[2] Frank had been working with Mowlem's in London but returned to settle in Swanage. He left a series of diaries, mostly concerned with his work, especially with the London sewers. In Swanage he first lived with his family at Handfast House on

64 Handfast House, Upper High Street. Francis (Frank) Burt, younger brother of George Burt, can be seen with his family in the front garden, c.1890. Following a fire, the house was demolished by Frank Burt and developed into Handfast Terrace. Fortunately the stone clasped hands over the door were re-erected on the east gable wall of the new buildings.

the upper High Street. Later he built Gordon Villas opposite and moved to no.1. He rebuilt the old house with a dismal brick terrace, but the clasped hands plaque was re-erected on the gable wall. His son Charles founded the well-known contractors, Burt & Vick of Poole.

Old Purbeck House and Osborne House

The opportunity came in 1857 when the owner, Miss Priscilla Edmonds-Cole died, another 'last of the line', and George Burt bought Purbeck House for £550. The original building, quite small and probably of the early 17th century, had been enlarged in 1810 when owned by Captain Joseph Edmonds R.N. (d.1818).[3] It provided six main rooms, a coach-house and outbuildings, standing on the High Street with a long garden, at the top of which was a circular stone-built summerhouse. Inside was a revolving table six feet in diameter, the top mounted on a stone-cart wheel, said to be the first one made by machine. This gave pleasure to generations of children, and still (2004) survives. Underneath is a large slate tank which supplied the house with spring water.

The local doctor, H.D.C. Delamotte, was the tenant at the time of the sale, but he and his family moved to Osborne House in Seymer Road which was advertised as a marine residence with three sitting rooms, nine bedrooms, a large garden and a coach-house; it was not shown on the 1838 Chancery map but must have been built soon after. It has a delightful front elevation and has since been converted into flats.

Durlston Park

John Mowlem Burt's coming-of-age was celebrated in 1865, and his father was hoping to loosen some of the London reins for his son. George Burt was turning his attention to property in Swanage, following his uncle's purchase of the Ilminster estate.

In 1862 Freeland Filliter, the Wareham lawyer, sold the Cliff and Sentry estate at Durlston to GB, who began to develop it forthwith. When he bought it, the headland was, if not a wilderness, a treeless expanse, some ploughed, with the abandoned quarries above Durlston Bay. What better than to turn it into a park with superior villas and terraces to enjoy the glorious views and pure air?

But first it needed a great deal of preparation. Broad roads were planned, but the priorities were providing piped water, gas and sewerage. The new Park Road rose above Marshall Row, and the crescents of Durlston and Peveril Roads were extended from the top of Seymer Road – shades of Morton Pitt and his unrealised crescents. Likewise, GB's plan for the development, also never achieved, is astonishing. There were to be continuous terraces of some 150 close-packed houses, though with long back gardens, extending to Durlston Head. Fortunately none of these were built, except for a few in the new Grosvenor Road, originally earmarked as 'stables'. Some two dozen large villas with extensive grounds are shown on the plan, and a few of these did get built, including 'Sentryfields', 'Hill Side' (later 'Steepways'), 'Peveril' and 'St Aldhelm's'. The alarming 'proposed road on the high land past Tilly Whim and Worth' never materialised: imagine a four mile motor road today, possibly with modern flats, overlooking the sea! The first Lord Eldon had often spoken of this road 'which would combine one of the finest drives and views in England'. GB was enthusiastic, but the later Lord Eldon was, fortunately, not in favour. We must be thankful that the Dorset County Council and National Trust are now the owners of most of this beautiful coast and that Purbeck was designated as an Area of Outstanding Natural Beauty in 1957. It almost became a National Park, and was rejected only because of its small size. But now its world-famous designation as the Jurassic Coast has finally safeguarded Purbeck.

The slow development of the Durlston estate was due to two facts: the distance from the nearest railway station (ten miles from Wareham) and the very steep access up Park Road (there were no motor vehicles for another 40 years). GB planned a new marketplace at the foot, and a few shops were built there, with little success. Slowly houses 'of a superior kind' appeared in Park Road where, later, a new church, St Aldhelm's, was built near the top, though not until 1892. Therefore this Victorian suburb took a long time to become, if it ever did, the 'New Town' of Swanage.

The scheme for a 'pleasaunce' had more rapid success. A zigzag was 'cut across the face of the cliff and kept in perfect order'. The new plantations, growing luxuriantly, soon needed to be thinned; 'high above the fuchsias waved the lordly Pampas grass.' This was the spot for a convalescent home, Dr Burrowes[4] thought, and 'with books or sketching apparatus, many an hour may be spent most delightfully; and most justly has the locale been named *La Belle Vue*.' Down the zigzag path revealed a cross-built stone shelter named 'All the year round' and a seat inscribed 'Rest and admire'. In 1881 a major landslide occurred, the zigzag was engulfed and several of the seats disappeared. 'Back to nature!'

Health and Sanitation

In an article 'Swanage as a Health Resort' from the *Medical Times*,[5] it was stated that the bathing was perfect and thoroughly safe. The air was remarkably fresh and exhilarating, and 'the weakest wight may be set on his legs, with food and exercise and an air which soon leaves its ozoniferous tints on the ruddy cheeks of the visitors.' However, the local men did not look robust, and 'all accounts speak of early marriages of cousins, of close apartments, of scrofula and pthisis, as concurrent facts. Although their water be as full of lime as possible, rickets and decayed teeth are very common.' Insanity was also said to be common, and whooping cough carried off many children. In spite of all this, epidemics were few and the populace was on the whole healthy. On the subject of food, it was considered that the meat, poultry and dairy produce was good, the bread indifferent and fruit scarce except for apples; fish was available (though sole and mullet only at London prices), but 'the lobster, traditionally abundant, is really almost extinct.' However. the famous 'Swanage lobster' continues to be available: at a price!

Sanitary conditions were still very poor and there was as yet no main drainage. GB was constructing a sewer from his 'new town' down to the sea, but 'drainage must be difficult because, if they allow water-closet sewage to be poured into the bay, the bathing will be spoiled. The Moule earth system[6] is clearly the one for a small place like this. The use of the sea as the outlet is morally wrong and physically nasty.' This main sewerage pipe was far from satisfactory for another hundred years.

Gas and Water

Swanage was now making progress with new buildings and new roads, and at no distant date it would be lit by gas. 'It is hoped that, following the example of Mr Mowlem and Mr George Burt, other well-wishers will strive to raise it to that high position which it intrinsically deserves.'

Following the construction of the gasworks near Prospect Farm, pipes were laid through the main street in January 1868. By the time of the lamented death of John Mowlem in March, the Mowlem Institute and some of the shops were lit, and installations in the church and chapels and the Durlston estate were proceeding. There was some anxiety as to the cost of supply, at 6s. 8d. per 1,000 cubic foot. GB had bought the gas company, and he reluctantly reduced the price. He obtained many redundant lamp-posts from London, some having inscriptions such as 'Grosvenor Place', 'Northumberland Avenue', 'William IV' and 'City of London'. Several handsome lamp-posts, which had formerly graced the front, were embossed with a representation of St George & the Dragon and with the words 'St George's Hanover Square'. After the Second World War, when the street lighting was changed from gas to electricity and inappropriate concrete standards were introduced, the old lamp-posts were removed by the council and sold to a scrap merchant. Some are believed to have found their way to America. So much for the councillors of the day. Fortunately there are still many London bollards to be seen in Swanage.

Soon after acquiring the Durlston estate, GB obtained an Act of Parliament in 1864 to supply it, and, he hoped, the whole town, with pure water. The original circular waterworks building behind Sentry Road survives (2004). The water was raised from an artesian well 113 feet deep to a reservoir 200 feet above sea level. Later a large tank was erected in a stone-built water tower at the top of Taunton Road and bears the date 1886.[7] Incidentally, this site was at first protected 'by a section of the railings pulled down at the famous Hyde Park Riot', which occurred in 1866 when thousands of people, denied admission to a meeting of the Reform League, tore down hundreds of yards of railings.[8] The water tower has now been converted into an interesting dwelling.

But by 1872 little more had been done to improve the water supply generally. A report by Dr Home[9] stated that some people had to take their drinking water from wells in their houses, which were all near cesspits and drains, while others took theirs from the Mill Pond, which was contaminated and, after rain, too foul to use; those who depended on this pond would then try to catch a little rainwater. The 'lake' at Carrant's Court was little better. At Herston, 'where fever

65   Children playing on a raft in Swanage Bay. How redolent of the Victorian age this scene is, with the children fully clothed even when paddling in the water.

66 The obelisk was erected on Ballard Down in 1892 by George Burt to commemorate the bringing of pure water to Swanage. It was demolished during the Second World War but was re-erected on 11 July 1973 (minus one damaged section) as part of an army exercise.

is so common', the dip-well used by some was within 10 feet of the road into which came house drainage. Dr Home hoped that the artesian well at Durlston, only so far supplying about fourteen houses, might be available for the whole town. Apart from this, 'it may be stated that all the inhabitants drink sewage-polluted water, or water imminently exposed to such pollution.' This was a damning report.

GB came to the rescue. A source of water below the chalk at Ulwell was found, a well was sunk and a reservoir was constructed on the hillside. To commemorate this event in 1892, he erected a monument immediately above it, a spot chosen upon a prehistoric round barrow. An obelisk of white Cornish granite, it stood near the Mansion House, serving as a giant gas lamp until GB brought it down from London. After the Second World War it lay in pieces, probably pulled down about 1941 as too prominent a landmark. The monument was re-erected in July 1973 by the Royal Engineers, as a 'Military Aid for the Civil Community' project, taking two days.

Mixed Bathing

Bathing in any form was generally not done. Was it not that Queen Elizabeth I's bath was but a twice-yearly event? Bathrooms were non-existent until the 19th century, and then only gradually introduced to the upper classes. In 1846 John Mowlem, somewhat of a fanatic about washing, was making a bathroom in 2 Victoria Terrace and enthused upon his 'new copper bath and shower' from London. His great-nephew was at Morgan's local school and 'all the boys went to bathe today, this is the second time this week. My namesake is frightened, he is badly taught.'[10] Many seamen never learnt to swim, which seems remarkable. But

67 Early bathing machines on the main beach at Swanage. The method of lowering and raising these large huts on wheels was via a capstan, of which you can see a crabstone by the wheels. See illustration 24 (p.42).

68   A Walter Pouncy picture showing two Sunday School teachers with their charges about to embark on a boat trip with George Rambler Chinchen, the longshore boatman.

69   Blatant disregard for Victorian modesty by the young girls paddling before the boat trip.

sea bathing became more usual, since George III entered the sea at Weymouth from a wheeled bathing machine to the accompaniment of 'God save the King'. In 1828 the *Manor House Hotel* at Swanage had regularly advertised safe sea bathing as well as warm and cold baths within the hotel itself.

In August 1877 George Stickland and George Clark, bathing machine proprietors, were summoned by the Swanage Local Board about the matter of sea bathing. The surveyor had observed several machines close together, two side by side about two feet apart. He had seen a lady get into one and a gentleman in another, and they had both bathed together. However, it appears that they were husband and wife! Mr Parsons told Stickland that he was breaking the byelaws, but Stickland said that he did not care. They were fined one shilling each and costs. It was 'Shiner', living at Ivy Cottage on the shore, who claimed that he first introduced 'Mixed Bathing' to Swanage about this time. Twenty years later there were still mixed feelings on the subject. The DCC reported (29 September 1898) that 'a most ridiculous prosecution has been brought against John Davis White about him teaching ladies to swim.'

The Wellington 'Clock' Tower

Thomas Docwra, another well-known contractor, 'of Balls Pond, London', was a friend of Mowlem and Burt and bought 'The Grove' in 1866. It was in his grounds that the Tower came to be re-erected in Swanage. It was designed by Arthur Ashpitel FSA as a memorial to the Duke of Wellington and originally adorned the southern approach to London Bridge where it was placed in 1854. The cost of the monument itself was £700, excluding the statue of the Duke, for which funds proved insufficient! There was an illuminated clock with four transparent dials, made for the Great Exhibition of 1851.[11]

Within a few years the monument was found to be 'an unwarrantable obstruction' because of the increase in traffic. Mowlem's offer to dispose of it without charge was accepted, and in 1867 the tower was carefully taken down, the stones numbered and packed, and brought in the *Mayflower* to Swanage. There it was presented by Burt to Docwra who rebuilt it in his garden at a cost, it is said, of £1,000. On the base is inscribed 'T.D.1868'. The clock never arrived; thus the 'clock tower' became another curiosity of Swanage. At the turn of the century the tower lost its spire: 'This old monument to martial glory has suffered of late, for its pinnacle has been blown down and replaced by a copper sheathing very like a dish-cover.'[12]

Docwra spent most of his time in London, but, when he retired to 'The Grove', he became another Swanage benefactor. In his 70th year he gave dinners at the *Ship* for his workpeople, lifeboat crew, coastguards and fishermen, then a 'Monster Treat' for all the Swanage children; about seven hundred and fifty including their teachers had an outing to Bournemouth on the *Empress* paddle-steamer, each child being given a bun. Docwra died in 1882, leaving over £120,000; by his will, his allowances to old people were to continue. He was survived by five sons and five daughters, his wife having died in 1878. His son Tom continued the extensive engineering firm and tendered for the later Swanage railway, without success.

Sir Charles Robinson[13]

Shortly after George Burt acquired Durlston, there appeared on the scene his only serious rival in Swanage, John Charles Robinson, art adviser to the South Kensington (later V & A) Museum founded under the auspices of the Prince Consort. He was knighted in 1887. At first they were friendly enough, sharing for instance the cost of fireworks (£5 each) for Swanage regatta. Robinson's first home was at the newly-erected 'St Aldhelm's' at the top of Park Road. It was built over abandoned quarry workings, and some years later collapsed in a cloud of dust, fortunately without loss of life.[14] Only recently have new flats taken its place, no doubt on firmer foundations. But in 1875 Robinson had moved to a more stately home, Newton Manor, the ancient domain of the former Cockram family. He proceeded to convert the large barn into a dining hall complete with a broad mullioned and transomed window. Introduced into various parts of the house and garden were Elizabethan, Queen Anne, French, Italian and Spanish works of art collected from all over Europe, unwanted, one presumes, by the Museum in London.

Robinson looked down on Burt, considering him to be lacking in taste. Sir Charles and Lady Robinson entertained the Crown Princess of Germany for the second time in three years (1887), while George Burt had to be content with the Lord Mayor of London: though indeed he had become Sheriff of London & Middlesex in 1878. When GB was finally able to supply water to the town, Robinson declined and built his own reservoir near the Priest's Way on his own land. Later there was friction over the layout of roads. However, they had to rub along together, particularly when the railway became a reality and both became directors.

70 A portrait of Sir J.C. Robinson, CB, FSA (1824-1913), who was Queen Victoria's surveyor of pictures from 1882 to 1901. He acquired the Newton property in 1873 and is in the Dorset section of John Grant's *Who's Who*.

Robinson soon embarked on acquiring more land. In 1875 he purchased the freehold of Eightholds from the Dean & Chapter of Exeter and proceeded to develop for building the northern part, which he called the Manor, Hedes and Eldon Hill estates. The new roads were named after earlier owners of the land. At the top, a new road connecting Burt's Durlston estate with his own was named Bon Accord, which promised good relations. However, Burt wanted to drive a road along Sunshine Walk, behind Purbeck House, to connect with Robinson's Manor Road, but it is said that the latter planted trees to prevent this. Soon, most of the terrace houses in Stafford Road had been built and also half a dozen larger villas including 'Rocklands' and 'Cluny', as named in the O.S. map of 1889.

In 1876 Robinson purchased 2 Victoria Terrace, formerly the home of John and Susannah Mowlem and later the Arbons, following the death of Susy (née)

71 Alfred Dawson's engraving of Newton Manor, *c.*1882.

Burt in 1871. It became the Post Office and also the H.Q. of the Isle of Purbeck Yacht Club, which had recently been established. The first Annual Yacht Regatta took place in August 1875. Charles E. Robinson, the eldest son, was the Hon. Secretary, and his yacht was the *Marion*. There was a luncheon at the hotel for members and their friends (by ticket only, Ladies admitted). C.E. Robinson MA, barrister-at-law, produced his handsome volume, *A Royal Warren or Picturesque Rambles in the Isle of Purbeck*, in 1882. His brother Edmund was an architect in partnership with James Clifton, but died young,

The Wild Wave

In the hazy darkness at 4 a.m. on 23 January 1875, the brigantine *Wild Wave*, bound for Poole with a cargo of coals, mistook the treacherous Peveril Point for the Foreland, and in a heavy sea suddenly struck the outer ledge, her mainmast instantly going by the board. The coastguards were alerted and quickly launched their four-oared gigs but could not get near the wreck. At the same time the rocket apparatus was brought into use, but all three rockets missed. At the sounds, people began to run to the Point including the Robinsons, father and son, who subsequently described and sketched the scene. By 5.30 it was discerned that five people were huddled on the deck which was constantly submerged by waves. Finally a small boat managed to draw up under the wreck, a rope was thrown, and four men and a little boy slid down into the rescuers' arms, whereupon the *Wild Wave* sank into deeper water and was lost to sight. The Swanage postmaster had sent a telegram for the Poole lifeboat, which arrived too late to do anything except to take the shipwrecked men back to Poole. The little orphan was taken into apprenticeship by a childless ship's painter. The gallant coastguards were presented with rewards.

This was the signal for the first Swanage lifeboat. J.C. Robinson wrote a full account to *The Times*[15] with a petition for a lifeboat and, following the publicity, the RNLI resolved that his should be one of the new boats with which private donors had endowed them. The lifeboat house was built by William Masters Hardy, and in September the new ten-oared boat, the *Charlotte Mary*, was launched. William Masters was appointed coxswain, and he appears in Thomas Hardy's novel *The Hand of Ethelberta* as Captain Flower.

In 1880 William Brown took over as cox, and the third boat, the *William Erle,* was launched in 1893. During a violent gale on 12 January 1895 it went to the aid of the Norwegian barque *Brilliant*. Suddenly the lifeboat was hit by several enormous waves and capsized but then righted herself. But the coxswain went overboard and was swept away. The body of William Brown was found next day at Studland. A fund was opened for his widow and family, the RNLI contributing £275. Bob Brown, a descendant, retired in 1966 after almost 50 years in the crew of the Swanage lifeboats, the last 24 years as coxswain, and was awarded the BEM. A new boat, the *Robert Charles Brown*, a Mersey class lifeboat, was launched in 1991 at a cost of £250,000 raised by private subscription. The first

72 The Swanage lifeboat, *Herbert Sturmy* (1918-28), the last of the 'pulling and sailing', on the old stone slipway.

motor-lifeboat was the *Thomas Markby*, on station from 1928 to 1949. More than 500 lives have been saved since 1875.

Storms and the Lighthouse

The sea and the weather have continued to take their toll of man and his works throughout the centuries. One Sunday in February 1866 the wind increased to hurricane force: even stronger, it was said, than the storm of 1824. People were blown over, a Kingston church window was blown in during morning service, and Afflington Barn was unroofed. Sixty-three large trees came down in Studland, 50 at Whitecliff, 30 at Godlingston, and many more at Encombe. At Corfe Castle the north-west octagonal dungeon tower collapsed, and a large part of it fell down the hill into the stream. At Studland several ships were driven ashore and at least 17 people lost.

But in most weathers a sound boat was safe as long as it could he steered well clear of the rocky coast. Sir George Biddlecombe, the retired naval sea captain, had written to Trinity House in 1857 recommending a beacon near Anvil Point, but it came to nothing because the new low-level lighthouse at the Needles was being constructed. However, following the wreck of the *Wild Wave* in 1875, approval was given for a lighthouse near Durlston Head. Delay and lack of funds saw more wrecks on the coast including the American *Constitution* near Handfast Point and the *Anna Margrette* who 'left her bones at Bollard Head, where the sea soon tore them into fragments'. Fortunately there was no loss of life in either ship. But at last the new lighthouse was built above Tilly Whim and was opened on 28 September 1881 by the President of the Board of Trade, who lit the oil lamp. In the evening the *Empress* made an excursion for 230 people from Swanage and Bournemouth to view the light. On the following evening Mr Docwra engaged the *Empress* to take all the women of Swanage over 15 and under 90!

However, the lighthouse was helpless one Saturday afternoon on April 1882. The pressure suddenly dropped and another hurricane quickly developed. The *Alexandrova* of Liverpool, 1,250 tons, with her sails in ribbons, was driven at full force against the cliffs about half a mile west of Tilly Whim. Coastguards from St Alban's Head were hurrying with life-saving equipment, but by now the ship was a complete wreck and no crew could be seen. On the next day a lifebuoy was picked up on the cliff with the name of the vessel. Bodies were seen floating in the sea, and others were jammed in the rocks. More than 20 perished, and eight bodies found on the shore at Swanage were buried in the cemetery. It was said that the phenomenal violence of the gale blew sea salt inland more than 100 miles and completely stripped young trees near the coast of all their leaves.

Thomas and Emma Hardy[16]

Thomas Hardy and Emma Glifford were married in 1874 and spent their honeymoon in France. After a short period in London they found their way to Swanage in July 1875, where Thomas completed his fifth novel *The Hand of Ethelberta*. They arrived on St Swithun's day, 15 July, from Bournemouth in pouring rain. Next day they found lodgings at West End Cottage, the home of a retired sea captain, William Masters, and his wife, and stayed until March 1876. Thomas was busy writing the story to keep up with the chapters appearing in the *Cornhill* magazine, though they 'walked daily on the cliffs and shore'. Hardy noted in his diary, 'Evening. Just after sunset. Sitting with E. on a stone under the wall before the Refreshment Cottage.' This building was a recent addition to the scene; later it became the Belle Vue restaurant, more recently the *Tilly Whim Inn*, which finally burnt down in 1972; on the site are now lofty flats.

73 The *Heather Bell* was acquired by George Burt and plied between Swanage and Bournemouth. He lost money on the project. The ship's bell was presented to the Swanage Museum by Kenneth Burt.

74 Sketch by Emma Hardy of her husband, Thomas Hardy, on board the steamer *Heather Bell*, in September 1875, for an excursion around the Isle of Wight from Swanage.

They both found time to sketch, and a small pencil drawing is titled 'Loading stone – Swanage, in 1875. T.H.' There is a lively sketch by Emma of people, including her husband, on the deck of the paddle-steamer *Heather Bell* which George Burt operated from 1871-76. Thomas and Emma went round the Isle of Wight on this boat in fine weather on 7 September.

While Thomas was writing, Emma sketched an old quarry entrance 'with its paved incline and black mouth festooned with ferns and flowers, the blackness of the depth showing each spray with distinction'. She was taken down the quarry 'by Mr A.'. She recorded in her notebook, 'This morning the men are talking in groups, the quarries all neglected. Mr R. has bought the land and raised the rent of the quarries. Five women went to meet the steamer, but he came by land to Wareham and got safely home.' This clearly referred to J.C. Robinson who had just bought Eightholds. It is said that when he tipped in a lot of potatoes growing round a quarry, the crowd started calling 'Taters!' after him. This nickname stuck for a long time.

There are extensive descriptions of Swanage in *The Hand of Ethelberta*: the old town, the new villas, the already rickety pier, and a wonderfully poetic view of the magnificent panorama from Nine Barrow Down. There are also amusing and sardonic accounts of both residents and visitors. 'Some wives of the village, it is true, had learned to let lodgings, and others to keep shops.' But the stranger found himself stared at suspiciously as an intruder. 'Everybody in the parish who was not a boatman was a quarrier, unless he were the gentleman who owned half the property and had been a quarryman, or the other gentleman who owned the other half and had been to sea.' But 'Knollsea had recently began to attract notice in the world. It had this year undergone visitation from a score of professional gentlemen and their wives, a minor canon, three marine painters, seven young ladies with books in their hands, and nine-and-thirty babies.'

West End Cottage is not shown on the 1823 Chancery sale map but appears in the 1838. It was apparently joined at one time to East End Cottage by a door, to accommodate the gardener of the hotel and his large family of 10 children. In 1986 West End Cottage was tastefully restored by a new owner, with a plaque by the front door recording the stay of 'Thomas Hardy, Author and Poet, July 1875 - March 1876'.

The new Purbeck House

The firm – Mowlem, Freeman & Burt – had so far not risen much above the level of London's sewers and pavements, well as these works were executed. In 1874, however, came the big chance when they won the contract to rebuild Billingsgate Fish Market at a cost of over £100,000.

After 17 years at his old house, George Burt decided to rebuild it as a more imposing residence for his retirement. One wonders whether he was spurred on by his rivalry with Robinson. He called in his architect friend Crickmay, and together they produced the extraordinary edifice which is Purbeck House. Its style has been described as 'Scottish Baronial' and it certainly has an air of rugged permanence. One critic thought it an irony that this building 'of which the aim was so obviously beauty, should have achieved so startling an ugliness', but after well over a century Swanage would hardly seem the same place without it.

GB's wife Elizabeth laid the foundation stone at the north-west corner of the tower on 27 December 1875. Underneath was deposited a Queen Victoria penny of that year and a Roman coin of the Emperor Vespasian, found while the firm was excavating at Billingsgate. The demolition of the earlier building, only 25 years old but inadequate for an expanding market, gave GB the opportunity to remove discarded items to Swanage including iron columns from the arcading which faced the Thames, and stone balustrading with decorative iron panels from the parapet. The porch at Purbeck House is of white Cornish granite, and the walls are faced with variegated granite chippings, waste material from the steps of the Albert Memorial in Hyde Park, where the firm had recently constructed the base of that famous monument.

75 & 76   Interior views of Purbeck House in 1875. The entrance hall floor was copied from a Roman pavement discovered by Mowlems below Queen Victoria Street in London. Illustration 76 shows the dining room. George Burt's monogram is over the Italian marble chimneypiece.

The design drawings for Purbeck House show that the gazebo with its handsome copper thistle, overlooking the High Street, was originally intended to surmount the octagonal tower. But the plan was changed so that the weather vane from Billingsgate, with its gilded flying fish, which had swung in the wind high above the Thames, should crown the tower instead. Many years later, when the house was empty and had become unsafe, the weather vane found its way to Newton Manor. A surprising feature in Burt's stable yard was the reproduction of a portion of the Parthenon frieze with its prancing horses, probably brought

77 High Street, *c.*1900, showing George Burt's new Purbeck House. It was designed by the architect Crickmay in 1875, as was the Town Hall to the right. The prominent gazebo was intended to surmount the Tower, as shown on the original plans, but Burt's acquisition, the flying fish weather vane (inset), was preferred to crown it, and is now at Newton Manor.

from one of the great London exhibitions.

During the formation of Queen Victoria Street in London, undertaken by the firm, a magnificent Roman tessellated pavement was discovered and was visited by 33,000 people over three days. The original is now in Guildhall Museum. GB, with typical zeal, had it exactly reproduced in the entrance hall of his new house. Italian craftsmen spent three years working on this and chimneypieces in Carrara marble. The inscription over the dining-room chimneypiece, 'Let Prudence direct, Temperance chasten, Fortitude support, and Justice be the guide of all your activities', was the motto selected by the Prince Consort for the interior of the dome of the Stock Exchange, built in 1853 but now sadly demolished.

The new house was built by London craftsmen with the assistance of WMH, and was occupied before the end of 1876. In 1881 GB purchased a large garden on the west of his grounds from the Church Land Trustees, and another on the east, enclosing the whole with stone walls. Many items of interest appeared in the grounds including a stone arch from Hyde Park Corner, railings from St Paul's, balusters from Thames bridges, a scale model of Cleopatra's Needle and an enormous jawbone of a whale. There were mementoes of Temple Bar, the Royal Exchange and the Houses of Parliament. Kenneth Burt remembered with amusement the 'two headless statues in the evergreens' said to represent Charles I and II; a robed figure nearby may have represented Sir Thomas Gresham. One of the finest pieces of stone is the tympanum of a pediment with richly carved crown, rose and thistle. Its provenance is unknown but it probably originated in the 17th century.

13

Local Authority and the Railway Age

The Local Board

An inquiry was held at Wareham in January 1873 regarding the desirability of adopting the recommendation that a Local Health Board be formed, at both Wareham and Swanage, following the Local Government Act of 1858. The medical officers of the Board of Guardians strongly condemned the sanitary state of both places. The Town Clerk of Wareham said that the ratepayers had taken no formal steps to adopt the Act, and there seemed to be strong feeling against it. In Swanage, too, there was opposition from the quarriers and fishermen to the formation of byelaws.

Mr George Burt reported that, following a meeting called by the Swanage churchwardens and largely attended by the ratepayers, a resolution to proceed sent to the Local Government Board was passed unanimously. Swanage was a parish supporting its own poor and keeping its own roads, of which there were six miles, in order; the cost of repairing them was under £200. There had been a good deal of emigration; young men went to London to work and returned when old. In summer the population increased by about five hundred. The Inspector said, to laughter, that if Swanage were to be made a nice watering place, a good deal yet remained to be done. GB said that some geologists had been knocking the place about some time ago. There was more laughter. The stone quarrying was decreasing. Mr Calcraft reminded the Inspector of the familiar saying in London some years ago, 'Polish your Purbecks!' The proceedings concluded.

So a Local Health Board for Swanage was established in 1873, and the first meeting was held in the Vestry, although this marked the end of centuries of both civil and ecclesiastical administration by the church and the subsequent division between secular and religious affairs.

The Town Hall

George Burt evidently considered that Swanage, though not by any means a borough, was by now a town, and deserved a Town Hall. A little below Purbeck House on the north side of the High Street stood some old cottages known as the Drong; one stuck out into the street and you could look into the bedroom not much higher than the pavement. In 1881 GB bought this church property and swept it away to provide the site for the new town hall.[1]

Meanwhile, in London, Cheapside was being widened, which involved the setting back of the entrance to the ancient Mercers' Hall, but it was stipulated that the original

78 (left) J.W.B. Gibbs' painting of the High Street, *c*.1870, showing old Purbeck House and, on the right, the Drong, which was later replaced by the Town Hall. The shops were replaced by King Alfred Place, built for J.C. Robinson.

79 (right) This facade from Mercers' Hall, Cheapside, was designed by Edward Jarman, a contemporary of Wren. It was brought to Swanage by George Burt and is now the frontage for the entrance to the Town Hall.

front designed by Edward Jarman, a contemporary of Wren, be incorporated with the new elevation. However, it was found that it was 'so thickly covered with "London black" that it would have cost more to restore it than to erect a replica'. That sounds extraordinary nowadays, but this was done, and thus it came about that George Burt acquired the original façade and removed it to Swanage where 'at this remote spot Nature's cleansers have perfectly done their work'. And so a feature of 17th-century Cheapside became the imposing entrance to King Alfred Hall, as it was at first called, no doubt, to perpetuate the memory of Alfred's 'great naval battle', as John Mowlem had done with his monument on the shore.

The land on the east side of the town hall, leading down to the public Frogwell pump erected by GB, was also named King Alfred Road, but the title was soon forgotten. The name of a row of shops to the east, again known as King Alfred Place, seems to have lasted rather longer.

The main building of the new Town Hall, into which was inserted the 17th-century entrance front, was a plain Victorian house, again designed by Crickmay and built by W.M. Hardy. There was a spacious staircase leading up to a large council chamber and gallery. There was a bust of George Burt and a canopy with the same words as at Purbeck House: 'Let Prudence direct ... ' etc. In the basement at the rear was an open shelter for the fire engine. Adjoining was the Blind House, moved for the third time, and opposite was the first police house.

In May 1886 the Local Board held their monthly meeting for the first time at their new offices in the Town Hall, which they had leased from GB for seven years at a rental of £50. However, they sublet two rooms to Mr Thomas Randell, solicitor; the Oddfellows, of which there were 150 members, were also renting a room for their meetings.

The attractive two-faced clock did not feature in the original design, but in June 1882 GB asked the opinion of the Board whether a clock should strike the hours; it was agreed that one should. The clock possibly came from a demolished City church.

Visitors and Residents

Two diaries relating to this period have been preserved. One, of 1874, gives accounts by the Thurston family of a six-week holiday in Swanage.[2] They were staying at no.2 Exeter Place where Mrs Farwell was charging 3½ guineas per week, including attendance, for

80 At work and play: North Beach, *c.*1890. A cart loaded with sand moves across the beach while the family in the foreground watch with idle curiosity. Note how uncluttered the beach looked before the groynes were built.

two sitting rooms and two bedrooms. The Thurstons made some good sketches of the bay and coastline. Mr Thurston considered that the lower road to Corfe Castle was not to be despised, as it was 'fully atoned for by some admirable views of the Castle through trees forming a complete arch across the road [now the A351]. Swanage was a place where you can do as one likes, as there is no promenade to make a swell appearance at, and where one can escape from the gaze of human beings.' There were some good shops but no band 'which is rather a comfort than otherwise. Since here is no railway, Swanage is not infested so much with visitors as other places are. The *Heather Bell* is a superior sort of vessel to the ordinary steamers. Swanage is an admirable place for walking, boating, excursions and every other amusement.' 'Playland' was a long way off in the future.

The other account was written by J.M. Falkner and consisted of her memories in Dorchester, 1859-70, including holidays at Swanage:[3]

> There was a fine open seafront with smooth and gently-falling sands, the beach strewn with wonderfully beautiful shells, and the country round famous for its wild flowers. There were no 'trippers', and lodgings were very few. My father took us for long days in the country, sometimes in a little Victoria, sometimes mounted on donkeys. He knew all about flowers, birds, weasels, hedgehogs, badgers, snakes and glow-worms. It was something of an adventure to clamber down to Tilly Whim, with its long-disused sea-quarries and a reputed 'underground passage' to Corfe Castle! What we enjoyed most was to climb the great downs which form the background of Swanage. On them lay a land of pure delight, close sward, thyme and harebells, little painted snail-shells, countless butterflies and bees ... Nine Barrow Down (what a name of incantation) could never fade from memory ... We filled baskets with bee-orchids which were uncannily so like bees that we were half afraid of them. They were halcyon days.

81   George Selby and his horse on Beach Road, returning home after a day's work on the foreshore, c.1890.

J.W. Tribbett first published his *Wareham & Isle of Purbeck* (Swanage Visitors' List) newspaper in the summer of 1879 and it continued until 1885. It has a wealth of information, giving names of owners of houses, many of whom offered accommodation, and often of the more 'genteel' visitors. In July 1880 Mr Thomas Docwra was still at 'The Grove', Mr R.F.D. Palgrave, of the Palace of Westminster, at 'Hill Side' (later 'Steepways'), and Dr Pearce at the Hydropathetic Establishment (this did not last long). The formidable Miss Julia Colson, secretary of the Shipwreck Society, remained at 'Belvidere' and Dr Delamotte at Osborne House. A recent arrival, Mr James Clifton, an architect who was to produce some good buildings in Swanage, was living at Bay View House. At Victoria Terrace, Charles Burt continued his shop at no.1, George Horlock at no.2 (Post Office and the Isle of Purbeck Yacht Club House), E.S. Harman (chemist and bookseller) at no.3. Of the inns, Bassum was at the *Ship*, Luker at the *White Swan*, Hoare at the *Anchor* and Vye at the *Red Lion*. Mr James Pope was the manager of Williams & Co's Bank.

Durlston

George Burt retired from the firm in 1886 and lost his wife Elizabeth in the same year; however, he still had his two daughters, Annie and Emma, at Purbeck House. In 1877 the three of them (Mrs Burt had not been well enough to accompany them) had made a tour of Greece and the near East. In Egypt they made an adventurous journey on camels, were caught in a sandstorm, and GB was in danger of assassination when, as an experienced stonemason, he started chipping off a piece of the Great Pyramid with the aid of his hammer and measuring rod. His privately published diary of the trip is as entertaining as his uncle's (JM) on the continent.[4]

82 George Burt's Globe, 1887. 'The great globe itself, yea all which it inherit, shall dissolve and, like the baseless fabric of a vision, leave not a rack behind.' This quotation from Shakespeare's *The Tempest* is the wording on the cliff face at Tilly Whim and tallies with the words set to music by Stevens and others, but the original reads: ' ... shall dissolve and, like this insubstantial pageant faded, leave not a rack behind'. In the play, the 'baseless fabric' line occurs later.

He now turned his attention to the embellishment of his Durlston estate. The most spectacular achievement was the building of the 'Castle' on Durlston Head with its fine views of Peveril Point and Old Harry Rocks. It was designed, as ever, by Crickmay, and was sturdily built by W.M. Hardy in 1887. At the entrance it resembles a pier pavilion: in fact it has always been a restaurant of sorts. The south side reveals a much finer prospect of rugged battlements and turrets. 'Here the castle rears its majestic head in all the grandeur of feudal character.'

The most arresting object in the park is the creation of the Great Globe, 40 tons of Portland stone and 10 feet in diameter. It was constructed in Mowlem's stone-yard at Greenwich and brought by sea in 15 sections to Swanage, where WMH set it up on a platform cut into the solid rock. It had a forerunner: in 1879 George Burt commissioned a granite globe 3 feet in diameter to he made under the direction of his friend Professor James Hunter of Aberdeen. Displayed in the garden of Purbeck House it showed the land areas in polished relief and marked by a gold line, with the seas and rivers coloured blue. It later overlooked the Beaulieu River where George Burt's grandson bought a house in 1933.

Now termed the Durlston Country Park and administered by Dorset County Council, it was then similarly 'most freely thrown open to the public by this benefactor': George Burt. At one time he employed 50 well-paid men to maintain the estate. For the visitor incised stones explained the mysteries of the universe; others bore admonitions such as 'No guns or sporting dogs allowed'. Another attraction was the opening of the long-abandoned Tilly Whim quarries, which he bought to afford access to the public. This was done by blasting a tunnel through the cliff and forming steps down to the old smuggling 'caves'. A ring of iron bollards from London encircled the Great Globe, with two slabs, each with the heading, 'Persons anxious to write their names will please to do so on this stone only'. Another tablet nearby read, 'The sea is His and He made it'.

During the early months of 1890 Lloyd's of London used the top storey of the castle as a signal station, but apparently it was not satisfactory. In 1897 they purchased an acre of land near the lighthouse, again as a signal site, but reconveyed it to J. M. Burt in 1902.[5] Marconi's early experiments in wireless telegraphy involved Durlston Castle. On 25 March 1898 his right-hand man George Kemp lay down in a snow storm, draping a long wire along the cliff. Covering the receiver with his mackintosh, Kemp put his ear to the tapper and read this message sent by Marconi from a house near Bournemouth Pier to their first wireless station at the *Needles Hotel* on the Isle of Wight: 'Mr Kemp carrying out experiments at Swanage'. Ten days later he repeated the experiment, sitting in the upper storey of the castle in the corner nearest to the sea.

The Railway Era

It was 'third time lucky'. The first attempt in 1847 came to nothing, and the second in 1863 got as far as an Act of Parliament, only to fail through opposition. But now George Burt and the other promoters were pressing hard for the realisation of the scheme, and Lord Eldon, who owned much of the land through which the railway would pass, said 'If your people want a railway, I will not oppose it.' The *Daily News* commented, 'Go to Swanage before the railway demon engulfs it, where the women still believe that a ride on a donkey's back to four cross-roads, or wearing a bit of hair clipped from the cross of a donkey's shoulders, as an infallible cure for whooping cough, and where the men rule themselves and believe themselves to be quite outside the regulations and laws of ordinary humanity.'

The Swanage Railway received the Royal Assent to the Act on 18 July 1881, and the moment of truth had arrived.[6] At a special meeting, the London & South Western Railway agreed to work the railway, with the option to purchase. Among the first directors were George Burt, John Charles Robinson and William Lansdowne Beale, the latter well known in Bournemouth. Following a re-survey of the line, invitations were issued and five contractors submitted tenders. The engineer's estimate was for £77,000 and the lowest was £76,646 from Curry & Reeve, which was accepted; this firm had recently constructed the Ilfracombe line. It did not include the cost of the rails which had already been purchased by the

83 Another timeless Walter Pouncy photograph of a stone and sand haulage cart with trace horses taking an early trip along the main beach, c.1890. See illustration 28.

84 (above) & 85 (opposite)   Loading seaweed (wrack). Unlike the two-wheeled carts used for loading stone, a four-wheeled cart is being used. Note the steamer at the old Pier, the Clock Tower, Marine Villa and The Grove in the background of illustration 84.

promoters.[7] In March 1883 the contractors were ready to commence the line and to put on 300 hands at Wareham, Corfe Castle and Swanage. In May the first cargo for the line was delivered from the pier by the Lord John Russell, and construction proceeded well.

In February 1884 a works locomotive belonging to the contractors was brought to Swanage by road from Wareham. It was hauled 'by 18 or 20 horses belonging to Mr H.W. Burt. The affair caused much excitement from its novelty, this being the first locomotive ever seen in this locality. It was put on the rails and it steamed and whistled for the first time.' It had to be taken up Kingston Hill as it might have been too heavy to cross the new stone bridges on the valley road.

This big undertaking was completed on time, and on 5 May 1885 an official inspection was made by the engineers of the Board of Trade accompanied by the contractors and railway officials.

> A great event in the history of Swanage occurred on 16th May, being the opening of the line of railway, which has at last connected this delightful watering-place with the system of the L & SWR … At 5.30 on Saturday evening merry bells were heard from the church tower, and crowds of people thronged the railway bridge and road adjoining the station, all anxiously awaiting the arrival of the first passenger train, an event naturally regarded with intense interest by every man, woman and child in the place. The whole town was en fête.[8]

The directors and other friends had left Waterloo in two special carriages at 2.30 and were transferred to the new line at Wareham, which was announced by telegraph at Swanage. A stop was made at Corfe Castle to receive the congratulations of that ancient

borough and the village band joined in the welcome. 'The "iron horse" made his first appearance at a quarter to seven, and as soon as the train came in sight the crowd rent the air with deafening cheers, and the band played with right good will "See the Conquering Hero Comes".'

On the arrival of the train, the party stepped down onto the platform whereupon warm congratulations were exchanged. In an address to the directors, it was said that the completion of the railway would prove a great boon for the district, both in the development of its trade and commerce and in the furtherance of its advantage as a seaside resort. The chairman of the project had achieved the long cherished desire of his heart.

George Burt replied:

We are delighted to come here among you and to bring the civiliser of the world so close to you ... I was only thinking today that the first time I went from Swanage I had to get to Branksea as best I could, and then get on board a Poole hoy – a vessel which was full of sheep and calves – and then, if lucky, we got to Portsmouth at night, slept there, and by coach the next day to London (laughter). And now to contrast that, 50 years on, with today's journey, which we have accomplished direct in four hours! (applause). In my opinion there is a bright future for Swanage.

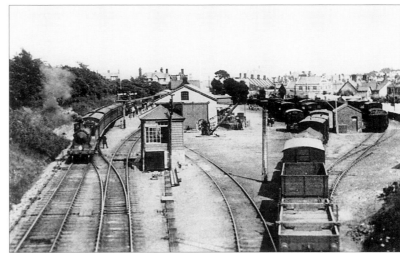

86   Swanage railway station in its heyday. The sidings have now been replaced by a supermarket, car park and health centre, but the goods shed survives.

But he wanted to impress on everyone that they must make use of this engineering skill. 'If you don't, someone else will be up and push you out.' He thanked everyone and, with loud cheers, 'God save the Queen' was sung. The directors then entered Mr Summers' four-horse brake and proceeded round the town with the band to Purbeck House, followed by 'splendid hospitality'.

The railway was opened for passenger traffic on the following Wednesday, 20 May, which was made a public holiday. There were five trains in each direction, the journey to Wareham taking 25 minutes and costing 2s., instead of 1½ hours and 5s. by road. There was no Sunday service at first. The line was worked on the 'one engine in steam' basis; the engine left Swanage with the first train at 7.20 a.m. and left Wareham with the last train at 9.10 p.m. to return to its shed. 'Swanage station remained a gem; dignified with its stone, quiet with its polite little tank engines.'[9]

Nuisances

It took some time for the railway to make its mark, but inexorably Swanage began to change. The rough road which led from the Mowlem Institute alongside the Brook and as far as Eastbrook farm (now the Recreation ground) was extended to the station, where the *Railway Hotel* was one of the first new buildings. It was not until 1899 that the brewery, though closed and taken over by Strong & Co. of Romsey, was demolished.

The Brook was still uncovered, but the level of the field on the south side – Tilly Mead – was being raised by masses of stone 'scars' in anticipation of building. George Burt had a scheme for laying out gardens on either side of the Brook, but the Mowlem Trustees owned the north side and there was a dispute. In the event Station Road became the shopping centre of Swanage, at the expense of the High Street, though not for some time. Before we decry the loss of the brook underground, it must be remembered that there was as yet no main drainage. In 1892 George Burt's plans for the first new shops in Station Road were passed. 'At the same time he is fast putting out of sight that most objectionable and disagreeable object, the Lake [a Dorset word for a brook] from the Brewery to the Institute.' But who owned the Lake? John Ernest Mowlem, who was now 24 and had inherited his great-uncle's estate, was asking whether he owned half of it and if so, whether he needed to pay half the cost if the Brook was being covered in by George Burt.

In passing, we may mention Mr Joseph Parsons, Inspector of Nuisances. Mrs White complained to him about the smell of Mr Horlock's cows. The clerk was to write to her saying that the Board could do nothing, and the Chairman said 'there was nothing more healthy than the smell from cows'. There were, however, much more serious nuisances: the register gives many instances of complaints about all forms of filth in back yards and more prominent places.

87 The scene in 1885: the brewery is still standing, with the new railway station on the right. The ground is being raised with scars to form the new Station Road area in the foreground, and the Brook is to disappear beneath it.

88   A view of High Street, near the Town Hall. Note Ashlar House in the distance, where the library now stands. On the right is the Curiosity Shop, which was demolished in 1959 as a possible site for a theatre and restaurant, but which became the Burr Stone Mead housing development. Note the lamp-post surmounting a London bollard.

    Sewers, or the lack of them, were a continual subject of indecision. The attitude was 'out of sight, out of mind'. There was a primitive brick drain in the lower High Street which discharged into the Bay. In 1888 it was to be cleaned out from Mrs Randell's house (Ashlar House) to the sea, but Mr Parsons said that they had never been able to get higher up the High Street than the pump by the *Ship*. George Burt complained of the privy cesspools below the Town Hall, and the clerk gave orders to the owners to fill them in and use earth-closets instead. On the establishment of the Local Board in 1873, there was talk of improving the drainage, but little had been done 10 years later. In 1886 George Burt offered to pay for preparing a scheme for main drainage by Francis Newman CE, and the Board was to apply for a government loan. Two years later there was another enquiry and in 1892 the Board was still discussing the proposals!

    At last the revised scheme was to be prepared and £6,000 borrowed. George Burt never saw the outcome of the main drainage. Mr Newman's plan was put in operation in 1894; the new flushing tank was completed and a 24in. iron outfall pipe was laid as far as the coastguard station.

The Bay

At last the bankers were doomed. A stone-yard (the 'Depot') was made west of the railway bridge with a siding, and the stone chugged away west instead of sailing away east. Under the 1881 Act, there was to be an extension of the railway to link with the pier, though no steam was permitted. This was never achieved due to opposition by one of the stone merchants. However, a short branch was made as far as Little Mead (now called Commercial Lane, from the present library) with a turntable for trucks. There are still two wall-stones marked 'WGW', the initials of William Grove White, stone merchant (Chinchen & White). Long after the removal of the branch, there remained a notice board on the wall of Commercial Road with the faded warning, 'To prevent accidents goods must not be left on or by the sides of tramway, 1893'.

Innovations included a 'gents' urinal by the pier and a drinking trough placed near the Institute in 1892; Mr Horlock suggested a notice board to remind people that the trough was for slaking the thirst of horses and not for washing fish or clothes.

George Burt envisaged a broad esplanade to sweep all round the bay as far as the pier, but Lord Eldon owned the foreshore on the south and Mowlem that on the north. He also had a plan for a pier and parade in Durlston Bay, but this came to nothing. The question of a 'Harbour of refuge' from the easterly gales had been talked of for half a century and more. In 1874 Charles Robinson proposed a new breakwater out on the Berry rock opposite the 'clock' tower to enclose a harbour with the existing pier. Needless to say, nothing came of that either. The pier had been badly damaged by storms, and a large portion was reconstructed in 1886. As a working pier, it was quite dangerous for the public as there were no railings; a girl was run over by a truck and knocked into the

89   The last of the Bankers, 1898-9. Clearance was necessary to make way for Mowlems' construction of the east side of Institute Road and, finally, the Parade area. The Mowlem Institute can be seen in the centre of the picture. The projecting stonework in the foreground still survives and is the top of the public slipway (see illustration 100).

90 A Walter Pouncy picture capturing an Edwardian summer, with the new pier attracting more visitors by paddle-steamer. This is the *Cambria* lying alongside. Notice the children around the sweet machine, *c.*1902.

sea. The loading cranes were removed when the number of paddle-steamers increased after the opening of the new Bournemouth pier in 1880.

If you wanted to hear Swanage news you only had to dally at the old stone quay where there was always a group of 'old salts' and quarrymen talking scandal and telling stories all day. There was news of unusual happenings: a large waterspout, some said 1,000 feet high, seen off the bay at about 9 a.m. in July 1875; 2,000 herring caught in one day and 30,000 in a week in 1886; a 5ft shark caught in 1889; the sad rowing-boat disaster on Easter Bank Holiday 1892 when three visitors were drowned in the bay. Then there were the elections for East Dorset when windows belonging to leading Conservatives, including George Burt, were smashed; it was said that their houses were marked with a red cross the night before: 'Swanage was under mob law'.

Secular and Sacred

George Burt saw little of the spate of building which was to follow in the path of the Railway and which brought loads of 'foreign' bricks, apart from his first row of shops, 'Peveril Terrace', built in the new Station Road in 1893. Before the impressive 'Trocadero' appeared in 1896 (as a bank but only briefly occupied as such), George Burt laid out the miniature 'Pleasure Gardens' on the sea side of the lower High Street. In front was a line of carriages ready to take visitors up to Durlston Park to view the wonders of nature (and George Burt); but first a ticket had to be obtained at the office in Victoria Terrace. Half way up was a stone column – another London curiosity – in the middle of the road to mark the boundary of George Burt's private estate, he having vested Park Road in the Local Board in 1882.[10] Carriages were permitted to enter his domain, but no merchandise.

It was in September 1892 that Thomas and Emma Hardy returned to Swanage. This month they attended a Dorset Field Club meeting where, in Hardy's own words, they 'were introduced to old Mr B—, "The King of Swanage". He had a good profile, but was rougher in speech than I should have expected after his years in London.' The party, including many gentry, clergy and 'quality', was conducted by George Burt from the station to Durlston Head, 'the owner of this magnificent property explaining points of interest' on the way. At the 'handsome restaurant erected on the very summit of the Head', George Burt gave them all lunch. Later, tea was taken at Purbeck House, with a hasty glance at the treasures there.[11]

91   A fisherman and quarryman exchange pleasantries over a pipe of baccy at the end of the day on the stone quay.

Changes took place in 1890 when the Williams family acquired 'The Grove' at Peveril, and two years later extended it. With further additions it became the *Grosvenor Hotel*. Two large red brick houses, 'Peveril Tower' (later 'Rockleigh') and 'Sunnydown' were built in the grounds. All are now gone.

On the ecclesiastical front, St Aldhelm's Church in Park Road was opened in June 1892, built by George Burt 'at his own expense'. It was consecrated by the bishop, and the church was leased to the Rector and churchwardens of St Mary's. It was not well attended on account of its position, high up the hill, and was demolished in 1973.

The Wesleyan Methodists, however, were flourishing, and in 1886 an impressive new church was built, set back from Jubilee Square. Pevsner says that 'the Gothic front with an overstressed octagonal steeple and flowering tracery is spectacular, the side anti-climatically utilitarian'. The architect was Mr Jennings of Bristol. Over the front entrance the faces of the Revd George Terry and Mr George Burt are carved in stone. The old chapel became the schoolroom until it was replaced by the large Memorial Hall in 1907. The steeple easily overtops the parish church tower, and perhaps was meant to. But George Burt was impartial in this respect. Although he gave a large sum towards the spire, remembering his grandmother's connection with John Wesley, he also paid for four new bells at St Mary's in memory of his wife; this brought the ring of bells to eight. The new rector was the Revd T. A. Gurney (1887-1901) who followed Duncan Travers and his 33 years in Swanage.

The 'King' departs

The curtain finally closed on Wednesday 18 April 1894 when, after a brief illness, George Burt died at the age of 77 in his Purbeck 'Palace'. He wished to be buried alongside his wife in Kensal Green Cemetery and the funeral to be without display. It took place in pouring rain early at 8.30 a.m. at the parish church, but nevertheless the procession was impressive. The carriages with the relatives, friends, county magistrates and councillors were followed by employees, members of the Local and School Boards, coastguards, lifeboat crew, lighthouse men, Masonic brethren, Oddfellows, Volunteer Artillery, and Cabmen. The Town Band played a Funeral march. The train left at 10.15 for London, with a saloon for the mourners.

Many tributes appeared in the press, including extensive accounts of his life, in the *Daily Chronicle*, the *Pall Mall Gazette*, and the *World*: 'You cannot help sympathising with Mr Burt in his efforts to persuade Lord Eldon to consent to the erection of the esplanade upon which he had set his heart. If the whole of his desires in regard to Swanage have not been realised, he has at any rate laid the foundation of another west of England resort.'

But Charles Harper wrote in 1905:[12]

It is not so certain that those who delight in quaint, old-world places ought to be grateful to the memory either of Burt or Mowlem, who are now gathered to their fathers; for largely to them is due that change from an old-world fishing and quarrying village to a modern seaside resort, which have quite succeeded in spoiling it. The curiosities of Durlston Park estate are alike the creation of the amazing Burt, in whose nature eccentricity and business capacity, and the instincts of the pedagogue, the philanthropist and the moneymaker seem to have been strangely mixed.

'The Cradle of a Poet'

Before saying farewell to George Burt, we should add a postscript, though it has a sting in its tail or, rather, tale. The semi-biographical book with this title by Elizabeth Godfrey (Jessie Bedford's pseudonym) appeared in 1910 but was withdrawn, presumably on account of threatened libel. Her identity is unknown to us, as the publisher, the Bodley Head, no longer exists, and enquiry has proved fruitless. Kenneth Burt (1908-88) knew nothing of the matter, which was surprising, though the legal action was no doubt conducted by the solicitors, possibly for Sir John Mowlem Burt.

Having tracked down and read a copy of the novel, David Lewer admitted that it was a good story and well written, but unfortunately a vicious and thinly veiled sarcastic criticism of the late George Burt. It is evident that the author knew Swanage and Purbeck House intimately. The book tells the story of a battle between a newcomer, Josiah Jerram, a retired solicitor and ignorant tycoon, and Chichele Harmon, an old-established stonemason. Jerram is hoping to modernise Stonedge [Swanage] by sweeping away the old stone-yard and replacing it with a new parade, but Harmon is not interested in selling it to him.

Harmon's son, Noel, is the hero of the tale, and is torn between becoming a poet, or a stonemason like his father. Noel and his childhood friend Theresa, daughter of Col Escombe [Encombe] are in love. They walk to Dancing Ledge and, being hungry, call reluctantly at Jerram's new restaurant, Ocean View [Durlston] Castle, 'a caricature of Carow [Corfe Castle]', and buy some hard buns and soft biscuits. At a cavern they notice an inscription: 'These caves are the property of Josiah Jerram, Esq. THE SEA IS HIS AND HE MADE IT'. They burst into laughter.

Jerram has just married his timid but wealthy wife and built his new, blatant mansion, clearly and derisively described as Purbeck House, although it is not named. He asks his wife what she thinks of their new home. She hesitantly says that she doesn't much like the nude statues, but he says that all the nobility and gentry have them. 'Culture, that's what's wanted – a grand thing!' He explains that 'Me and Walter [Crickmay] chose them all; Walter knows what's what, him having designed all this beautiful place – under my direction of course – and taking all the medals he did at Muddleport School for Design.' Maria says she would prefer a small dressing room upstairs for her sitting room. Josiah snorts, and trusts that she will sit in this drawing room, not in a box-room, otherwise the servants will not think much of her. 'People will suppose we must have made our money if we don't know how to enjoy it.' She hastens to say that they will entertain company downstairs, but ladies of position have a small boudoir upstairs to rest and do their sewing. 'Oh a BOUDWAH of course. Well, give your orders, only let it be handsome!'

Maria congratulates Josiah on the completion of his task.

> 'Now you have done it and have nothing more to do but sit down and enjoy it.' He was still tramping up and down, and he stopped short in front of her, spreading out his chest, his thumbs in his waistcoat pockets, 'Nothing more to do! Don't you believe it M'ria; why, I haven't scarce begun yet. Do you know what I'm going to do? I'm going to *make* Stunnidge. I tell you I 'old this town in the 'ollow of my 'and. The names of Stunnidge and of its benefactor Josiah Jerram shall go down to posterity together.' It was not often that Josiah's carefully acquired aspirates forsook him, but in moments of strong excitement they unhappily relapsed.

And so on. No wonder the book was withdrawn. By the way, after many vicissitudes, Noel publishes a volume of verse, returns to his quarry and marries his lady-love.

14

Urban Swanage; The Steamer People

It was after the death of George Burt that Swanage was ready to face the approach of the 20th century. By 1895 the first decade of the railway had passed. Illustration 89 shows scaffolding for the building of the first shops on the east side of Institute Road. Digging for the foundations began in the winter of 1898/9. The bankers were still there, though abandoned, and before long a short length of the Parade took their place: here a terrace of houses was built with balconies overlooking the sea, anticipating the need for more visitors. Swanage was progressing.

But was it progress? Some thought not, though it was inevitable. Charles Harper wrote:[1]

> Thomas Hardy's picture of an out-of-the-way place remained, very little blurred by change, until well on into the '80s. With the opening of the railway, the primitive houses, and the equally primitive people who lived in them, suffered a change almost as sudden as though a harlequin had waved his wand over their heads. There was indeed something exceptionally primitive in the Swanage people. They were chiefly quarrymen, and like all quarry folk, mining the great blocks from mother earth, a strangely reserved and isolated race.

They were known as 'Swanage Turks', and a Poole sailor, when asked about the derivation, answered, unfairly: 'Tarks, we al'us carls 'em, 'cos they know nawthen about anythin'.' But things had changed.

The trouble was that development had been too rapid. Hotels and boarding houses were springing up: 'a change from the time when a simple glass of ale and a crust of bread and cheese at a rustic inn was all one wished, and certainly all one could have got.' Mrs Panton hated the hideous new houses; 'old-world Swanage had died a horrid death'. So there it was. If the town had had more of a prosperous past, with fine Georgian terraces, such as those at Weymouth, the change might not have been so drastic. And the authority for a sympathetic architect – 'planning' had not been heard of – guiding the development of the town, instead of piecemeal building, might have produced a more attractive face. But Edwardian Swanage could hardly avoid Edwardian England.

A *new pier*

It was perhaps the completion of the new 'parade pier' in 1897 which really set the scene for 'seaside Swanage'. Unlike the old one, its chief use was for bringing visitors to Swanage from mushrooming Bournemouth, on board the increasing number of paddle-steamers; more than 10,000 'trippers' came over on Bank Holiday Monday that first year. Those on

92 Edwardian ladies in the height of fashion disembarking from
the paddle-steamer *Brodick Castle* in 1906.

holiday in Swanage, and residents too, were also able to enjoy sea excursions to Lulworth
Cove, Weymouth, Torquay, the Isle of Wight and even occasionally to Cherbourg. Some
of the most remembered and popular boats included the *Monarch*, the *Majestic*, and
Brodick Castle (Cosens Co. of Weymouth), and the *Balmoral*, *Stirling Castle* and *Lord
Elgin* (Southampton Co.). It was fascinating to watch the strong, gleaming pistons in
action below: coal-fired, of course, in those days.

The pier was open to pedestrians on Sundays but there were no steamer services until
as late as 1929. The entrance charge to the pier was 1d. and the cost of a return fare to
Bournemouth in 1899 was 1s. 6d. Just 7s. 6d. would buy a return to France. The old pier
was relegated to coaling and cargo for the ships, and a new brick building was erected
for coal and fish. It is said that it was used occasionally as a morgue for the not unusual
number of bodies washed up on the shore over the years. In 1902 Mrs Millward fell off
the pier when disembarking from the *Monarch*. Mr Ward, the steamship agent, and Dick
Graham, a young steward, jumped in and saved her. In 1907 a medal was awarded to
Richard Grant by the Royal Humane Society for rescuing Walter White from his yacht
after its collision with the *Brodick Castle*.

The new pier was designed by R. St George Moore of Westminster, the contractor being
the well-known pier builder, Alfred Thorne.[2] The first pile was driven on 30 November 1895

and the last on 25 July 1896. The pier was opened to all traffic on 29 March 1897. During the summer the town band played on the pier in the evenings. Soon after, the tramway was reduced from standard to 2ft gauge. Flat waggons were used for coal and fish but no longer for stone; there were still one or two in the 1920s, though the old pier was gradually falling into ruin. It had been repaired in 1902 by Mowlem's to create an extra berth for overnight steamers.

After the First World War, deterioration of the new pier at sea level was found to be increasing, so in 1928 'surgical engineering' had to be undertaken. The problem was that the Greenheart tropical hardwood piles, 14ins. square, were being attacked, not so much by the teredo or shipworm beetle, as at Bournemouth pier, but by the marine borer *Limnora* (or gribble). In 1927 divers found that 145 of the 170 piles were affected, some very badly. The solution was to encase the zone in concrete 'muffs', strengthening the timber piles above and below the wave points. The successful operation was recommended by the consulting engineer DuPlat Taylor.

The Urban District Council

The word 'urban' indicates the change which came over Swanage: from being a rural village to becoming a town. When the Local Government Act of 1894 came into force, the Local Boards were abolished. 'The vote was given to all county and parliamentary voters, thus creating a more democratic form of government.'[3] Only the School Boards and the Boards of Guardians were still outside the local government system. The surrounding villages became part of the new Wareham & Purbeck District Council, Dorset itself having been provided with a County Council. The U.D.C. met for the first time on the last day of 1894, and Swanage was still to manage its own affairs to a considerable extent, including approving building byelaws and drainage improvements. These responsibilities were removed from the U.D.C. when a new Act came into force in 1974 and Swanage became a Town Council: little better than a Parish Council. When it was shorn of much of its authority, the U.D.C. acquired a Mayor with chain instead of a Chairman, and revived the Town Crier: perhaps attempts to preserve its dignity.

It is surprising to note from the council's minutes as late as April 1908, regarding a discussion on the rates, that 'overseers are appointed by the U.D.C. and not by the Vestry': the lingering vestige of ecclesiastical control.

There had been much concern over the loss of sand from the beach by the action of the sea, and a sea wall was discussed by the council in 1898. However, a counter proposal was made to build 26 stone groynes. Great controversy followed and James Day, a local worthy, resigned over the matter, having been called a 'troublemaker' by J.M. Burt. But

93 The Swanage football team of 1926/27, with James Day, JP, seated in the centre. He was a local greengrocer and benefactor, as well as being a member of the S.U.D.C. and a county councillor. Day's Park and Day's Road were both named after him.

94   Construction of the new sea wall and the widening of Shore Road in the 1920s. Ocean Bay was built at the far end and the *Grand Hotel* can be seen on the right. In the foreground is a quarr cart and just behind the workmen a two-wheeled horse cart.

he asked, 'Why spoil the best bathing ground on the south coast?' When it was learnt in 1900 that the Board of Trade would not support the scheme, the 'anti-groynes' won. After the First World War a series of timber groynes were constructed, and the beach was considerably improved.

The sea wall and promenade were constructed by Burt & Burt in sections, the middle part being the last. The foundation stone was laid by John Mowlem J.P. on 25 February 1904, it being on his estate, but by now it is illegible. He gave a half-crown to each workman. The road halfway along the front was narrow, so Ivy Cottage was rebuilt and set back into the cliff, enabling the sea wall to be straightened. Cliff Cottage above was given a long sloping access path. At the far end of the parade the Beach Café (Ocean Bay Stores) with its castellated roof, designed by Bournemouth architect Thomas Grimes, was built in 1908. A shelter, the first of three, was constructed near the monument in 1908 and there were complaints that the cabmen, often in trouble, were using it. The cab stand was moved northwards, and soon some of them were driving motor-cabs, about which they had complained to the council not long before. Drinking fountains on the front were erected by J.E. Mowlem, and were much appreciated.

New Developments

William Masters Hardy, builder and local historian, said in the preface to his book *Old Swanage* (1908):

> Natives of Swanage like myself, while proud to see the natural beauties and advantages of our town as a health and pleasure resort being duly recognised, and while gratified at the rapid growth and

95 The north end of the beach before the Ocean Bay building was constructed and the widening of Shore Road. The original deeds of Shore Villa, seen on the left, refer back to 1805. It is now a retirement home.

development of this new residential watering-place, which is springing up like the prophet's gourd, yet cannot at the same time help feeling pangs of regret at the disappearance of one familiar landmark after another, landmarks associated with the intimate and tender recollections of childhood and youth. Old Swanage, in short, houses and roads alike, is fast being improved away, and the inhabitants too now bear every year less and less resemblance to those – hardy, shrewd, independent, and witty – of bygone days, the days, for instance, when I was a boy.

Before the coming of the railway there had been development, it is true, up the hill on the south side of the town, planned by Burt and Robinson. A second 'New Swanage' northwards towards Ulwell had begun, and now rows of modest terraces were appearing both north and south of the High Street. The new King's Road stopped abruptly before reaching Newton Farm, but showed every intention of continuing to Herston, which it did in due course. On the Mowlem estate, plans were afoot for setting out new roads there.

96 An early view from the working quarries at Townsend. This photograph, taken by Walter Pouncy c.1890, shows the Victoria Avenue area through to New Swanage before development started. Northbrook Road can be seen in the distance.

A plan was prepared by the ever-willing Crickmay for the laying out of more than a hundred plots of varied size.[4] It was to include a dozen large villas with extensive gardens overlooking the sea, each with a 118ft frontage, on Marine Drive (i.e. Shore Road), and a large hotel at the corner of Victoria Avenue. Fortunately none were built.

In contrast Northbrook Terrace was to consist of 20 houses, each only 15ft in frontage! In fact the plan was altered, Rempstone Road alone surviving in name. Sunnybank Road became Gilbert Road (an old field name); Guernsey Road disappeared, becoming Cranborne and Ilminster Roads instead. After many years of standing in splendid isolation in de Moulham Road (later renamed Victoria Avenue), de Moulham Villas were joined by other villas and boarding houses. It seems a pity that Rempstone Road did not become the new shopping centre, rather than Station Road, for then the Brook (after cleansing!) could have run through public gardens, as is the case in Bournemouth, thus avoiding later flooding. On the other hand, the High Street shops would have become isolated. As for the proposed Marine Drive, the site of Eastbrook Farm remained vacant until after the First World War, when the council acquired it for a recreation ground, adding a graceful bandstand.[5] Less happy was the encroachment recently on a part of the recreation ground for a car park, as happened years ago on the Downs. But thankfully Swanage's front remained almost free of buildings.

Losses and Survivals

And so 'a new red brick Swanage' appeared, though still often completed with local stone quoins, lintels and other embellishments. Development gathered pace. In Station Road most of the south side was built up by the time the new Post Office opened there in 1908, where it remained until 1973. The fishermen's (and smugglers'!) cottages on the north side, nearest the shore, were the last to go in 1914. The shops on the east side of Institute Road were completed in 1905; when the foundations were being prepared, old stone groynes and a beach were revealed, showing that the sea had retreated.

The Square, the ancient Albion Place, in which John Mowlem's father had his shop a century ago, was rebuilt in brick by WMH in 1896, relieved by the attractive verandahs. The old Round House remained until 1928 when it was rebuilt, albeit in stone. The *White Swan* survived, though threatened in 1881 by road widening. The Old Bank House, with its additional shopfront (1907) as Swanage Dairies, also survived until it was demolished by a bomb, as did the *Ship Inn*, which was partly rebuilt after bomb damage. Victoria Terrace is still there (2004) but not the quaint buildings beyond: the renowned Brown's fish shop, the old Straw Basket Works and Hixson's House Agency. After the demolition in 1908 there

97 Lower High Street in 1905, showing the *Purbeck Hotel* (formerly the *White Hart*) and Victoria Terrace. The old building left of centre is Brown's fish shop, and further along is Hixson's House Agency and the Strawplait Basket shop; all of these were demolished. The *Royal Victoria Hotel* can be seen in the distance.

98   The *Grand Hotel* was built in 1898 and remains the only first-class purpose-built hotel left in Swanage.

were complaints about the vacant site: 'Anything better than nothing!' came the cry; similar sentiments were heard again, following the demolition of the *Grosvenor* and *Corrie* Hotels, before the recession of 1990 which stopped redevelopment 'for the duration', a term also used in the War.

Up the High Street, the row of old shops on the south side gave way to the new Bank in 1896. Another old building, used by Pouncy's photographic studio from 1888, soon went. The smithy opposite was auctioned at the *Ship* in November 1903 following the death of Charles Smith, the blacksmith, but was not demolished until 1927. The *Red Lion* and the *Anchor* survived, as did the *New Inn*, which was partially rebuilt in the 1850s; it continued later as the *Stonemason*, until closed by the brewers in the 1970s. The *Black Swan*, the *Globe* and the *Royal Oak* continued, but the youngest public house at this time, the *Railway Hotel* (1886) closed its doors in 1981. No.1 Victoria Terrace, having been Robert Burt's residence and Burt's Restaurant, eventually became the *White Horse Inn* after it was badly damaged by fire in 1947. The *Purbeck Hotel*, successor to the *White Hart*, survived as a worthy 18th-century hostelry, but has been spoilt of late by ill-considered replacement bay windows. Interesting remains of the old inn behind were demolished a few years ago.

The Architects

We have seen much of Crickmay, the Weymouth architect and friend of JM and George Burt, who designed, among other buildings, the Mowlem Institute, Purbeck House, the Town Hall and Durlston Castle. Now we come to J.E. Clifton FRIBA. It seems that Charles Robinson introduced James Clifton to Swanage; he was articled with Edmund Robinson, a younger son of JCR, and they went into partnership. The distinguished

Lloyds Bank building (originally Williams & Co., then Wilts & Dorset Bank) was designed in 1896. Clifton can be glimpsed, cane in hand, walking up the High Street in an early picture postcard.[6] He also had an office at no.2 Victoria Terrace where he was the agent for JCR's Manor (Eightholds) Estate development. Moreover, he designed 'Harberton' in Rempstone Road.

John Ernest Mowlem, heir to his great-uncle's estate, qualified as an architect and came under the wing of the older James Clifton. They were devoted friends and neither married. Clifton later moved to 'Northbrook', the old farm, while Mowlem continued to live at de Moulham Villas – the left-hand one – in Victoria Avenue, where his two sisters Susannah and Louisa also lived; they, too, never married, and once again, the three were 'the last of the line'. Their father, Thomas Joseph Mowlem, had died there in 1892 when his son John Ernest was 24; their mother Elizabeth survived until 1910. Her father William Rabling was agent for the estate, and a road was named after him. John Ernest was said to have been dilatory, rarely finishing anything, and he bred terriers. However, he was something of a scholar and printed privately his valuable book, *Moulham – the Place and Surname* (1934), which took considerable research.

Mowlem, Robinson and John Mowlem Burt did not get on with one another and there was much friction. There was a lawsuit concerning a footpath from Darky Lane to Ulwell Road; someone defied the closure, so it was said, and was sent to prison. Clifton too, when chairman of the council, brushed with Burt.

The imposing Trocadero range of buildings opposite the *Ship* was designed by George Silley of the Strand in London and was built in 1896 for the Wilts & Dorset Bank who only briefly occupied it. The Post Office took its place from 1901-8. The extensions to 'The Grove', which became the *Grosvenor Hotel*, were designed by Walter Hickson of Nottingham and built between 1901 and 1905. The *Grand Hotel* on the cliffs of New Swanage was opened in 1898. The unusual and delicate Arcade (see illustration 112) over the pavement in the High Street was designed by Crickmay as a row of seven shops, but only one was built; the date 1896 can be seen above. He had also designed the four shops in King Alfred Place, below the Town Hall, for J.C. Robinson in 1877; he seems to have been at home with 'classic', 'rustic' and 'gothic', the latter shown in his St George's church, Langton Matravers (1875). Scar Bank House, in a delightful position at Durlston, was designed by the well-known architect Morley Horder in 1930.

Churches and Chapels

Much ecclesiastical activity took place in Edwardian days. The new Congregational church was opened on 4 July 1901, the foundation stone having been laid on 22 August 1900 by Stephen Collins M.P., a former Swanage quarry boy who, like John Mowlem before him, made a successful career in London. He provided the stone for the front of the building and collected over £1,000 for it among his London friends. 'He was one of Dorset's most loyal sons, a devoted Congregationist, a staunch Liberal and a keen Temperance Reformer.' He did much good work at the LCC and as M.P. for Kennington (1908-18). He was knighted in 1913 and was President of the Society of Dorset Men, 1913-15, dying in 1925 at the age of 78.[7] The architect of the new church was Tom Stevens of Bournemouth; the builders were William and George Hardy. The 'old meeting' (1837) became the schoolroom. The beloved minister, the Revd Thomas Steer, retired in 1908 after 28 years, and during his time a great spiritual revival had taken place. The SUDC did him the honour of naming a road at Herston after him.

Many years earlier, and during an unhappy period when there was a split in the congregation, a new chapel called the 'Mission Hall', under the leadership of Thomas

99 Artist Francis Newbery poses for the photographer during the painting of 'The Annunciation' in the side chapel of the Roman Catholic Church of the Holy Ghost. Helen Muspratt, the renowned photographer, was the model for the angel. Mary Spencer-Watson was one of the other models.

Seavill, was erected in the High Street and opened in 1872. Differences were resolved, and it was at first let and then sold, in 1937, to the Salvation Army. On 27 August 1906 'the town was covered in bunting on Monday for the visit of General Booth who gave an address at the Wesleyan Chapel.' A little Mission Hall was erected at Ulwell in May 1905. It was taken over by the Congregationalists in 1912 and the building was extended in 1930.[8]

The foundation stone of a new Roman Catholic church was laid on 10 February 1904 when some hundred and fifty members and clergy attended. It was built in Victoria Avenue near the shore and was completed in July. Well-proportioned and built in Purbeck stone, it was designed by Canon Scoles.[9] The impressive triptych and baldachin were painted by the distinguished artist Francis Newbery, of Glasgow School of Art and later of Corfe Castle.[10] The subjects are St Aldhelm, St Edward and St Elgiva, Abbess of Shaftesbury. The decoration in the sanctuary is in art nouveau style and was carried out by Newbery's wife. The adjacent Priory was completed in November 1907 and occupied by the new prior, the Revd Cuthbert McAdam.

It was now the turn of the Wesleyans. Their spacious church had been built in 1886, but in 1907 the old chapel of 1807, latterly the schoolroom, was demolished to make room for the much needed Centenary Memorial Hall opened on 14 November 1907.

Both the population of Swanage and the number of visitors were growing. This pressure led to an extension of the parish church, for which Sir J.M. Burt gave the necessary land on the north side of the building. The architects were Clifton & Robinson, the builders H. & J. Hardy. The cornerstone for the new north aisle was laid on 10 October 1907 by the daughter of the Rector, W.H. Parsons; she was presented with an engraved trowel. The churchwardens were G.C. Delamotte and C.W.T. Dean. The extension nearly doubled the size of the church, resulting in a somewhat unhappy duality. One advantage was the omission of pews, and the three-manual organ was resited at the new east end; it was built by Vowles of Bristol in 1900, rebuilt in 1928, and after the war completely restored by Harrison & Harrison.

The Baptists had a temporary chapel in King's Road. Their new brick building in the High Street beyond Court Hill was opened in 1921. A fine new, airy, C of E church, All Saints, designed by Robert Potter, was opened in 1957 in Ulwell Road. The beautiful font of 1751 came from Melcombe Horsey. A spacious hall, attached to the church, has recently been built.

The Schools

Little has been said about the schools in Swanage since the days of Andrew Bell and T.O. Bartlett, but Margaret Emms has given us a detailed account of the subject in her paper 'Education in Swanage'.[11]

Schooling was at a low ebb until the Revd Duncan Travers became rector in 1854 and did a great service by promoting education. The school he established at Herston has been touched upon; in Swanage the National School was built behind the existing infant schoolroom to the west of Upabout Lane. The site was on glebe land given by the Rector. Built in 1857, it was cramped and overcrowded with a tiny playground. Dr Home's report on Swanage sanitation in 1872 added:

> The very worst seen by me were those attached to the National School, used by about 200 children. I was told that these privies were connected with a road drain, but I doubt this. Jammed into an unventilated corner, and close to the school building, their position is the worst which could be chosen, and their neglected state is evidenced by an inconceivably sickening stench.

The school was eventually used for other purposes, including the Labour Hall, and survived until the 1970s.

In the 1850s there had been a British School on the site of the present Congregational (URC) Church, under the pastor, the Revd Thomas Seavill, who established day and evening classes, but it did not survive for long.

The Elementary Education Act of 1880 said that all children must attend school until at least 10 years of age; this was raised to 12 in 1890. There must be a new school in Swanage soon. The Rector, T.A. Gurney (1887-1901), was in favour of continuing the voluntary school, speaking of the 'evil to the town religiously and financially' if a Board school were to be established, but the Revd Thomas Steer, the Congregational minister, supported it. There had been a good school attached to his church which had now lapsed. The government inspector in 1887 observed that the population of Swanage as a whole was mainly Nonconformist. It seems that local church people were apathetic about retaining their school, and the Swanage School Board was formed in 1894.

The new school at Mount Scar above Queen's Road (Upabout Lane), costing £6,000, was opened on 28 October 1897 by John Ernest Mowlem, the first chairman, with a silver key now preserved in the Swanage Museum. It had a short life as a Board School as, under the Education Act of 1902, both Board and National schools were abolished, the new County Council being made responsible for both elementary and secondary education. Swanage Grammar School in, Northbrook Road, was opened as a mixed school in 1929 and attained considerable distinction. After the Second World War, with a new Education Act, Mount Scar became a First School when a fine new Middle School was built at Herston with a spacious playing field. The Grammar School was regretfully closed, and senior pupils were then transported to the postwar Purbeck School at Wareham, which has also achieved a high standard in its many departments.

Private schools in Purbeck could occupy a chapter by themselves. From 1874 until at least 1878 there was a 'small select school' in the Mission House (later the Salvation Army Citadel). A 'Ladies College' was opened at no.5 Park Road in 1885 and the first preparatory school for 'young gentlemen' was Purbeck College, opened in 1890 by the Revd Thomas Russell Wright; most of the boys were boarders and came from outside the area. It seems to have continued thus until the turn of the century, when it became Durlston Court School in 1903.

Headmasters of private schools began to be aware of the benefit of 'ozone' for their pupils, and there was a general movement to the south coast, not least to Swanage. A school was started in Oldfeld House in Cranborne Road; it moved just before the First World War to a new red brick building, again called Oldfeld and set prominently on a knoll north of the town.[12] For many years its adjacent modern windmill was a familiar sight as one arrived by train at Swanage. At the outbreak of the second war, part of the school was evacuated to Canada and did not survive in Swanage. It then became the boarding-out department of the Grammar School until both sections were closed. As Harrow House, it became a centre for sports and visiting foreign students.

Brookfield House, another 'prep' school, was established in Victoria Avenue in 1910 and moved to Northbrook Road in 1913. It was built by George Hardy to the design of Hart & Waterhouse of London for Hugh Saunders. When it was taken over by Rohan Chadwick in 1919, it took the name of Forres, formerly in Northwood, Middlesex. The chapel was added in 1933 and later damaged by a bomb. The school returned after wartime evacuation and remained in Swanage until it moved away to Fordingbridge in 1993.[13]

None of the several other preparatory schools remained in Swanage. Among them was Durlston Court School, where the comedian, Tony Hancock, was educated during the '30s. 'Hill Crest' school was founded in 1911 and later moved to 'Carthion', formerly the residence of Sir J.M. Burt.

Swanage Hospital[14]

There had been for some years a primitive hospital in converted cottages in the High Street. Emma Rust Burt was secretary from 1890 and continued as such for the new hospital until her death in 1910. She, her sister Annie, and brothers John Mowlem and George, made their great contribution to the welfare of Swanage by their creation of the Cottage Hospital in Queen's Road as a memorial to their parents, George and Elizabeth Burt, whose likenesses may be seen in the ornate chimneypiece in the entrance hall.

Although George Burt desired that his estate should be managed for 21 years after his death, his will enabled the family to purchase the land for the hospital. It was on glebe land and almost the only area free of quarry working. The new Cottage Hospital for 14 beds was designed by Walter J. Fletcher of Wimborne and was described as 'picturesque', more like a villa than a cottage, and an improvement on the usual dismal appearance of hospitals. It was built by local labour, superintended by Mr Cooper, foreman of the Durlston Park Estate.

The opening ceremony took place on 26 September 1895 using an ornamental key turned by the Bishop of Salisbury, with the Rector, the Revd T.A. Gurney, the donors and many other members of the Burt family present. When Emma died, Annie took over as honorary secretary. The hospital was extended in 1912 as a memorial to her sister and included an operating theatre. At her own death in 1918 she bequeathed to the hospital £2,000 and a large plot behind it. In her memory the future house 'Everest' next door was bought, which became a maternity home and later the outpatient department. Sir John Burt also left a legacy at his death in 1918; he had been Chairman of the hospital committee.

In 1909 Rothelstone House at Herston was acquired by the Local Authority as a 'Sanitary Hospital' for infectious diseases; it was closed in 1929. In 1919 the Red Cross Children's Hospital in Peveril Road was opened as a War Memorial by the Bishop, assisted by Thomas Hardy who came over from Max Gate.[15] It was closed in 1954 when a new children's ward was set up at the cottage hospital.

In spite of generous support, the hospital was running at a loss in 1934. At least Polly, the parrot at the *White Swan*, was doing her bit, spending most of her time outside,

100 The Parade during the floods of 1935, with the water pouring over the public slipway (see last of the Bankers, illustration 89).

collecting hundreds of pounds for the hospital and other charities; she was later at the *Greyhound,* Corfe Castle, until she was killed by a dog. Hospital Day and concerts continued to provide support, and in 1945 a good sum was raised from the 'Victory Dance' and 'V.J. Dance' at the *Grosvenor Hotel.*

1948 saw the advent of the National Health Service and an end to the payment of fees at the now officially named 'Swanage Hospital'. There were then 21 beds including five at 'Everest'. Since then there have been splendid improvements, with a new operating theatre, X-ray and therapy departments and a large dayroom, not least due to the help of the League of Friends. By 1984 the local population had contributed £160,000 towards the £500,000 improvements. 'The sustained support of the people of Purbeck for their hospital reflects the measure of their esteem.' In the 1960s there was the possibility of closure, but fortunately wiser counsel prevailed.

Floods and Disasters

As ever, there was often news of exceptional weather. A strong gale in 1896 brought down Old Harry's wife, leaving only the base. A phenomenon occurred in 1903 when a sandstorm hit the town one Sunday and a thick yellow fog rained down from the southwest; the pier was left coated in red sand.

The trouble from periodic floods in Swanage following heavy rainfall arose from the combination of inadequate draining and high tides. Often the floods were of short duration, but sometimes the damage was done in a matter of minutes. There were serious floods in the lower part of the town in 1895 and 1896, but the most notable ones were those of March 1914 and November 1935 when, on both occasions, the lower High Street, Station Road, King's Road and Eldon Terrace were underwater, and boats were used in the streets. Extensive damage was done to shops and houses. Perhaps the most spectacular photograph taken in 1935 was of the 'Niagara falls', showing the flood pouring from the Square over the sea wall.

Disasters at sea included the wreck of the Norwegian brigantine *Netto* on Peveril ledges in 1900; fortunately the captain, the four crewmen and the ship's cat were brought ashore by breeches buoy; the cat was taken home by the local photographer, Thomas Powell. More serious was the wreck off Old Harry in February 1908 of the French ketch *Esperanza,* which ran into fog, with the loss of a sailor and the 15-year-old cook. One of the saddest tragedies occurred in July 1911 when the paddle-steamer *Stirling Castle* and *Osiris* collided in the bay. Annie Watson, her son Walter, aged five, and daughter Isabel, aged seven, together with a manservant, Robert Brown, aged 16, were drowned when their rowing boat capsized. Mr Watson arrived in Swanage by train, only to read the news in the paper.

To turn to the menace of fire, a serious blaze arose at Parry's ironmongery in the High Street in June 1914, during which Thomas Powell[16] took some dramatic photographs. The fire brigade used a garage next to Gilbert Hall in King's Road. A Powell photograph of the new appliance, the Swan, with the brigade in 1907 also shows the police station, in Argyle Road, completed in 1899.

National Events

In July 1896 bad weather forced many boats into the Bay, including the German Emperor's yacht, which caused much interest on shore. Queen Victoria's Diamond Jubilee was celebrated in June 1897 when a procession made its way from Church Hill, down the High Street and along the shore to a field where maypole dancing took place. All council workers were given the day off. Later hundreds sat down to a tea in the Drill Hall. After covering the cost, £173 was raised for the new hospital. The *Royal Victoria Hotel* was decorated with the dates 1837-1897, and Mr J. Vye's butcher's shop was adorned with effigies of cows surrounded by fairy lights. By now electricity had appeared.

The Boer War raised much patriotic sentiment, and concerts were held for the war fund in 1900. News of the end of the war in June 1902 brought more festivities, decorations and bell ringing. By coincidence, the top section of Prince Albert's memorial was dislodged on 19 January 1901 during a heavy gale, a few days before the death of Victoria. On the day of the funeral, all shops and public houses were closed and a memorial service was held to coincide with the London service. Over three hundred men marched from the *Royal Victoria Hotel* to the parish church. James Day proposed that an avenue of trees, paid for by public subscription, should be planted along the de Moulham. Road and for it to be called Victoria Avenue, and this was done. It is surprising to note that, on 19 September 1901, 'the flag has been flying at half-mast in respect of President McKinley's assassination'.

August 1902 brought the celebrations of the Coronation of Edward VII. There was a procession round the town, an old folks' tea, and an ox was roasted above Shore Road, the gift of J.E. Mowlem. It was followed by 'a grand fireworks display which illuminated the entire town, and a vast bonfire'. Similar celebrations have since overwhelmed Swanage, which has been decorated for the coronations and jubilees of George V, George VI and Elizabeth. It was reported in the DCC (21 July 1904) that 'the German fleet passed by at 2 o'clock on Wednesday'. In October 1905 flags were displayed at the White House in commemoration of Trafalgar and Nelson's death.

15

The Great War; Seaside Swanage

The effect on Swanage of the First World War was much less, visually, than that of the Second, but at least as great with regard to human sorrow. Much of the action took place in France, of course, and the slaughter was devastating. During the years 1914-18 telegrams arrived continually, at thousands of homes throughout the land, with news of dead or missing loved ones. The Swanage war memorial is something of a curiosity, but entirely appropriate: a pile of weathered Purbeck stone stands ruggedly on the highest point of the recreation ground overlooking the sea. It bears the names of 99 Swanage men who did not survive. Mermond Place, off Station Road, was named in memory of

101 Whitecliff and Swanage Bay, showing the development of an army camp during the First World War in the middle distance, now Ballard Estate.

102 High Street, 1919, and the visit of the Royal Navy. The sailors are marching up to Purbeck House, past the Town Hall. Virginia House, in the left foreground, has since been demolished, as indeed has Ashlar House, which was pulled down in 1938, but the stone arcade, at the far end of the street, still survives.

Merton and Osmond, two sons of the Rose family, local watchmakers, who were killed during the First World War.

At the outbreak of war Swanage went about its business almost as usual. One item of note was the sinking of the SS *Kyarra*, which was torpedoed, off Durlston. The relief lifeboat *Zaida* was on service during the war but the station had to be closed temporarily in 1917 as so many local men were away, having been conscripted.

There was one major change below Ballard Down. For many years Swanage had been the scene of the annual volunteer camps at Whitecliff; now, in 1914-15, five vast camps, extending to Ulwell and Godlingston, were built by the local builders Parsons & Hayter and George Hardy for the War Department. After the war the hutments near the Bay became the Ballard Estate, with many of the huts converted to, or rebuilt as, comfortable homes. The guardhouse still exists (2004) at the entrance, though much altered. Troop trains were a great feature at Swanage Station; in the forecourt 'horses and limbers were assembled and the troops mustered before marching to the camps at New Swanage.'[1] Extensive training took place there, and early biplane aircraft were seen in the fields below Oldfeld School. The end of the War was commemorated by the annual 11 November two-minute silence, but this was not the end of war. On the war memorial 65 more names were added after the Second World War (1939-45).

Farewell to Purbeck House

Following the death of George Burt, the house became quieter. His two daughters continued to live there until their deaths. John Mowlem Burt, their brother, first built red-brick 'Craigside' opposite Purbeck House in 1900, replacing the old Spring Hill House and WMH's builders' yard, who moved their business down to Central Works in Mount Pleasant Lane; there it flourished under his son's direction as 'George Hardy', only closing in 1985 after four generations.

Sir John Mowlem Burt, knighted after the Coronation of Edward VII for services to the Government by the firm, built a new house, 'Carthion' at Durlston in 1909. After his death in 1918 it became a school, renamed 'Hill Crest', and since the War has been converted into flats. But both Sir John and his son Edwin John Burt (1875-1946), who finally succeeded to Purbeck House, were mostly living in London in order to conduct the affairs of the firm. Their nephew and cousin respectively, Sir George Mowlem Burt (1884-1964) later became chairman of Mowlem's. Kenneth Burt, great-grandson of GB, was the last director in the firm, and at his death in 1988 the connection with the family was severed.

Kenneth recalled:[2] 'I well remember as an urchin of five years, when we stayed with my great-aunt Annie Burt, being taken by my mother to say Goodnight to her, and there was my great-aunt poring over the hospital accounts and saying to my mother, "Minnie dear, I have lost a penny!" – but with a twinkle. She seemed a little formidable then, but as I grew to know her better she was in fact a kindly soul and was fond of children, despite that she never married.'

In 1919 an impressive swan-song was arranged by Major E.J. Burt, as he then was, on the occasion of the visit to Swanage of two large warships, the *Warspite* and *Valiant*, anchored in the Bay. A large contingent of men and a band marched up the High Street to the grounds of Purbeck House where the sailors were joined by many local people. Photographs were taken in the garden, with Rear-Admiral Clinton-Baker (*Valiant*), and the three commanders, together with the Burt family, the Rector, the Revd W.R. Parr (1916-34), and old William Masters Hardy, who died in 1921 aged 85.

This was almost the end for the Burts of Purbeck House. Sir John, Emma and Annie were all dead. In accordance with GB's will, the great sale of the estate took place in 1921 conducted by Fox & Sons of Bournemouth. Some of the land and buildings fell into private hands, but the sale of Purbeck House was withdrawn by Major Burt in 1923, though he continued to live in London. A keen sailor, he had a large motor yacht and in 1933 bought a house and grounds overlooking the Beaulieu River. He then offered Purbeck House to the town but the Council felt unable to undertake such a burden during the depression, though it would have made an excellent library, offices and public grounds.

Finally the Convent of Mercy, a Roman Catholic order of teaching nuns, acquired it in 1935. Buildings on the west side became a successful junior school. The house and grounds were well maintained; the chief alteration was the conversion of the billiard room into a well-loved chapel. In 1994, with a change of policy, Purbeck House was put on the market once again after nearly sixty years, except for the school, which was to continue under the wing of the Local Authority as before. Burt's mansion is now the *Purbeck House Hotel*.

Bucket and Spade

Most people came by train for their family holiday. Luggage in advance, whereby it was waiting

103 Major E.J. Burt (back row, top left) and his family pose with the Revd W.R. Parr, rector of Swanage, and naval commanders at Purbeck House in 1919. William Masters Hardy (1836-1921) is seated in the front row on the far right.

for you at the station when you arrived, cost a shilling or two; for a little more it could be delivered to your lodgings. In the 1930s a few wealthy people stayed at the *Grosvenor*, the *'Vic'* or the *Grand*. More stayed at the growing number of small 'private' hotels or guesthouses, but many lodged with a local family. You had your own meals, probably in the parlour, and if it was wet you could play indoor games, but often mother would go shopping after breakfast, for the landlady was supplied with the food and would cook the dinner.

Once on the beach, you retired into a bathing-hut to change into your one-piece costume; after your swim you might sit in a deck-chair (still with us!), but there were no windbreaks or pedaloes to hire, though there were rafts in the bay. The children made sandcastles, as ever, and there were donkey rides along the sands. Punch & Judy came rather late: an application to the council was made in April 1908 by Prof. G. Day, which was greeted with laughter. Anxiety was expressed that there was not enough room for such a show, and that the beach should be kept 'select'. Before the First World War there would be a good number of nursemaids looking after the children of the 'upper classes'. Bed and breakfast was unusual: at about 12.45 the beach was suddenly deserted as everyone went home for midday dinner. In the afternoon, perhaps, you might go on a ten-seater charabanc tour to Corfe Castle or further afield through the 'Hardy Country'. If it rained, a large concertina-like hood was brought forward over the passengers and driver. The Swanage Motor Company was established in 1919 and started from the pier.

If you went for a walk over Ballard to Old Harry rocks and Studland, you might come back along the quiet road and meet the welcome 'Walls man' on his box-tricycle – 'Stop me and buy one' – 2d. for an ice cream, 1d. for a 'snowfruit'. The first ice-cream parlour was opened in Station Road in the 1930s. Penny-in-the-slot amusements were established earlier: all mechanical, of course.

Sports and Entertainment

The results of cricket matches appeared regularly in the DCC in mid-Victorian years. Mr Thurston, a visitor in 1874, gave a good account of local matches in his diary.[3] A football club existed well before the turn of the century, as it was reported in the DCC (8 October 1898) that a meeting took place at the *Ship* with the purpose of restarting the Club. In 1903 the Albion football club dinner was held there. Rugby football flourished before the last war, perhaps influenced by the many 'prep' schools, and in the 1950s the club used the old Tithe Barn, adding galleries and, of course, a bar! This now forms the counter of the Museum. Day's Park was opened for these sports in memory of James Day, the well-known greengrocer, councillor and revered benefactor.

The first annual Swanage Lawn Tennis Tournament was held in 1903 at the Durlston Park courts. There was a fine pavilion in the grounds, but the courts

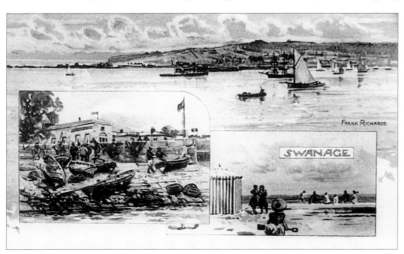

104 Victorian montage by Frank Richards showing the bay with its typical collection of fishing boats, nets and pots.

105   A Punch and Judy show on the beach before the First World War.

no longer exist. The Council created tennis courts and bowling greens in the recreation ground; more recently they were moved to the extensive Beach Gardens, together with putting greens. The creation of the interesting mini-golf course above the pier provided a very popular amenity until it suffered the fate of the marina development, which itself was overtaken by the 1990 recession. The Isle of Purbeck golf course at Studland, delightfully overlooking Poole Harbour, was established in 1892. Enid Blyton of Noddy fame was a director. Originally a nine-hole course, it was doubled in 1921.

   With the splendid facility of the Bay, yachting was naturally popular from early days for those who could afford it. The Isle of Purbeck Yacht Club was inaugurated in 1875, while the modest Sailing Club was first established in 1935 with Dr G.W.S. de Jersey at the helm.[4] The clubhouse at Buck Shore was in the old Amusement Arcade, formerly filled with gaming machines to 'catch' the passengers landing from the paddle-steamers. In 1948 the Club was affiliated to the (later Royal) Yachting Association. It is interesting to note that Dr de Jersey surveyed the Bay for the possible construction of a breakwater. The Swimming Club was well supported, and the old pier was used by divers, often watched by many onlookers, until it became too decrepit. More recently, an underwater diving centre was established at the present pier and proved popular with divers from afar. In 1903 a rifle range was opened at Ulwell. Perhaps it helped to overcome complaints made about the shooting of gulls in the bay which caused distress to visitors on the steamers (DCC, 1 September 1898). 'One wonders how one can call this a sport in our 19th century civilisation.' It was reported (17 July 1902) that 'a pair of Peregrine falcons have been spotted off Swanage'.

106   Swanage Town Band, *c*.1890.

On King's Road the Gilbert Hall was opened in 1907, becoming the Chuch Hall from 1920.[5] The first cinema show was held there in 1912.[6] The Swanage cinema in Station Road was opened in 1916 as the new Electric Theatre. From 1932, when 'talkies' were well established, there were two cinemas next to one another: the Swanage Cinema and the Grand, formerly the Pavilion, which had been converted from an army hut and used for First World War concert parties. Freddy Beck and Dorrie Dene performed there and, also, at the open-air 'concert pitch' on the front. The Mowlem Institute was not used for public entertainment until after the First World War, when the 'Savoy Follies' performed there; other concert parties followed. The bandstand was always popular during the season, with the Town Band and other visiting players performing. Except for the war years, the Regatta has continued for a century and a half, with the traditional 'greasy pole' and 'miller and sweep' entertainment at the Quay, and fireworks after dark. There was often a visiting fair and occasionally a circus. Once two young elephants were led into the sea for a bath near the Institute, and they refused to come out, squirting water everywhere from their trunks, much to the glee of those at a safe distance.

Transport

The opening of Swanage to the rest of the world via the railway was enhanced by the construction of the Sandbanks 'floating-bridge' and toll road from Studland in 1926, and by the inaugural bus service to Bournemouth, which included Sundays, introduced in 1927. This no doubt encouraged the steamers to run a Sunday service to Swanage pier in competition. The 'Londoner' in the *Evening Standard*[7] wrote of the desecration of one of our most ancient, wild and beautiful heaths, a natural haven for many rare birds and flowers: 'the heathland and seashore strewn with fairy palaces made of mother-of-pearl shells … With Lulworth in the grip of the War Office and Studland Heath in the clutches of the speculative builder, what will be left to us of Thomas Hardy's land?' Fortunately, Studland remained practically undeveloped, thanks to the Bankes Estate and its successor the National Trust. The Heath is now a National Nature Reserve and, even with the discovery of oil reserves beneath, BP have carefully guarded the area during operations.

In 1905 there had been a scheme to link Swanage with Bournemouth by a tramway across the Haven point, but it was soon abandoned. The plan would have included a transporter bridge, raising the tram to cross Poole entrance at high level. In the 1950s there was a proposal to build a high-level road bridge, but fortunately this came to nothing. With the giant cross-channel ferries entering the Harbour in the 1990s, we are even less likely to see a bridge. Buses have always been carried across on the chain ferry.

Bus services from Swanage to Langton, Worth and Kingston began in the 1920s.[8] The last bus would wait at the cinema for the last performance and was usually packed

107   Outside C.H. Parsons' Alderney Dairy in King's Road East, *c.*1930. Note the full transport fleet: from pushbike to motorised vehicles.

with people as it drove off. The Hants. & Dorset and Southern National bus companies later provided services to Corfe Castle, Wareham, Weymouth, Poole and Bournemouth as well as special excursions in the summer.[9]

Sunday trains were introduced in the summer of 1901, despite opposition, and a winter service followed in 1904. At that time the railway was kept busy with the transport of volunteers to and from the camps, and the movement of troops during the wars. After the First World War, the railways were amalgamated into four main groups, the London & South Western becoming part of Southern Railway. The heyday of the Swanage branch came in the 1930s. There was a winter service in 1931 with 13 trains in each direction. In the summer there were even more, and on Saturdays complete trains full of holidaymakers, hauled by large, named locomotives, arrived from Waterloo via the original Wimborne route, avoiding Bournemouth. Swanage station was rebuilt and extended in 1938, except for the stationmaster's house, which remained as before. The goods service, with its large shed, was excellent: a local builder could order a small consignment of material from Poole, and delivery was sometimes on the same day.

The impact of the internal combustion engine was beginning to be felt. At the regatta in 1907 a cycle carnival also accepted motorcars, though only one was entered. Sir

108   The Swanage Garages, Dean and Son, recently demolished.

Charles Robinson was complaining about speeding motor vehicles in the High Street, and a man was summoned for driving a car down the wrong side of the street. As early as 1903 Sir John Burt suggested that a lamp-post and 'Keep to the Left' sign be erected at the Round House junction. One-way traffic was not introduced in Institute Road until 1937-8. It was complained that 'Tarmac is appearing everywhere!'

Swanage Art

The Isle of Purbeck has for many years attracted prominent artists. Turner must have visited Swanage as he mentioned in his notes, when painting on the south coast, that there was no pier there; unfortunately he did not paint the Bay. George William Joy (1844-1925) exhibited his painting *Christ and the Little Child* (based on Luke, chapter IX) at the Royal Academy in 1898, where it was regarded as his most important work. It was executed in the empty Swanage brewery, just before it was demolished, during visits to his friend Sir Charles Robinson. Models for the principal subjects were, Hugh Hume, a popular coastguard, as Christ, Master George Joy, who fell in the First World War as the Child, and John Gotobed as the figure with a wicker basket across his back.[10] The work of the distinguished artist Francis Newbery is described on page 148. Studland Bay was painted by both Vanessa Bell and Roger Fry (1911). More recently Arthur Bradbury made a fine watercolour of a *View Across to Old Harry*, and Augustus John, a frequent visitor to Worth Matravers, painted *An Hour at Swanage*. George Spencer-Watson R.A. was living at Dunshay Manor, and his daughter Mary became equally distinguished as a sculptress in Purbeck stone. Elizabeth Armsden excelled in etchings of local scenes. Alfred Palmer had a studio in Swanage during the Second World War where he painted local quarrymen at work and bombed cottages, with spring blossom hinting at resurrection. John Craxton did a mysterious drawing of Swanage in black crayon (1944), recalling Paul Nash's[11] well-known semi-surrealist painting of Ballard cliff with a large shell on the shore. During 1934-5 Nash stayed first at Whitecliff and then at no.2 The Parade. He was struck by the varied geology, the white chalk cliffs, the black Kimmeridge shale and the Purbeck stone at the quarries. His *Dorset Shell Guide* was published in 1936.[12] After the War, Graham Sutherland made an ethereal painting of the Durlston Globe. Swanage has continued to be a centre for many fine artists.

The Clearance Orders

Early in 1937 a bombshell (perhaps a foretaste of the real thing) dropped on Swanage in the form of a decision by the UDC to demolish 54 houses in the oldest part of the town, including the Narrows and the well-known and admired Mill Pond cottages. This was on the grounds that they were unfit for human habitation and did not comply with modem byelaws, following a report after a visit by a Ministry of Health Inspector. It was possible that another 100 houses would be under review.[13] Mounting opposition to the proposal, including that of the inhabitants of the cottages who seemed to be healthy and happy, culminated in a Public Inquiry by the Inspector, a Ministry of Health architect, in July which lasted for three days. Extensive statements given by representatives of the Society for the Preservation of Ancient Buildings and the Dorset branch of the Council for the Preservation of Rural England were reported widely in the Press. The Rector, the Revd H. V. Nicholl-Griffith, stated that 'the tenants desired to remain in their present houses and as a body they had petitioned the Ministry of Health to this effect. The owners were also anxious to preserve these properties, and in order to do so would recondition them. Therefore, as far as the tenants and owners were concerned, there was no call for demolition.'

It was true that the traditional cottages, mostly of the 18th century or early 19th century, had, in the main, no special architectural features, apart from old Purbeck stone roofs and walls and what we now call 'group value'. The most picturesque group at the Mill Pond were the cottages next to the parish church, which belonged to a local architect, Fred Walsh, who presented a scheme of restoration. A photograph of the Mill Pond had appeared in *The Times* in March and caused widespread concern among the many artists and visitors to Swanage over the years. A question about the subject was raised in the House of Commons.

The upshot, after another inquiry and a long delay, was that the cottages would not be demolished, on condition that they were repaired and improved. But it was less than two years to the outbreak of another war, and Hitler finished off the work more quickly.

109   A peaceful scene at Swanage Bay in the late 1890s. Note the lamp standard. The last of the elms was cut down in 1898. In the distance are the Mowlem Institute and the doomed stone bankers.

16

War and Recovery

When Chamberlain gave the grave news on the wireless on 3 September 1939 that Britain was at war again, the sirens wailed immediately. It was a false alarm, but we were half expecting bombs at any minute. In the event, the 'phoney war' continued into the next summer, with little happening in that way until after the fall of France. But preparations for war steadily mounted. The Congregational Church's schoolrooms were requisitioned, first as a reception centre for evacuated children from the big cities and then as a 'British Restaurant'. The White House information centre was taken over by the War Department, to act as the Home Guard HQ, and was protected with a wall of sandbags. Swanage was then declared a Designated Defence and Prohibited Area, along with the whole south coast. A mass of steel scaffolding was erected along the length of the bay some distance from the shore, concrete 'dragons' teeth' were placed at short intervals along the promenade, and barbed wire entanglements appeared on the cliffs. A section of the pier was removed as a precaution against invasion. Life continued in Swanage as best it could, with rationing and without visitors, but with much military and secret activity. Once again many of the younger men were called up, and older people had to take over essential tasks. No more evacuated children came to Swanage, and most of the private schools moved inland or elsewhere, some never to return. Several school buildings were occupied by soldiers, and the Americans were well remembered by the local children for their generous supply of sweets and doughnuts; their infantry regiment stationed in Swanage suffered heavy losses in the 1944 'Overlord' Invasion.

Much has been written about the story of the birth of Radar in Swanage, Langton and Worth Matravers, and of the hurried evacuation of the Telecommunications Research Establishment (TRE) to Malvern that followed. 'It was the nerve centre of our entire radar system, where the boffins carried out their experiments.'[1] In 1942 there was a Commando raid on Bruneval to capture German radar equipment. Then it was known that a bombing and parachute raid on the Purbeck TRE was imminent, and a decision was made that it must be evacuated before the next full moon. When convoys of cars and lorries left Swanage, 'it was one of the biggest moving jobs in history, involving the Army, Navy, RAF and the Ministries of Food, Labour, Transport and Works & Buildings.' So there was no parachute raid, though Swanage was bombed that month.

Bombs on Swanage[2]
The first high-explosive bomb was dropped near Durlston Castle on 20 September 1940 and the last on 3 February 1943, when four HEs fell in Station Road, King's Road, Chapel

110   The Swanage beach defences during the Second World War.

Lane and Church Hill, except for an isolated raid on 24 April 1944 when 392 SD1 bombs fell in the New Swanage area. Altogether 60 HEs fell, 37 of them on land. There were 20 people killed, 28 seriously injured and 96 slightly hurt. Fourteen houses were totally destroyed, 58 had to be demolished as they were beyond repair, 61 were evacuated and 778 slightly damaged, not including broken windows. There were 2,596 warnings of all colours, of which there were 965 'Red' and 7 'Crash Red'. The total length of 'Red' warnings was 39 days, 15 hours, 59 minutes. Surprisingly there were more 'Red' warnings in Swanage than in London (900) though of course the damage sustained was not to be compared. Nevertheless Swanage bore its share.

The worst raid occurred on 17 August 1942 when the Westminster Bank, opposite the present bank, received a direct hit from an HE, killing eight people and seriously injuring a further 11. Other heavily bombed areas were Cornwall Road, Station Road, where five were killed and 21 wounded, Springfield Road, Park Road, High Street (Chapel Lane and the Narrows), and Church Hill. Several well-known buildings were destroyed, including Wesley's Cottage, Newton Cottage and Swanage Dairies, with the west wing of the *Ship*, where five were killed and nine wounded. A bomb entered the Congregational Church at the apex of the south wall, passed through it and demolished the north wall, completely

111 Bomb damage in Cornwall Road during the Second World War. This raid, on 20 April 1942, also badly damaged Station Road and killed five people.

destroying the organ. It exploded in the old graveyard below, blew out all 14 windows in the parish church opposite, bringing down some of the stone roof-tiles there and more at the Tithe Barn. The Methodist Church was also put out of action. Many of the old cottages due for improvement in 1937 were too badly damaged to repair.

On 16 October 1942, two Messerschmit planes 'buzzed' the town, but one was brought down at Durlston. Mrs Banfield remembered playing on the beach as a child of nine (there was a gap in the barricade) when, from nowhere, an aeroplane appeared, flying along the shoreline. 'My companion threw himself on top of me, as the plane passed overhead, machine-gunning the beach and then went on to drop bombs on the town. We had great difficulty in getting home.'[3]

It is more than sixty years since D-day, 6 June 1944. Before the Invasion, there was a rehearsal on 18 April at Studland Heath and Bay. Major Trefusis records that preparations were made at the *Grosvenor Hotel*, when without warning the King and F.M. Montgomery walked in. The next day they were taken to a pillbox to observe the rehearsal.[4] On 5 June Studland Heath was alive with men and machines. Churchill and Eisenhower were 'on duty' on the ramparts, the concrete bunker 'Fort Henry' overlooking the Bay. There was a flotilla of landing crafts and ships in Studland and Swanage bays and then, when they left for Normandy next day, Purbeck was suddenly empty.

Mercifully VE Day came on 8 May 1945, and VJ Day followed on 15 August after the atom bomb had dropped. The Union Jack was flown at half-mast on the church tower, and the Last Post sounded in remembrance.

Swanage slowly recovered from its battering. Buildings were repaired or rebuilt, defences removed, and thousands of both exploded and live shells on Studland Heath were cleared by the army. When the ferry reopened, notices on the road warned of the possibility of remaining missiles. A great tragedy happened in 1955 when five boys from Forres School were killed near Sheps Hollow at the north end of Swanage Bay. An object which they found in the cliff turned out to be an unexploded mine, missed by clearance and probably exposed by erosion. In 1994 a rocket was seen sticking out of the ground in the dunes at Studland, and it is still well to be aware of danger even now.

Holidaymakers reappeared in 1946, and the White House reopened as the Information Centre once more. Forres School returned, and Newton Manor was opened as a girls' boarding school, only to close in 1980; the grounds were redeveloped for housing. At the 1951 census the population was 6,866, little more than in 1931, but ten years later it had increased to 8,120.

All the war-damaged buildings on the south side of the Narrows were cleared away, making it the widest part of the High Street. On Church Hill a new rectory took the place of the bombed cottages, appropriately in long-forgotten 'Paradise'. The remaining picturesque group next to the church tower and mill pond was reconstructed sympathetically by the architect Fred Walsh who, as surveyor to the local authority, also produced some award-winning stone council houses in Priest's Road. Not so attractive was the extensive Greyseed (Greasehead) Herston estate: it was decided that stone would be too expensive, and raw bricks were chosen, though the terraces fronting the main road were rendered.

The new Mowlem and Library

Early in 1960 the Council met to discuss alternative schemes for a theatre or a restaurant, either in place of the Old Curiosity Shop opposite the Town Hall (presumably without a car park), or on the old concert pitch, also taking the place of the White House and Cabin Café. In the event, neither of these came to fruition, and the new 'Mowlem' was officially opened in 1967, replacing the old Institute. This caused much controversy and many people were against the idea, though the trustees obtained permission from the Charity Commissioners for rebuilding. At one stage there was a proposal to adapt the original building to create a new library; however, a library was built 'as new' on the site of Ashlar House (demolished in 1938) in the High Street. This modern dodecagonal design by the County Architect proved to be a successful building and sits pleasantly next to the *Anchor*. The present Mowlem building, typical of its time, has a spacious restaurant overlooking the sea. It is not mentioned by Pevsner, perhaps intentionally, but he describes the Day Centre (1959) in the former Narrows as 'an overgrown bungalow, whose generous lawns break up the texture of the old High Street'.

Swanage Railway

The branch became part of British Rail in 1948 and continued to bring holidaymakers to Swanage and to carry local people to work in Poole. But with the rapid

112 The dodecagonal library, designed by the county architect J.Hurst in 1965, with Crickmay's 1896 arcade and the ancient *Anchor Inn*.

113 An early advertisement for James Smith & Son, drapers, who still occupy part of the same building in the High Street. The business originally started at Langton Matravers.

increase in car ownership, the number of passengers steadily declined, though steam had been replaced by diesel in 1966. Dr Beeching had not recommended closure of the branch in 1965, but British Rail had second thoughts and proposed closing it in September 1968. Local opposition was successful for a while, but the writing was on the wall, and the last passenger train left Swanage on 1 January 1972 'from a station little more than a ghost, with the siding long gone, the turntable overgrown, and only the fine stone station to remind one of the great days when only the best was good enough'.[5] However, there were many people who were not prepared to confine their activities to mourning. 'The preservationists were soon in full cry, with the blessing of Sir John Betjeman, for whom Swanage must surely have represented the epitome of pre-war family holiday-making which he was recalling so forcefully in print and on television.'

The Swanage Railway Society came into being, to be followed by a professional group operating, with the Southern Steam Trust, the Purbeck Line, which would eventually connect Swanage with Corfe Castle and Wareham once more.

May 1985 saw celebrations of the Centenary of the Railway, with the re-enactment of the Opening Ceremony at the station. 'Mr George Burt', 'Mr Meikle, Chairman of the Local Board' and the Town Crier were, with many others, on the platform, all in Victorian dress. There were boat, carriage and steam rides, a Music Hall event and a Centenary Ball.

Durlston Country Park

In 1970 George Burt's Durlston Park was in a sorry state, still showing wartime scars, with old Nissen huts, a great deal of rubbish, overhead cables, barbed wire, broken walls and neglected trees. For a while there was a strange 'aviary' as a sort of offshoot from the owner's amusement centre in the town. The Great

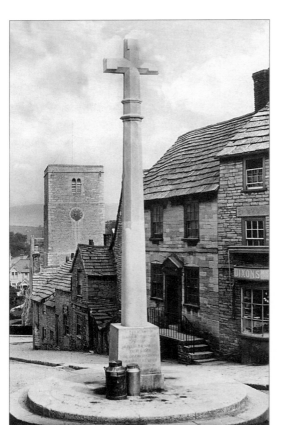

114 The Palgrave Cross. The cross was erected on the site of the Town Pump by the family of Sir Reginald Francis Palgrave CB after his death in 1909. His house was Hill Side (later Steepways) in Durlston. He was a friend of Sir Charles Robinson and was clerk of the House of Commons for 40 years. His more famous brother was Francis Turner Palgrave, poet, who edited the much esteemed *Golden Treasury*. The cottages further down the hill were demolished after the wartime bombing.

Globe was masked by a concrete wall and wire fence to prevent people seeing it, except by payment at the Castle.

The area was steadily improved when the Dorset County Council acquired 261 acres in 1973 which became the Durlston Country Park, as part of the Heritage Coastline. The problems were stated then, and still apply:

> As leisure hours have increased, more and more people have taken to their cars to visit the countryside, and, despite its apparent remoteness, well over half a million people live within thirty miles of Durlston. Indiscriminate driving of cars began to wear away the grass, not only producing ugly scars, but seriously disturbing the wild plants, animals and birds.[6]

An excellent information and exhibition centre was built on the site of the former radar station, and the old camp was landscaped with parking bays. The grass recovered well when access to the lighthouse by car was barred. The wardens have done wonders with the Park; nature walks are frequently arranged, not least for children, who are all-important for the future prosperity and safekeeping of the coast. There is now a 'dolphin watch', as these fascinating creatures can often be seen off Durlston Head.

The Great Globe became 100 years old in 1987, and on 5 July there was another grand celebration around it with maypole dancing and the arrival, once more, of 'George Burt' in the person of our long-standing journalist George Willey – formerly of the defunct *Swanage Times* – who has been an excellent watchdog.

115   A crowded beach scene in Swanage Bay, typical of the Victorian and Edwardian eras.

17

To The Millennium

As has been seen, talk of a 'harbour of refuge' has continued for 150 years without result. Swanage is well-sheltered except when the east wind rises, and then the boats in the bay are in trouble. In 1988 it looked as though a harbour would at last materialise. The *Grosvenor Hotel* was demolished for redevelopment in conjunction with a proposed 'yacht haven', which was to include a substantial breakwater encompassing the existing pier, and berthing facilities for 252 boats.[1] There was intense interest in the scheme, with half the population in favour and half opposed. A referendum was taken and the opposition won the day. It had also to receive Parliamentary approval but the House of Lords turned down the application. Meanwhile the first phase of an ingenious plan for 32 'waterside homes' had been approved and built but, with the sudden onset of the recession in 1989, the scheme collapsed leaving three more phases incomplete. The Marina therefore came to nothing.

Wessex Water

Perhaps the greatest change in the appearance of Swanage Bay since 1990 has been the sewerage scheme carried out by Wessex Water. The *Grosvenor* had been demolished; also gone were the swimming pool and car park above Marine Villa, which fortunately was not included in the plan and still survives; it has been restored as a Marine Museum.

There have been long-needed improvements to Swanage's drainage. After various suggestions, it was decided to acquire the *Grosvenor* site and install up-to-date works to deal with the sewage problem at Peveril Point, taking in all the shore frontage from the Pier entrance to the Berry rock opposite the clock tower. Looking down from Folly Knap above, people could observe the massive excavations beneath the former hotel and the subsequent construction of a series of deep treatment tanks designed to convert the effluent sewage into an acceptable condition for conveyance out to sea. The long outfall pipe beyond the Point, which hitherto was in a state of collapse, was also enclosed. During the excavations, seams of Purbeck Marble and Burr Stone were encountered, along with ancient quarry workings and cavities that required tons of infill. Eventually the new works were covered with a flat concrete roof, and they were completed with planting. On the elevations towards the sea, the new walls having been faced with Purbeck Stone, the bastion appeared almost like a second castle. The actual works were designed to be controlled remotely from headquarters in Bath, with regular inspection all that was necessary on site. It was indeed a huge achievement, resulting in one of the best sewerage schemes in Europe.

116   Aerial view of the *Grosvenor Hotel* before Wessex Water's developments saw it demolished.

Floods Persist

The problem of Swanage floods has been difficult to overcome. The spectacular 1914 and 1935 floods were mentioned earlier. More recent ones occurred in the 1960s, and in 1990 Victoria Avenue was under water. With hindsight, much less damage would occur had Station Road, Eldon Terrace and Kings Road never been built, and the Brook been left uncovered. As part of the new Swanage Sewage works, extensive work had to be carried out in order to conduct some of the treated effluent away to holding lakes, in the vicinity of Prospect Farm, a mile away. To allow for a pipe six feet in diameter, the subsoil was excavated below and across the centre of Swanage, beneath the Square and other buildings, to the Station and beyond. This large pipe carries surface water, and a smaller one within it takes away foul water. In addition to all this, another new pipe was constructed

117   The same coastline today, with the sewage works on the site of the *Grosvenor*. Note the stumps of the first pier.

below Victoria Avenue to take flood water, bypassing the Brook and to discharge into the sea. Rather than having this stream spill on to the beach, the notorious jetty 'Banjo' was constructed in 1993. Although well built, and forming a pleasant extension from the Promenade, many considered it an intrusion into the sweep of the Bay. There was also apprehension about the effect it would have on the sand. This proved to be a problem as sand piles up on the south side of the projection but is denuded on the north. There was also concern about the state of the Parade wall as a result of the loss of the beach,

118   The lighthouse immediately above Tilly Whim Caves, showing the Portland Stone series of the Jurassic Coast.

the most important feature of Swanage Bay. The suggestion to build massive stone groynes has reared its head once more, as it did in 1898 (see p142), but a paragraph in the *Swanage Times* on 26 January 1939 reads interestingly.[2]

Recently fisherman Roger Marsh pointed out that the 'Banjo' stops the sand from swilling around the Bay. The pre-war timber groynes have done their job adequately and they might be renewed if necessary.

Peveril and Stone Quay area

With the prospect of the restoration of the Pier and the completion of the Wessex Water project, plans for the enhancement of the Peveril waterfront and downs continued into the Millennium. The scheme was carried out under the direction of the Planning Department of the Purbeck District Council. It included extensive repaving of the Parade, resetting the former narrow-gauge railway tracks, and restoring the western end of Burt's Market (the brick-built fish and coal building). The stone-built lavatories were demolished, and the site was then replaced by Burt's original 'Pleasure Gardens', now with attractive seats and decorative paving. Similar enhancement was carried out at the entrance to the downs area, formerly the site of the popular mini-golf course (the loss of which was regretted by many). The planners wished to maintain a wide public access to give maximum visual appeal across the Bay, which admittedly was achieved. Finally, at the eastern end, the Prince Albert Gardens were formed, incorporating a circular paved area for performances (weather permitting!). But where was Prince Albert, now banished from his monument in the High Street? Two Ionic columns resurrected from the former *Grosvenor* forecourt completed the Gardens.

The Pier Restoration

The old Pier of 1859 had all but disappeared and there were only a few stumps remaining. The new Pier (1897) had steadily disintegrated since 1966 when the last steamer, *Embassy*, still called on a regular basis. A hovercraft between Swanage and Bournemouth came into service during the late 1960s and early 1970s while the Pier was still usable, but was then discontinued. Not having been maintained for six years, a combination of wood rot, marine-borer attack and storm damage had left it in a dilapidated state.[3] Finally the Pier became dangerous and was closed, even for the fishermen, in 1982. The last pier master was Ken Bird and the Pier was owned by the Hotel Grosvenor Company. Although the Pier was Grade II listed, nothing was done about its state of repair until its proposed incorporation into the Marina project of 1986. Re-decking began, only to stop with the financial collapse of the scheme in 1989. Strong appeals to save the Pier then came from all directions. Eventually the Purbeck District Council acquired grants for the Swanage Pier Company; applications for Heritage Lottery Fund Grants were also successful. Decking of the walkway was resumed, partly assisted by the many residents and visitors who donated small brass plates, which were set in the wooden planks of the deck, to the memory of their loved ones; this resulted in several hundred plaques on either side. It was now possible for boats to land and take passengers once again. The last ocean-going paddle-steamer, *Waverley*, resumed her periodic visits. Finally the upper deck at the seaward end was repaired, the shelter (which had disappeared) was rebuilt, and railings and handsome lamp-standards were put in place. One of the best remaining Victorian Piers was now restored to its former splendour. There is, of course, the problem of continual maintenance costs, to which the many visitors only contribute a small entrance fee. It is hoped that some amusement for them can be provided on the Pier in a profitable way. The Diving Centre here was established many years ago and continues to flourish. A fine new Sailing Club was built in 1999 and sits agreeably adjacent to Marine Villa.

Industry and Building

Change has come steadily since the war. When petrol rationing ceased, goods began to be transported by vans and lorries rather than by rail. One prominent feature of Swanage that could formerly be seen, especially from the train on approaching the Station, was the large gasometer, now long gone. The gas is now delivered from afar, as is the mains water. At the entrance to the old Gas Works, north of the railway bridge, the foreman's villa still stands. Beyond it the Victoria Avenue Industrial Centre and Business Park was developed with a growing number of workshops and stores.

Building increased rapidly after the war: first with the repair, or replacement, of bombed areas, later due to the demand for flats, some as second homes. In this way Edwardian villas have been disappearing, as have boarding houses and hotels, large and small. Several old established building firms ceased operation, but these were replaced with many small establishments run by fewer than half a dozen men.

Quarrying was resumed: some in Swanage, but mostly beyond the Parish on the Kingston road, and at St Aldhelm's Head Quarry. The long-established Brick Works at Godlingston continued to flourish, producing superior bricks destined for important buildings far and wide.

Recent buildings of prominence include the Post Office, on the site of the Old Drill Hall, and the Health Centre, both built in brick; the rest – the Co-op Supermarket, All Saints Church Hall, St Mary's Rooms, the Sailing Club and the new Sewage Works

119 One of two murals painted by Phyllis Mapley in 1974, both of which are displayed at the Swanage Hospital.

120 Phyllis Mapley's other mural, depicting the Jurassic Coast.

– are all in Purbeck Stone. Swanage Hospital has again grown in size and reputation. The outpatients department, the formerly converted 'Everest' house, has been demolished due to the continual settlement of the foundations, and a new wing on the hospital itself has opened.

Shopping

The first small supermarket was created by the conversion of the Co-op Grocery Stores below York Terrace in the High Street, seen in illustration 84. It was carried out by George Hardy, builders in the mid-fifties, and was called the Food Hall. In Institute Road there were the International, Home and Colonial shops, and in Station Road were Boots (still there) and Montague Purchase (excellent grocers). When Robsons Grocery Stores closed, the High Street was no longer the main shopping centre in Swanage and several old-world shops such as haberdashers had gone, though Smiths the Drapers remain there (illustration 109).

The first large supermarket came after the closure of the cinema in 1959, taking its place together with that of the adjacent dress shop, and is now, in 2004, one of the Somerfield's chain. A much greater change in Swanage came later when the new Co-op supermarket and car park were built on the site of the Station Goods Yard, and the Brook Garage alongside King's Road closed. As part of the new Conservation Area it had been intended to become an 'open green lung' but the Town Council thought otherwise.

At first it was suggested that the Co-op occupy the station itself, and the terminus be moved to the west of the bridge. Fortunately this did not happen, but there was still great opposition to the whole scheme, particularly because at the same time it was proposed that an additional car park be built on the site of the Recreation Ground, thought to be sacrosanct as per the deeds when the Urban District Council acquired it. However, the pre-war Bowling Green had already been moved northwards to the Beach Gardens, so it was easier to claim this area. Public meetings and appeals against the Planning Permission were of no avail and redevelopment proceeded. Already the post-war new Fire Station was situated beyond the Co-op, and there was also a bus park behind it. So much for the 'open green lung'.

The Farms

The war revolutionised farming.[4] With no exports or imports, and with the introduction of rationing, great changes took place. The Purbeck Hills were ploughed and, on a smaller scale, lawns disappeared to make way for vegetable plots, urged on by the 'Dig for Victory' slogan. Many more people took up allotments. Working horses vanished, to be replaced by tractors. Haystacks and stooks disappeared from the scene; instead arrived combine harvesters, and baling, silage and milking machines. The use of fertilisers greatly increased.[5]

After the war there were yet more changes with the resumption of trade and foreign imports. Containers took the place of goods wagons and, with the introduction of supermarkets, fruit and vegetables began to be flown in from all over the world. The effect on Dorset farms was great. Flocks of sheep had long disappeared. Very few people now worked on the land, and a Victorian farmer would be bewildered by the modern farming scene.

Many farms within Swanage ceased to exist, such as White Hall at Peveril, which was swept away by Pitt as early as 1820 to provide greensward for the Manor House visitors. Carrant's Court Farm was swallowed up for building development a century ago, and it was followed by Eastbrook, Northbrook, Townsend and Newton. Of the remaining farms, Whitecliff, Godlingston, Currendon and Verney are still active. The rest, Ulwell, Swanage Farm, South Barn, California, Belle Vue, Cauldron Barn and Prospect, are not. Some of these are occupied by caravans (seven such sites are marked on the O.S. map). On a few acres, ponies are kept, and 'Horsiculture' is now using more acres in Purbeck than dairying. Some farms are being cropped or grazed by neighbours. Another sign of the times is the conversion of barns into residences. Knitson, just outside the parish boundary, is farmed intensively, but is also used for summer camping. A retired farmer there has written a fascinating paper on the history of his farm:

> Knitson is an excellent example of the general trend in farming of the area, with five comfortable modernised homes replacing three collapsing leaking near-derelict houses, a redundant cow shed and a prefabricated Arcon shed. In 1947 every farmhouse and cottage along the Underhill Road between Corfe Castle and the sea was dark, damp and seriously in need of repair. Now every dwelling and some former barns have been modernised, extended, beautified and landscaped. Tourism-money has made possible the modern homes at Knitson and city money from many sources has improved others. This appears to be the foreseeable future of the countryside.[6]

Recreation

Above Herston, and operated by Swanage Town Council, is the Vista Complex and Bay View Holiday Park. It includes a large indoor swimming pool, a 'Trimnasium', an indoor bowling green and many other attractions. There is a large hall and stage. The

Council also owns the Swanage Boat Park at Peveril Point. In the Anvil Point area official cliff climbing is permitted, supervised by dedicated people; many others from all the churches and schools also run programmes. In Victoria Avenue stands the handsome stone entrance to King George's Playing Fields, built after the war but sadly neglected as the result of the large, extended car park. But plans are on course for a 'face-lift' for the Fields to include new changing rooms and provision for the latest demand: a skateboard park. To the west, a 'pitch-and-putt' golf course has been created on a former Prospect farm, but, being quite flat, it lacks the attraction of the hilly mini-golf course that was formerly above the Pier.

The Railway may count as recreation due to the success of many journeys to Corfe Castle, as does the Park and Ride at Norden enjoyed by hundreds of holidaymakers, young and old. But great strides continue to be taken by Swanage Railway to achieve the connection to Wareham. The track and the signalling are in place, and recently a Virgin train made the journey to Swanage from the main line: the first to do so since the closure in 1972. Before long, no doubt, there will be a regular service of trains to Wareham and perhaps beyond.

The annual Regatta, dating almost from time immemorial, combined with the Carnival after the war and together they grew steadily in extent, including the length of the procession. There were several marching bands at intervals between the competitively decorated floats mounted with tableaux; these culminated, of course, with the float of the Swanage Queen and her attendants. In its time the Tithe Barn members entered many commercial scenes including Princess Victoria in her carriage, walking London bollards, ancient dancing skeletons, a trundled bawdy bathing-hut and Swanage Hospital's travelling (and bloody) operation! Meanwhile on the recreation ground the genial George Willey, that prince of journalists, conducted races and competitions, hardly needing his loudspeaker. In the Bay one would watch the rowing races, with entrants from home and afar, and further out to sea the many handsome yachts. A spectacular firework display always ended the evening. In the 1980s a spontaneous fancy dress New Year's Eve Carnival in the lower High Street was brought into being by Swanage enthusiasts. This grew in size, becoming well known far and wide, with revellers pouring in from around the surrounding countryside and even from London. Of recent years, however, the numbers at this annual gathering have gradually dwindled. On the other hand the annual Jazz Festival has flourished, drawing many well-known musicians to Swanage. In addition, Morris dancers appear regularly, visiting town bands play at the charming bandstand in the summer, as they did of yore, and other performers take part in the recently created Prince Albert Gardens. The Mowlem Theatre continues with both cinema and live shows all the year round; local performers include the Swanage Choral and Operatic Society.

Tourism

Since the war, tourism has overtaken farming to become the most important industry in Purbeck. This was primarily the result of rapid growth in car ownership. Even in the 1950s many visitors were still coming by train, spending most of their holiday on the beach. There had always been the dedicated hikers, but now many more people were able to tour Dorset, with still more visiting Swanage for a day out; all were in their cars, however, and needed somewhere to park. This had an effect on the landscape. On entering Lulworth Cove for instance, the astonishing view of the huge, prominent car park caused dismay to many. Entering and leaving Swanage became an increasing problem, particularly at weekends, when stationary cars stretched for miles along the A351, but this was relieved considerably by the removal of the railway crossing at Wareham Station, and the bridge that replaced it. The problem at Studland grew worse, too, with lines of cars parked off the road on the approach to Sandbanks Ferry, even though the National Trust created large car parks at the entrances to the beach. On Sundays these were often overflowing. Swanage itself has several car parks including a well-designed one at the Durlston Country Park. Shore Road, between the Mowlem and Victoria Avenue, is closed to traffic in the summer months. In the winter at weekends there are often closely lined cars along the whole length of the Parade, many people not even leaving them for a breath of fresh air! More facilities more visitors appeared. In addition to the White House Information Office the new Heritage Centre was created from the western part of the former coal and fish building on the front; it opened in 2000. Operated by the Purbeck District Council, the centre has displays covering Swanage's geology, landscape, quarrying and natural history, and also recounts the history of the Mowlem and Burt Families in Swanage.

The Swanage Museum and Art Centre

Swanage Rectory included gardens, an orchard and the ancient Tithe Barn. The whole property was sold in the 1920s to the long-established Parsons family, subsequent rectors living in their own homes until the new Rectory was built on Church Hill after the war. In 1976 Tony Parsons was about to sell the Rectory and leave for Australia to spend his last years. David Florence was anxious to establish a Museum in Swanage, while Phyllis Mapley was equally keen to set up an Art Centre. Mr Parsons offered the Barn for these purposes and for the benefit of the town, on a 99-year leasehold at a peppercorn rent, but a decision had to be made within a week. A hurried meeting was arranged with other interested people and a deal was signed by Trustees. The building, though Grade II listed for preservation, had been empty for some years and much work was needed before it could be opened to the public. Volunteers were soon at work, and ever since the museum has continued to prosper with the help of its many members. Among its attractive features are the forecourt and garden. The museum includes displays on quarrying and sailing ships, with many photographs of old Swanage. In the summer there are art exhibitions, and changes are made to the displays. The local Family History Centre has become well established. The many schoolchildren who visit the museum while staying in Swanage are an important element in its life.

The remainder of the old Rectory grounds was developed to become Church Close, which is part of the Swanage conservation area extending to the church, mill pond, and lower High Street.

Durlston Castle

Henry Charles Burt continued to run the shop at 1 Victoria Terrace, which later became Burt's Corner House and Restaurant; it is now the *White Horse Inn*. He had also taken over the Castle, which he ran as a restaurant in conjunction with the shop. Remarkably two of his children were born there: Bruce Durlston, in 1902, and Donald Jago, in 1907. The others were born in Victoria Terrace. After HC's death in 1922 his wife gave up the Castle, and new tenants came to continue the restaurant. The Castle was sold in 1936, but after the war it continued under various tenants until 2003. After closely guarded negotiations in that year, the Dorset County Council bought the Castle, to everyone's satisfaction. 'The DCC, in partnership with the South West Regional Development Agency and other partners, intend to make Durlston Castle a flagship gateway to the World Heritage site. It is also intended to restore the Castle to its prominence, making it the centre of the Country Park's activities. It hopes to develop its catering and interpretation facilities to provide a hospitable welcome to a wide range of visitors of all ages and

121   Durlson Castle, immediately above the Purbeck Portland cliffs, now destined to become the Jurassic Coast World Heritage Visitors Centre.

abilities. It is also hoped to restore those visionary elements of the Park, created by George Burt to inspire wonder at nature's bounty, and to further develop his vision of the world through special features and an on-going Arts Programme.'[7]

The Jurassic Coast

In the new Millennium designation of the East Devon and South Dorset Coast as what would be the first World Heritage site created in England was deemed to be of paramount importance, ranked alongside the Grand Canyon, and achieved worldwide fame. East to West the coast starts from the sands of Studland at Redend Point and continues to the chalk cliffs of Old Harry and Ballard Head. Beyond the Wealden Bay of Swanage, and Cretaceous Marble at Peveril Point, the Jurassic Beds come into their own: at Durlston Bay, Durlston Head, Anvil Point and Tilly Whim, all the way through to St Aldhelm's Head, and beyond. Here, however, we must confine discussions of the spectacle to the coast of Swanage itself, which is described in more detail in Chapter 1. The Jurassic Coast has now been advertised intensively both at home and abroad. Commercial enterprise has inevitably come to the fore, although this is to the advantage of tourism in Purbeck. Some people have complained that, since it was designated an area of outstanding beauty, the landscape has been subject to overly rigid controls, leaving it in an unnaturally tidy condition. But nobody could object to the extensive rebuilding of many of the collapsed drystone walls carried out by the National Trust! Perhaps it was all more 'natural' in the past but now, with the all-pervading car and consequent ease of approach for one-day trips from the next door conurbation (which stretches from Upton 20 miles through Poole, Bournemouth and Christchurch to New Milton), there is a need to manage the landscape carefully. However, with the National Trust owning the cliffs to the west of the Country Park, and with Ballard Down and Studland Heath to the north, Swanage is well protected from being swamped by large-scale development. It is also perhaps fortunate that access to the Jurassic Coast necessitates a good walk!

Looking Ahead

Oil rigs were seen beyond the Bay and tests for oil south of the town fortunately proved negative. Swanage has in fact benefited from British Petroleum's support for several local projects. But it seems that the search for oil on shore in Purbeck has not produced any increase, for the oil is now retrieved offshore under Poole Bay. The Gathering Station is still the largest onshore unit in Europe.

Traffic and parking in Swanage continues to be a problem. Eventually there will have to be further restrictions. None of the traffic entering the town is passing through and therefore it must be accommodated in the future. Both Poole and Dorchester have pedestrianised their own shopping streets to great advantage, and one hopes that the planners still have a scheme for Swanage that will be put into action.

The 2001 Census gave the population of Swanage as 10,138 (4,727 male, 5,411 female). Is the parish spiralling? Paul Hyland, in one of the best books on Purbeck,[8] wrote:

> Swanage is the craziest town I know. It has the sublimity of long history, the charm of a fishing village, the ambition and pragmatism of a port, and the calculated grace of a watering place.
> It sports the artistic pretension of a poor man's St Ives, the garishness of a funfair, and the red brick boredom of a retirement haven. It contains modern buildings of flair like the Library, as well as the block-busting monstrosities like the Mowlem Theatre.

What of the future? The superb Bay and the outstanding beauty of its surroundings will surely endure. The quality of the town, both of its environment and its life, is the keynote of its future well-being. But that is easier said than achieved in a changing world.

122   Tilly Whim Caves, showing the majestic Purbeck Portland stone series of the Jurassic Coast.

Notes

1 *Rocks and Dinosaurs, pp.1-8*

1. The 'Isle' of Purbeck is bounded on the south and east by the sea, by Poole Harbour and the River Frome on the north, and on the west by a small stream, Luckford Lake, which flows north into the Frome from its source only a mile north of Worbarrow Bay.

2. Since 1964 The Institute of Geological Science has accepted that the Cinder Bed is the new time zone. All beds of stone below the Cinder Bed are known as the Lulworth Beds, and those above, as the Durlston Beds. Natural Environment Research Council, R.V. Melville, MSc and E.C. Freshney, BSc PhD, *British Regional Geology. The Hampshire Basin and adjoining areas* (4th edn).

3. The O.S. designation of the Purbeck Hills is strictly confined to the western chalk ridge between Corfe Castle and Worbarrow, although the eastern range of Nine Barrow Down and Ballard (the 'Bollard') is usually included.

4. The County Museum at Dorchester houses an extensive and informative geological display.

5. J.B. Delair, the Proceedings of the Dorset Natural History and Archaeological Society, No. 84, 1963, pp.92-100; also P.C. Ensom, No. 105, 1983, p.166.

6. J.B. Calkin, MA, FSA, *Ancient Purbeck*, 1968.

7. M.P. King, *Beneath your Feet*, 1974.

8. In 1876 William R. Brodie died at the age of 46 and was buried in Swanage cemetery.

9. Samuel Husbands Beccles FRS, FGS (1814-90).

10. Etching by R.P. Leitch from a photograph by F. Briggs (see page xii). Beccles' project cost £390, which included £200 for labour, £150 for rent of the house and £40 for the purchase of Brodie's specimens. Beccles' Purbeck collection was eventually sold to the British Museum. See notes by Ken Woodhams at the Dorset County Museum.

11. C.E. Robinson, MA, *Picturesque Rambles in the Isle of Purbeck*, 1882, p.98, with reference to Willett's excavation.

12. J.F. Nunn, 'A geological map of Purbeck Beds in the northern part of Durlston Bay', Proc. DNHAS 113, 1991, p.145.

13. In a letter of 1961 to Tom Hardy, of the Swanage builders George Hardy, Kenneth Burt wrote, 'Yes, it is sad to hear of the Durlston landslip. I remember my father telling me that when he was quite young he spent some time with his grandfather, old George Burt, on the estate, and father told his grandfather that he would never be able to build a road round Durlston Bay because the geological formation of the cliff was constantly on the move, and in the event he was right – I remember the useless bridge below the 'castle' as a child.'

14. W.J. Arkell, MA, D.Sc, 'The Geology of the Country around Weymouth, Swanage, Corfe and Lulworth', HMSO, 1947.

15. Cunning and Maxted, *Coastal Studies in Purbeck*, 1979.

16. Arkell, *op. cit.*

17. An alternative name is *La Trenchye*.

18. Thelma Woolf, *Purbeck Shore*, 1973.

19. L. Forbes Winslow, MB, DCL, MRCP, Physician to the North London Hospital for Consumption.

20. 'Sunnydale' is the Durlston sheltered valley where George Burt planted a 'pleasaunce', *c.*1870.

21. Thomas Hardy, *The Hand of Ethelberta*, 1876, chapter 43.

22. The water table below the chalk hills was probably higher than now, affording more hillside trees such as those of the north-facing woods that still remain west of Corfe Castle.

2 *Settlers and Invaders, pp.9-17*

1. Proc. DNHAS 17, pp.48, 67 and 74. See also J.B. Calkin, *Some Archeological Discoveries in the Isle of Purbeck*, 1953.
2. Proc. DNHAS, 101, 1979, p.140.
3. Grimsell, *Dorset Barrows*, 1959.
4. There have, however, been suggestions that the stones were boundaries and not ancient (ref. East Dorset Archeological Society).
5. J.B. Calkin, *Discovering prehistoric Bournemouth and Christchurch*, 1966, p.31.
6. Pevsner and Newman, *Dorset*, 1972, p.242.
7. Christopher Taylor, *Dorset*, 1970.
8. P. Vinogradoff, *The Growth of the Manor*, 1920 (3rd edn).
9. W.M. Hardy, in his *Old Swanage*, 1910 (2nd edn), discusses 'The Old Lake' at length.
10. Nigel Sunter, *Romano-British Industries in Purbeck*, DNHAS monograph, 1987, no.6.
11-12. Peter Salway, 'Roman Britain', *Oxford History of Britain*, 1988.
13. Calkin, *Ancient Purbeck*, p.55.
14. Proc. DNHAS 97, 1975, p.67 and RCHM Dorset SE, pp.598-9.
15. Proc. DNHAS 98, 1976, p.54 and 113, 1991, p.173.
16. Local archaeologist Tony Brown discovered a small Roman altar near Kingston barn in 1960.
17. Calkin, *op. cit.*, p.29.
18. Proc. DNHAS 87, 1965, p.142.
19. Calkin, *op. cit.*, p.28.
20. Peter J. Cox, Proc. DNHAS 110, 1988 (a full report with illustrations).
21. C.E. Robinson, *Picturesque Rambles in the Isle of Purbeck*, 1882, p.104.
22. *Swanage Times*, 9.4.1981.
23. John Beavis, 'Purbeck Marble in Roman Britain', Proc. DNHAS 92, 1970, pp.181-204.
24. Roger Peers, 'Prehistoric and Roman remains', Pevsner, p.68.
25. Salway, *op. cit.*, p.59.
26. John Blair, 'The Anglo-Saxon Period', in OHB, p.65.
27. *Dorset Year Book*, 1925.
28. Blair, *op. cit.*, p.68.
29. F.P. Pitfield, *Purbeck Parish Churches*, 1985, pp.2 and 39.
30. David A. Hinton, 'Minsters in SE Dorset', Proc. DNHAS 109, 1987, p.47.
31. Thomas Bond, *Corfe Castle*, 1883, p.63.
32. Laurence Keen, 'The Towns of Dorset' in J. Haslam (ed.), *Anglo-Saxon Towns in S. England*, 1984, pp.203-48.
33. The same battle in a painting by Herbert A. Bone, exhibited at the Royal Academy in 1890 and presented by the artist's daughter to the Russell Cotes Gallery, Bournemouth.
34. Dennis Smale, 'The Battle of Swanage – Hypothesis of The Battle with the Danes by King Alfred the Great A.D. 877', *Dorset Life Magazine*, 240, March 1999.
35-36. Blair, *op. cit.*, p.68.

3 *Domesday, pp.18-27*

1. Ralph Arnold, *A Social History of England*, 1967.
2. Sue Weeks, *Domesday in Purbeck*, 1986, Tithe Barn Museum, Swanage.
3. E. Ekwall, *Oxford Dictionary of English Place names*, 1960 (4th edn). A. Fägersten, *The Place Names of Dorset*, 1933. A.D. Mills, *The Place Names of Dorset*, 1977.
4. Swanage Tithe Map, 1839, DRO.
5. Studland Tithe Map, 1840, DRO.
6. T.V.H. FitzHugh, *Dictionary of Genealogy*, 1985.
7. W.E. Tate, *The Parish Chest*, 1983 (3rd edn).
8. W.M. Hardy, *Old Swanage*, 1910 (2nd edn.). Hardy put forward interesting theories but overstated his case. There may well have been a shallow inlet as far as Herston, noting the alluvium shown on the geological map. But, for instance, Treswell (1586) in his Purbeck map indicates only a brook at Swanage, as now.
9. See Susan Edgington, 'An Anglo-Norman Crusader' in *Crusade and Settlement*, 1985.
10. The name derives from the Centaur Chiron, famous in Greek mythology, for his skill in medical herbs. Culpepper (1616-54) said, 'They grow ordinarily in fields, pastures and woods. The herb is so safe you cannot fail in the using of it, 'Tis very wholesome, but not very toothsome.' The Saxon herbalists prescribed it largely for snakebites and other poisons, and as a cure for fever – hence it also being known as Feverwort. 'The herb formed the basis

of the once famous Portland Powder, which was said to be a specific for gout.' See Mrs M. Grieve's *A Modern Herbal*, 1931, Penguin 1980.

11. Court rolls of Eightholds, DRO.

12. Survey of Eightholds by Clarke, 1806, DRO.

13. 'Steinschmatzer' (The German for Wheatear, a bird often seen on stone walls) observed, 'The most incomprehensible name is Tilly Whim. Sir Walter Scott, after describing a place called Tully Veolan, says one part of it would have turned the brains of all the antiquaries in England had not the worthy proprietor pulled it down. Such a prank with Tilly Whim could not be played with impunity, and so it will perhaps continue some time longer, a darksome cave, and rather damp.' Steinschmatzer was an unofficial 'reporter' to the *Poole & Dorset Herald* in 1848-9. He refers to his 'perch at Peveril' and must have been living there when he contributed a series of entertaining and knowledgeable letters to the newspaper.

14. Martin Bond, of East Holme, who has written *A brief history of the Bonds*, has preserved Denis Bond's original 'Chronology'.

15. Photograph by G.H. Cox on p.114 in WMH's *Old Swanage*.

16. In the DRO is a 'Court Book, 1785-1809, with rentals also diagrammatic plans of land in Langton, Swanage and Herston belonging to the Serrells, and notes on their ownership, 1721-1813'.

4 *Manors north of the Brook, pp.28-36*

1. Durand also held Afflington (Corfe Castle), worth 6s., and Wilkswood (Langton Matravers), worth 10s.

2. H.M. Colvin (ed.), *The History of the King's Works*, vol. 1, 1963.

3. Moulham manor, DRO.

4. John Homme, Rector of Worth and Swanwich, 1437-73.

5. Jean Bowerman, 'Godlingston Manor', 1970 in W.G. Hoskins (ed.), *History from the Farm*.

6. The Godlingston Roll, DRO.

7. *Poole & Dorset Herald*, 13 May 1847.

8. James Rattue, 'An Inventory of Ancient, Holy and Healing Wells of Dorset', DNHAS 114, p.267: 'Owl Well, SZ 020808. Ulwell not from "holy well", as Hutchins thought. Saxon burial ground nearby'.

9. C.E. Robinson, *Picturesque Rambles in the Isle of Purbeck*, 1882. It includes a drawing of the Ulwell millwheel by Alfred Dawson, which is also shown in *John Mowlem's Swanage Diary*.

10. It is not known whence the originals were obtained, or where they are now. They were dated 1557-71 when Humphrey Walrond was lord of the manor, and 1674, 1688-9 and 1705 when the trustees of the Free School of Ilminster were the lords. The rolls refer to Carrant's Court lands, including Northbrook, Cauldons, Mylhams (Moulham), Holecroft etc. In the early roll of 1557, Richard Moleham, Christian, his wife and John Moleham, his brother, are mentioned. Marion Dale also informed J.E. Mowlem, when working on a common plea roll, that she had noted in a document that John Fytelton had been appointed attorney by Walter atte More v. John Moulham of Dorset in a plea of debt in 1366.

11. RCHM, Dorset SE, 1943 survey notes.

12. Vestry Minutes, 1824.

13. Hutchins.

14. Swanage Chancery Sale, 1823.

15. F. P. Pitfield, *Purbeck Parish Churches*, 1985.

5 *The Marblers, pp.37-46*

1. D. Lewer and R.Dark, *The Temple Church in London*, 1997.

2. G. Drury, *The Use of Purbeck Marble in Medieval Times*, Proc. DNHAS 1948.

3. Observation by Treleven Haysom of St Aldhelm's Head Quarry.

4. John Blair, 'Purbeck Marble', in *English Medieval Industries*.

5. H.M. Colvin, *The King's Works*, HMSO.

6. Dorset Record Society, vol. 4, 1971.

7. R.A. Griffiths, *The Later Middle Ages*, OHB.

8. C.H. Dundas, *St Nicholas, Worth Matravers*, 1947.

9. Purbeck Society Year Book, 1948.

10. Dundas, *ibid.*

11. Illustration 23, of the ancient key, is in Purbeck Society Papers, 1852-69, p.164.

12. John Guy, *The Tudor Age*, OHB.

13. Rachel Lloyd, *Dorset Elizabethans*, 1967.

14. Joan Brocklebank, 'The Dollings of Dunshay' – Essay, 1983.

15. K. Merle Chacksfield, *Armada 1588*, 1988.

16. James Hankinson ('Clive Holland'), *Pearson's Gossipy Guide to Bournemouth and District*, 1903.

17. Chacksfield, *op. cit.*

18. John Braye (ed.), *Swanage*, 1890.

19. Dennis Smale, *A Short History of Quarrying in the Isle of Purbeck*, 1984.

20. C. Cochrane, *Poole Bay and Purbeck*, 1970.

21. A.T. Buffery (personal communication).

22. It was realised that a larger organisation than the PSQPG, which had no access to public funds, should become involved for the long-term survival of the quarry workings. Bob Stebbings, the noted Bat Preservation Officer, suggested that the then Dorset Naturalist Trust would be the best contact. Miss Brotherton of the DNT was interested in the conservation of the quarries for bat hibernation during the winter period. An agreement was reached whereby an exchange of letters between the DNT and the PSQPG would not only save the underground quarry workings for future Industrial Archaeology but also for the conservation of rare bats in Dorset (ref: Dennis Smale, PSQPG, John Burry, Hoburne Company, New Milton; Miss H.J. Brotherton, OBE, DNT.)

23. Information from T. Haysom.

24. D. Smale, *op. cit.*

25. Christopher Dalton, *The Bells and Belfries of Dorset*, forthcoming.

26. Observations by T. Haysom, D. Smale, D. Haysom, H. Tatchell and D. Lewer.

27. F.P. Pitfield, *Purbeck Parish Churches*, 1985.

28. J.H. Bettey, *Dorset*, 1974.

29. See Audrey Pembroke's *Maid of Purbeck*, 1994, a convincing pro-royalist historical novel, introducing the Cockrams of Newton and Whitecliff, and the Bankes of Corfe Castle.

6 The Restoration, pp.47-54

1. C.N. Cullingford, *A History of Poole*, 1988, p.85.

2. Leonard Tatchell, *Swanage Congregational Church*, 1951.

3. William Rose Jnr was christened in March 1669 and was buried in woollen in November 1700, aged 31.

4. Quoted in Southey's *Life of the Revd Andrew Bell*, 1844.

5. Daniel Defoe, *A Tour thro' the whole Island of Great Britain*, 1724-6 (Peter Davies, 1927).

6. Mary E. Palgrave, *Under the Blue Flag – A Story of Monmouth's Rebellion*, n.d., p.49.

7. At a meeting of the Dorset Natural History and Antiquarian Field Club, 9 September 1896 (Proc.18, 1897).

8. WMH, *Old Swanage*, p.143: 'One of the condemned men was sent to be hanged, and the account of the execution was to be seen in the vestry records in the early part of the last century, but it has long since disappeared'. K. Merle Chacksfield, *The Dorset and Somerset Rebellion*, 1985, p.87.

9. Tatchell, *op. cit.*

10. DRO, original in PRO.

11. Plan illustrated in the RCHM Volume (SE Dorset).

12. Quoted in Hutchins, 3rd edn, App.I, p.682.

13. This seems incredible, though WMH says, 'I have seen quarrymen carrying stones on their backs from the quarries to pay for their beer, 'baccy' and other commodities.' But this refers to Swanage stone pennies (12 lbs) and shillings (144 lbs), tendered to merchants and shopkeepers in lieu of coinage.

14. Cullingford, *op. cit.*

15. Hutchins' mistake probably arose from the sale in 1664 of part of Carrant's Court by Onesiphorus Bond to Thomas Chapman.

16. As described in an Indenture, 3 April 1789.

17. Hutchins also said that Sir William Phippard bought Centry in 1700 and sold it to John Chapman in 1701. Chapman would then have been only 20 years of age, but there is evidently an error in the main text, for in the Appendix the date is given as 1721.

18. Little is known of the details of this venture, at which time many of the stone merchants amalgamated but then dispersed. It is suspected that any records were destroyed.

19. Indenture, 3 April 1789.

7 The Sea; Boney's Threat, pp.55-64

1-3. Thomas Hardy, *The Hand of Ethelberta*, 1876.

4. Charles Kingsley, in *Illustrated London News*, 1857.

5. 'Evidence respecting the Quay', a document of *c.*1842.

6. W.M. Hardy, *Old Swanage*, 1910.

7. Leland, the 16th-century antiquary, described 'a fishar town called Sandwiche, and there is a peere and a little fresh water.'

8. Philip Brannon, *Guide to Swanage*, 1858.

9. Tablet in Wesleyan Methodist Church: 'In memory of Robert Burt died 13 March 1825 aged 75 years, also of Mary, wife of the above, who died 13 March 1826. Having walked to Salisbury, and brought the Revd John Wesley on his first visit to Swanage, she became one of his followers and remained so until her death, a period of 50 years.'

10. Leonard Tatchell, *Swanage Congregational Church 1705-1951*, 1951.

11. Renamed *The Stonemason* by the brewers in 1971 but closed soon after. There is some evidence in the records of the Purbeck Marblers that this inn was known alternatively as *The Stonemason* over a century ago.

12. A Swanage stone merchant/sculptor and his wife. The tombstone is illustrated in David Lewer, *The Story of Swanage*, 1986.

13. An article by E.W. Horncastle in the *Swanage Times*, 29 November 1954.

14. WMH, *op. cit.*, says that on the west side of the Church Hill 'stood a very ancient cottage, in which was carried on a school by Dame Brown in the early part of the 18th century'.

15. WMH says of John Mowlem, 'his father and his three brothers and himself were the last gang of quarrymen who worked at Tilly Whim'.

16. David Lewer (ed.), *John Mowlem's Swanage Diary*, 1990.

17. From the Tithe Map Returns of 1839 it appears that Robert Burt Jnr occupied a considerable area of the Common Fields, including one or more quarry shafts.

18. *WMH's Old Swanage*. The photograph at p.1 is headed, 'A Bit of Old Swanage; The Author's Birthplace – This Picturesque Cottage was pulled down in 1908'. It was also the birthplace of George Burt – later the 'King of Swanage'.

19. Mowlem's old shop at Albion Place is shown in *John Mowlem's Swanage Diary*.

20. 'General View of the Agriculture in the County of Dorset': a Report for the Board of Agriculture and Internal Improvement, London, 1793.

21. G.A. Cooke, *British Traveller's Guide to Dorsetshire*, several editions of which appeared in the first decades of the 19th century. Cooke says that there were upwards of 60 quarries in the parish.

22. Frank Baines, 'History of John Mowlem & Co.' (Unpublished).

23. Report on the Coast of Dorsetshire, 1798, drawn up and transmitted to HRH the Duke of York by William Morton Pitt (DRO).

24. Summary from Lyme to Lilliput Chine (9-pounder). Serviceable, 43. Peveral Point has 7 serviceable. Guns: Unserviceable, 23 guns (the highest concentration at one point). Wanting, 19.

25. Their contents, with facsimile reproductions, were collated and published by J.E. Mowlem FSA.

26. 'Mrs Toop's house to be taken for the establishing a Rendezvous @ 15/ – a week.' (Swanage Vestry minutes, 10 April 1803). The arrangement was discontinued after 12 June.

27. Dated 8 April 1810 and in the possession of the Haysom family.

28. Thomas Masters Hardy's analysis of names and numbers in families, compiled from Nathan Chinchen's 1803 census sheets (DRO 286/11).

29. John Dampier of the Great House, Swanage.

30. Thomas Webster made the pioneer survey of the Isle of Purbeck and the coast westward in 1811-12, and produced a remarkably accurate geological map and several engravings, all of which appear in Sir H.C. Englefield's *Picturesque Beauties of and around the Isle of Wight*, 1816. See Plate 3: 'Tilly Whim ... that in which the excavation is represented, is the only one worked'.

31. Letter from C.E. R[obinson] in *Tribbett's Wareham Advertiser*, 27 May 1881.

32. J.C. Robinson purchased Eightholds in 1875.

8 *Andrew Bell, Rector, pp.65-74*

1. Robert Southey, *The Life of the Revd Andrew Bell*, 3 vols. 1844. Volume 2, by his son, the Revd Cuthbert Southey, 'contains the Swanage material, largely gathered and prepared by Dr Bell's amanuensis Mr Davies, who made a special visit to the town for the purpose'. See also: *Andrew Bell* in DNB, and J.T. Graham, 'A Rector of Swanage', *Dorset Year Book* 1952-3. The DNB adds, 'Southey's *Life of Bell* is the most tedious of biographies ... A short Life, *An Old Educational Reformer*, by Prof. Meiklejohn contains everything of importance'. Inspired by others, with Bell's enthusiasm, Wordsworth and Coleridge encouraged him, and Southey 'had the most extravagant belief in him'.

2. The 1803 Invasion census gives a total of 1,173 persons in Swanage, but this does not include the whole parish; Herston and Whitecliff are listed as separate tithings.

3. WMH, *Old Swanage*.

4. Hutchins records that 'In the bridge at Westminster (finished 1750), over the soffit of each arch built with Portland block, was another arch of Purbeck, bonded in with Portland stone'. This first Westminster Bridge of 15 arches, was erected 1739-50 and rebuilt 1854-62. A stone inscribed, 'This pedestal was work from the stone of old Westminster Bridge, built AD 1747 taken down 1860', stood in the garden of 'The Mount', Durlston, formerly the home of the Revd H. Nicholl-Griffith, Rector of Swanage, who placed several curiosities there.

5. Diary, 24 December 1846. John Mowlem married Susannah Manwell in 1812.

6. In the Vestry minutes of 22 November 1815, the irregularity of the church clock was discussed, and it was decided to erect a sundial.

7. Southey, *Life of Bell*.

8. WMH, *op. cit.*

9. In 1822 Mr and Mrs Stickland settled permanently in Swanage.

10. Articles by L. Stockwell published in the *Swanage Times*, 21 October 1953 and 23 May 1968 respectively.

11. E.M. Wallace, *The First Vaccinator*, 1981. Benjamin Jesty's son, Benjamin, was also an enthusiast, and in 1809 vaccinated great numbers, keeping a register. The family flourished near Dorchester and later held some of the largest farms in the county.

12. Graham, *op. cit.*
13. DNB.
14. DNB.
15. Southey, *op. cit.*
16. Graham, *op. cit.*
17. Southey, *op. cit.*
18. Frank Baines, 'The History of John Mowlem & Co.' (Unpublished.)
19. 'Whatever advantage might accrue to Dr Bell from his appointment to Sherburn Hospital, it certainly was somewhat extraordinary that the Bishop of Durham should have sought to make it a matter of exchange when it was discovered that it was untenable with a cure of souls – especially as it placed Dr Bell under the necessity of requesting it as a personal favour from Mr Calcraft that the Bishop's nominee might be presented to the living of Swanage.' Southey, *op. cit.* Calcraft of Rempstone was patron of the living.
20. Mrs A. Murray Smith, *The Roll-Call of Westminster Abbey*, 1902.
21. The frontispiece of Southey's *Life of Bell* gives a portrait of Bell by R.A. Owen. Another portrait appears in Nicholas Bentley's *The Victorian Scene*, 1968 (acknowledgment to the *Radio Times* Hulton Picture Library).
22. Report of Education Commission, 1861, p.98.
23. DNB.
24. Graham, *op. cit.*

9 Swanage in Chancery, pp.75-89

1. 25 June 1826: 'Letter from my father [Thomas Bartlett, Attorney and Town Clerk of Wareham] with matters finally agreed with regard to the Livings of Swanage and Worth, William and myself being now in for life'.
2. His grandson R. Grosvenor Bartelot FSA (who changed his name from Bartlett) made extracts from the original diaries and added, 'Two or three earlier volumes were destroyed by the ladies when packing up to leave Thurloxton Rectory, 1904'.
3. Henry Digby Cotes Delamotte (surgeon), Swanage doctor and registrar (1796-1874). He was followed similarly by his son, Dr George Cotes Delamotte (1829-1922).
4. Princess Charlotte had married Prince Leopold of Saxe-Cobourg, and died in childbirth at the age of 21, thus breaking the royal descent. Her uncle became William IV. For a balanced and entertaining account see J.B. Priestley, *The Prince of Pleasure*, 1969.
5. On Christmas Day there were 93 communicants. 'The Revd Mr Collins, the Independent minister, and the Revd Mr Hyde, the Westleyan [*sic*] minister, attended with many of their people. The church uncommonly crowded.'
6. The Revd John Dampier's unattractive likeness may be seen among the portraits and photographs of incumbents of St George's, Langton Matravers, collected there by R.J. Saville. A deed of 1815 refers to the Dampiers, 'now at the Great House in Swanage', after he had sold Leeson to George Garland in 1808.
7. Colson v. Dampier, PRO, c13 2147/4. The evidence makes a heavy roll more than six feet long, tied in rope, which was brought into the Land Registry Office from Ashridge, and daunted David Lewer on examination in 1970.
8. Twenty-one Lots in all, but no.VII was a cottage at Wareham and no.XXI was a meadow at Lynch, Corfe Castle.
9. 'The Mill wheel stands on part of the last-mentioned premises, for which 20s. a year is paid by the owner of the Mill.' (Chancery Sale Particulars.)
10. This plot was on the east of Church Hill. According to the 1828 rate book this brewery was in the occupation of William and Joseph Ellis.
11. It would seem that the mansion, or Great House, first came to be called the Manor House following this sale of 1823; it may be noted that although Lot VIII was described as 'the Manor, or reputed Manor, of Swanage', the house itself is not actually called the Manor House in the sale particulars.
12. Pitt's first wife died in 1818. He married his second wife, Grace Amelia, daughter of Henry Seymer of Hanford, in 1819: hence Seymer Road, Swanage.
13. Hutchins (3rd edn) and WMH. The east wing appears to have been converted into a large ballroom.
14. Mary Bartlett, not yet aged four (born 12 March 1821).
15. The crescents did come, but not until George Burt bought Durlston in 1864.
16. Among early distinguished visitors were the families of Lady Mary Ann Sturt, Lady Charlotte Sturt, Henry Seymer, Lady Barbara Ponsonby; also Lady Anne Brudenell, the Rt. Hon. Lord Bessborough, Admiral Hanwell, Sir James Hanham, the Hon. Frederick Noel, Sir Archibald Murray, the Revd Francis Close, the Revd Morton Colson, George Bankes Esq., Sir Richard Colt Hoare, Bart., etc.
17. Perhaps the promoters had been inspired by the brilliant meteor which passed over the Purbeck Hills in November 1825, 'vividly illuminating the country'.
18. W.M. Hardy, *Smuggling Days in Purbeck*, 1906. Also see Roger Guttridge, *Dorset Smugglers*, 1987 (2nd edn).
19. *Salisbury & Winchester Journal*, 4 October 1824. DCC: 2 November 1826, 24 June 1830 and 6 November 1834.
20. Thomas Hardy made some notes for a performance of *The Distracted Preacher* at the Corn Exchange, Dorchester, in 1911: 'The Preventive man (they were not called excisemen) each carried two pistols in his belt which were fired to give the alarm, and then a blue light was burnt. The smugglers carried heavy sticks. These pistols, blue lights and sticks would add to the picturesque and truth of the play if introduced.'

21. The parish was reunited with the see of Salisbury in 1837, as it had been before the Reformation.

22. Notice displayed in the parish church.

23. DCC reported (31 October 1833) that a standard pear tree in the Swanage rectory garden had this year borne 2,121 pears: about ½ ton. One pear weighed 2 lbs 2½ oz.

24. His tombstone describes his wish to be buried in the south graveyard, which he himself obtained for the church. The stone has been removed to the north churchyard for its better preservation.

25. Annuity shares by subscribers to loan, the shares increasing until, as subscribers die, the last survivor gets all. The originator was Lorenzo Tonti, c.1653.

26. This Thomas Hardy was said to have been a kinsman of the famous Thomas Hardy, OM.

27. Hutchins (3rd edn) says October 1835 but, for some unexplained reason, was incorrect. A full report was given in the DCC of 15 August 1833. See R. Bartelot, *Princess Drina comes to Swanage*, 1983. There is also an account in Ida Woodward, *In and around the Isle of Purbeck*, 1908.

28. Sir Tresham Lever, *The House of Pitt*, 1947.

29. In Chancery, Davis v. Pitt (between the Revd John Davis and others, Plaintiffs, and William Grey Pitt and another, Defendants).

30. Lot 21: Seven Tontine debentures, Lots 22-30: Pews in Swanage Church, Lots 31-9: Norden clay pits, Fordington and elsewhere.

31. Daniel Asher Alexander 'of Exeter' (1768-1846). Lord Eldon bought the hotel and Peveril in 1849 from DA Alexander's son, Philip.

32. John Scott of Encombe, 1st Earl of Eldon and Lord Chancellor, died in 1838 at a venerable age. The 2nd earl died in 1854.

10 *The Return of the Native, pp.*90-101

1. David Lewer (ed.), *John Mowlem's Swanage Diary, 1845-51*, 1990.

2. There were in fact seven children of Robert and Laetitia Burt; the first, Ann-Cole (b.1813) died at two months.

3. An annotated copy of the 1838 sale catalogue, marked 'Thos. Phippard Esq., Wareham, with Mr Coombs compts. with plan'.

4. James Arbon of Hyde House, Kingsbury, Middlesex. It is said that the surname was 'made up', being an acronym of 'A Rothschild Born Of Nathan' (who was an illegitimate son of the Rothschilds of Luton Hoo). James and Susy's eldest son, John Mowlem Arbon, is described as 'Farmer, Kingsbury Farm' in his marriage certificate, and later lived at Colindale as Huntsman to the Baroness Alfonse de Rothschild of Tring. He died having been thrown from a dogcart. It is also said that he gambled away the front of Swanage with a pack of cards with fuchsias on the back, and was kept by his wife as a sad example to their children. But the 'front of Swanage' never belonged to the Arbons and remained part of the Mowlem estate. It may have been some banker land in front of Victoria Terrace, formerly belonging to Robert Burt, that was lost in this way. George Burt's wife, Elizabeth Hudson, was brought up by her uncle, William Rust, also of Hyde House. Perhaps Susy Burt first met James Arbon there, or at Mr Rust's London residence.

5. Charles Castleman, solicitor of Wimborne, was the driving force in establishing the original Southampton/Dorchester railway which twisted and turned through the New Forest.

6. Alpha Cottage is something of a mystery, as it did not appear in the 1823 sale catalogue or map, although it was for sale in 1838 and was described as being next to the Shrubberies. It was purchased by Mr Coventry. His new house, The Grove, did not incorporate Alpha Cottage, as the latter appears to have been some way east of the Shrubberies. It does not seem to have been mentioned after 1838 and was evidently demolished. A view of the Bay c.1830 shows a substantial house which must have been Alpha Cottage (illustration 46).

7. Tablets in the parish church: 'Mrs Coventry of the Grove, Swanage, d. 30 September 1865 in her 70th year. She fell asleep at Swanage where she had desired.'
   ... 'to her daughter Louisa d. 1841 in her 18th year'.
   ... 'to her eldest child Capt. Fredk. Coventry, d. in India 1846 in his 26th year of age'.
   ... 'to Matilda wife of Revd T. G. Clarke, d. 1862 aged 38'.

8. Brewery sale particulars given in the Eldon Papers, DRO.

9. In her book, *Fresh Fields and Green Pastures*, Mrs Panton said that Cmdr Dr Marston, on succeeding to the Rempstone Estate, burned priceless historical records in the stable yard. He denied it and she had to pay him £250, which he gave to the Wareham Coal and Clothing Clubs, and to withdraw the book from publication to avoid an action for libel. An extensive and entertaining account is given in the DRO, ref: D86/L 11.

10. Mrs Melmoth, hearing cries of 'Murder!', drew the poor 'Bobby' into the house, locked the door and tended to his injuries. She was later presented with an inscribed silver-gilt cup.

11 *A New Rector, Church and Pier, pp.*102-112

1. Family trees of Mowlem and Burt are shown in David Lewer's *John Mowlem's Swanage Diary*, 1990, p.10.

2. See Margaret Emms, *Education in Swanage 1787-1902*, Proc. DNHAS 113, 1991.

3. See F.P. Pitfield, *Purbeck Parish Churches*, 1985.

4. Another version (DCC, 8 September 1859) suggested that the tramway would 'pass under the main street by an arch, on which it is proposed the arms of the chairman and other emblematic designs should be carved'.

5. A study of Philip Brannon was made by A.T. Markwick who provided a note headed 'Versatile Victorian' about him in *Country Life* (11 July 1980).

6. DCC (27 November 1856).

7. It was a replica of an obelisk erected at Ludgate Circus. Ref: Lewer & Calkin, *Curiosities of Swanage*, 1999.

8. The Mowlem Institute is shown on the cover photograph.

9. The field called 'Mowlams' (ref: sz 025798) belonged to the Revd S. Serrell at the time of the Tithe Map, 1839.

12 *King of Swanage: George Burt, pp.*113-125

1. Sister Liam Cummins, M.Ed.ACP, 'Climbing the Social Ladder – the Story of two Victorian quarryboys' (unpublished thesis, 1970).

2. There has been some confusion over the many Burts who were in Swanage at that time. George Burt, though a contractor and stone merchant, had no quarries here. Four brothers, Henry Weeks Burt, 'Guvnor' of the 'Depot', George Burt, known as 'Boss Burt' of the Cowleaze quarries, Bill Burt of the Herston quarries, and Charles Burt, who went to Liverpool and later worked on the new cathedral there, were all sons of William Burt, a stonemason, and only distantly related to GB.

3. The plan survives at Crickmays' architects office.

4. E.D. Burrowes LLD, Vicar of Kimmeridge, *Swanage*, 1873. Dr Pearce's Hydropathetic Establishment did not last long. It was stated that plots for buildings of a superior class were on lease for 999 years, or to be sold. 'G.R. Crickmay, Architect, Weymouth.'

5. Quoted in the DCC.

6. A glorified mechanical earth closet invented by the Revd Mr Moule of Fordington.

7. 'The artesian well was sunk to a depth of 60 feet and bored to a further 53 feet. The water was raised by two eight hp gas engines, and was stored in tanks capable of holding 5,737 and 22,000 gallons respectively. The bottom of the bore is 78 feet below high-water mark, and the top of the well is 35 feet above, while the tanks are about 200 feet above HWM.' Mrs Panton, *Guide To Swanage*, 1885.

8. The Land Agents' Record (6 June 1891).

9. Dr Home.

10. David Lewer (ed.), *John Mowlem's Swanage Diary, 1845-51*, 1990.

11. Lewer and Calkin, *Curiosities of Swanage*, 1999.

12. C.G. Harper, *The Hardy Country*, 1925.

13. H.E. Danes, 'Sir John Charles Robinson', 1992. For D.Phil.Oxford (copy at V&A Library). 'Robinson was argumentative, obstinate, cantankerous and quarrelled with Henry Cole of the Musuem. Sir Austen Layard, MP and Trustee of the National Gallery, despised Cole even more than Robinson did, but regarded the latter as offensive, bumptious and devious. I may say that the more I hear of Mr Robinson the less I like him. He is nothing but a dealer and up to every trick in the trade.' Robinson retired to Swanage, dying at Newton Manor in 1913. A catalogue for the sale of the house and contents is housed at the Dorset County Museum.

14. *Curiosities, op. cit.*

15. *The Times*, February 1875.

16. David Lewer, *Hardy in Swanage*, 1990.

13 *Local Authority and the Railway Age, pp.*126-139

1. Lewer & Calkin, *Curiosities of Swanage*, 1999.

2. Red House Museum, Christchurch.

3. DRO.

4. George Burt, 'Notes of a three months' trip to Egypt, Greece ... etc.', 1878.

5. Researched by Harry Spencer, with acknowledgements.

6. R.W. Kidner, *The Railways of Purbeck*, 1973.

7. J.H. Lucking, *Railways of Dorset*, 1968.

8. DCC, 21 May 1885.

9. Kidner, *op. cit.*

10. *Curiosities, op. cit.*

11. David Lewer, *Hardy in Swanage*, 1990.

12. Charles Harper, *The Hardy Country*, 1925.

14 *Urban Swanage, pp.*140-152

1. Charles Harper, *The Hardy Country*, 1925.

2. Lawrence Popplewell, *Stone blocks and Greenheart*, 1988.

3. Margaret Emms, *Swanage Local Board of Health 1873-1894*, Proc. DNHAS 107, 1985.

4. Crickmay & Son, Plan of Building sites: De Moulham Estate, 21 May 1985.

5. The bandstand ironwork is marked 'W. Macfarlane & Co. Glasgow'. This recalls the huge 'Saracen' Foundry of Macfarlane's works which once sent its products to all parts of the Empire. 'Macfarlane's "Kits-of-Parts",

in fact, provided many arcade roofs, station awnings, pissoirs, and other artefacts of the Victorian scene.' J.S. Curl, 'Aspects of Scottish architecture and townscape' in *The Architect*, May 1974.

6. No.57 in David Haysom and John Patrick, *Swanage in old picture postcards*, 1992.
7. Obituary of Sir Stephen Collins, *Dorset Year Book*, 1925, p.140.
8. Leonard Tatchell, *Swanage Congregational Church*, 1951.
9. Pevsner and Newman, *Dorset*, 1972, p.410.
10. Francis Newbery (1855-1946) of Bridport had been Director of the Glasgow School of Art, and retired to Corfe Castle. See Peter Davies, *Art in Poole and Dorset*, 1987.
11. Margaret Emms, *Education in Swanage 1787-1902*, Proc. DNHAS 113, 1991.
12. Information from Mr and Mrs Mark Helfer.
13. Information from the Revd Peter Chadwick.
14. Margaret Emms, *The History of the Swanage Cottage Hospital*, privately printed, 1990.
15. Hardy built his house, Max Gate, in 1885 and died there in 1928.
16. Thomas Powell was assistant to W. Pouncy in the High Street in 1888. He then had his own shop in Shore Road. His son William continued there until his retirement in 1956.

15 *The Great War,* pp.153-161

1. Photograph *c.*1916. David Haysom & David Bragg, *Swanage & Purbeck in Old Photographs*, 1991, p.132.
2. Margaret Emms, *The History of the Swanage Cottage Hospital*, privately printed, 1990.
3. The Thurston Swanage diaries, at the Red House Museum, Christchurch.
4. Information from Peter Hancock.
5. Gilbert Hall was demolished in 2004 for redevelopment as flats.
6. Haysom & Bragg, *op. cit.*, pp.74-9.
7. Quoted in the *Dorset Year Book*, 1925, p.118.
8. The 'Blue Comfy Cars' and Len Nicholls' bus operating from Langton Matravers.
9. Colin Morris, *History of Hants & Dorset Motor Services Ltd*, 1973, p.106, 'The Swanage Outstation'. Photograph of the Ferry, p.120.
10. Information from Squadron Leader NVOP Healey, 1993.
11. Pennie Denton, *Paul Nash in Swanage*, 2002.
12. Peter Davies, *Art in Poole and Dorset*, 1987.
13. Full accounts given in the *Swanage Times, passim*.

16 *War and Recovery,* pp.162-167

1. Capt. Spencer Mitchell CBE, *Production Under Fire*, 1967.
2. Information from John Dean, taken from his father's notebook. Capt. R.C.W. Dean was Air Raid Prevention Controller for the area.
3. Mrs Jennifer Banfield, letter in the *Swanage Times*, 5 December 1974.
4. K. Merle Chacksfield, *Swanage at War*, 1993.
5. R.W. Kidner, *The Railways of Purbeck*, 1973.
6. Dorset County Council, Planning Office, 1976.

17 *To the Millennium,* pp.168-177

1. Durrant Developments, Christchurch. Architects: Cheshire Robbins Design Group Ltd, Christchurch.
2. 'Although Swanage suffered little or no damage, it has – for the time being – lost the bulk of its beach. This, of course, is a more or less annual occurrence and few take notice of it, knowing that in time the sands will come back. This time, however, the beach seems to have been denuded to a greater depth by the prolonged scour and heavy ground swell. From the Mowlem Institute to Victoria Avenue the sands have been almost entirely swept away, leaving behind a beach of shingle, rubble and rocks. But it is further along the promenade nearer the Beach Cafe that the biggest scour seems to have taken place and here the beach has been lowered to a depth of about four feet. The most serious feature is that the foundations and underpinning of the sea wall have been laid bare and at the mercy of the ravages of future storms. Several times this week the southern half of the promenade has been strewn with large quantities of shingle thrown up by the waves while the opposite gutter has been filled with thrown sand.'
3. Lawrence Popplewell, *Stone Blocks and Greenheart*, 1988.
4. J.H. Bettey, 'Man and the Land', *Dorset Farming 1846-1996*, DNHAS, 1996.
5. Dorothy Kerridge, 'A Brief History of Agriculture in the Isle of Purbeck' in Trudi Miller (ed.), *Course Study*, Leeson House Field Studies Centre, 1989.
6. Mark Helfer, *The History of Knitson* (forthcoming for the Langton Matravers Coach House Museum).
7. Dorset County Council Planning Department.
8. Paul Hyland, *The Ingrained Island*, 1978.

Bibliography

Arkell, W.J., *The Geology of the Country around Weymouth, Swanage, Corfe and Lulworth* (1947)

Arnold, R., *A Social History of England* (1967)

Austen. J., *Purbeck Papers* (1852-69)

Bartelot, R., *Princess Drina comes to Swanage* (1983)

Beavis, J., 'Purbeck Marble in Roman Britain', DNHAS no.92 (1970)

Benfield, E., *Purbeck Shop* (1940)

Benfield, E., *Southern English* (1942)

Bettey, J.H., *Dorset* (1974)

Bettey, J.H., *Man and the Land* (1996)

Bond, M., *A Brief History of the Bonds* (n.d.)

Bond, T., *Corfe Castle* (1883)

Borrett, S., *Swanage in the 1920s and 1930s* (2002)

Bowerman, J., 'Godlingston Manor', in Hoskins, W.G., *History from the Farm* (1970)

Brannon, P., *Guide to Swanage and Isle of Purbeck* (1858)

Braye, J., *Swanage* (1896)

Brunsden, D. (ed.), *Dorset and East Devon Coast* (2003)

Burrowes, E.D., *Swanage* (1873)

Burt, G., *Notes of a three months' trip to Egypt* (1878)

Calkin, J.B., *Ancient Purbeck* (1968)

Calkin, J.B., *Archeological Discoveries in the Isle of Purbeck* (1953)

Chacksfield, K.M., *Swanage at War* (1993)

Chacksfield, K.M., *Armada 1588* (1988)

Chaffey, J., *Illustrated Guide to the Dorset and East Devon Coast* (2003)

Claridge, J., *Agriculture in the County of Dorset* (1793)

Clark, G.C. and Harding, T.W., *The Dorset Landscape* (1935)

Cochrane, C., *Poole Bay and Purbeck*, 2 vols (1970 and 1971)

Colvin, H.M., *The History of the King's Works*, Vol.1 (1963)

Cooke, G.A., *British Traveller's Guide to Dorsetshire* (early 19th century)

Cox, P.J., 'A Roman-British Cemetery at Ulwell' DNHAS no.110 (1988)

Cullingford, C.N., *A History of Poole* (2003)

Cunning, A.D. and Maxted, K.R., *Coastal Studies in Purbeck* (1979)

Dain, S.J., *Mary Burt went for a Walk – the Story of Purbeck Methodism* (1974)

Damon, R., *Geology of Weymouth, Portland and Coast of Dorsetshire* (1884)

Davies, G.M., *The Dorset Coast, a Geological Guide* (1956)

Davies, Peter, *Art in Poole and Dorset* (1987)

Defoe, Daniel, *A Tour thro' the whole Island of Great Britain 1724-26* (Peter Davies 1927)

Delair, J.B., Proceedings of the Dorset Natural History and Archaeological Society, DNHAS no.84 (1963)

Denton, Pennie, *Paul Nash in Swanage* (2002)

Dorset Natural History & Archaeological Society (Proceedings & Monographs)

Dru Drury, G., *The Use of Purbeck Marble in Medieval Times* (1948)

Dundas, C.H., *St Nicholas, Worth Matravers* (1947)

Edgington, Susan, 'An Anglo-Norman Crusader' in *Crusade and Settlement* (1985)

Emms, Margaret, 'Education in Swanage, 1787-1902', DNHAS no.113 (1991)

Emms, Margaret, 'Swanage Local Board of Health, 1873-94', DNHAS no.107 (1985)

Emms, Margaret, *The History of the Swanage Cottage Hospital* (1990)

Englefield and Webster, *Geological memoirs of the ... Dorset Coast* (1816)

Ensom, P.C., 'Geology in 1983', DNHAS no.105 (1983)

Farr, G.E., *Wreck & Rescue on the Dorset Coast* (1971)

Foss, D., *Lionheart, The Story of Leo Exton 1887-1960* (1985)

Godfrey, Elizabeth (Jessie Bedford), *The Cradle of a Poet* (1910)

Graham, J.T., 'Dr Bell, Rector of Swanage', Dorset Year Book (1952-3)

Grimsell, L.V., *Dorset Barrows* (1959)

Gutteridge, R., *Dorset Smugglers* (1987)

Hardy, W.M., *Old Swanage* or *Purbeck Past and Present* (1910)

Hardy, W.M., *Smuggling Days in Purbeck* (1906)

Hardy, Thomas, *The Hand of Etheltlerta* (1876)

Harper, C., *The Hardy Country* (1925)

Haysom, D. and Bragg, D., *Swanage and Purbeck in Old Photographs* (1991)

Haysom, D. and Patrick, J., *Swanage in Old Picture Postcards* (1992)

Heath, S. and Hazelhurst, E., *Swanage and District* (c.1910)

Hinton, D.A., 'Minsters in S.E. Dorset', DNHAS no.109 (1987)

Holland, C., *The Gossipy Guide to Swanage and District* (c.1905)

Hutchins, J., *History and Antiquities of the County of Dorset* (1874)

Hyland, P., *The Ingrained Island* (1978)

Kidney, R.W., *The Railways of Purbeck* (1973)

King, M.P., *Beneath your Feet* (1974)

Kingsley, C., *Swanage* (1857)

Legg, R., *Purbeck Island* (1995)

Legg, R., *The Jurassic Coast* (2002)

Lever, Sir T., *The House of Pitt* (1947)

Lewer, D., *The Story of Swanage* (1986)

Lewer, D., *John Mowlem's Swanage Diary* (1990)

Lewer, D., *Hardy in Swanage 1875* (1990)

Lewer, D. and Calkin, J.B., *Curiosities of Swanage or Old London by the Sea*, 4th edn (1999)

Lucking, J.H., *Railways of Dorset* (1968)

Markwick, A.T., 'Versatile Victorian' (Philip Brannon) in *Country Life* (11 July 1980)

Mills, A.D., *The Place Names of Dorset* (1977)

Mitchell, V. and Smith, K., *Branch Line to Swanage* (1986)

Morris, C., *History of the Hants & Dorset Motor Services Ltd* (1973)

Morris, J., *The Story of the Swanage Lifeboats* (1984)

Mowlem, J.E., *Moulham – a Dorset Place and Surname* (1934)

Nunn, J.E., 'A Geological Map Purbeck Beds in the Northern part of Durlston Bay', DNHAS no.113 (1991)

Oppé, E.F., *The Isle of Purbeck* (1964)

Oppé, E.F., *Swanage Bay AD 877* (1959)

Palgrave, M.E., *Under the Blue Flag – A Story of the Monmouth Rebellion* (n.d.)

Panton, J.E., *Fresh Leaves and Green Pastures* (1909)

Parsons, 'J.F., Princess Victoria in Dorset, 1833', *Bournemouth Local Studies* no. 734 (n.d.)

Payne, D., *Dorset Harbours* (1953)

Peers, R., 'Prehistoric and Roman remains' in Newman, J. and Pevsner, N., *Dorset* (1972)

Pembrook, A., *Maid of Purbeck* (1994)

Pitfield, F.P., *Purbeck Parish Churches* (1985)

Pitt, W.M., *Report of the Coast of Dorsetshire* (1798)

Popplewell, L., *Stone blocks and Greenheart* (1988)

Pushman, D., *Purbeck Underground* (n.d.)

Putman, B., *Roman Dorset* (1985)

Rattue, J., 'Ancient Holy and Healing Wells of Dorset', DNHAS no.114 (1992)

Reed, T.D., *The Rise of Wessex* (1947)

Robinson, C.E., *Picturesque Rambles in the Isle of Purbeck* (1882)

Short, B.C., *The Isle of Purbeck* (1967)

Smale, D., *A Short History of Quarrying in the Isle of Purbeck* (1984)

Southey, R., *The Life of the Revd Andrew Bell*, vol.2 (1841)

Stanier, P., *The Industrial Past* (1998)

'Steinschmatzer', series of accounts of Swanage in *Poole & Dorset Herald* (1848-9)

Stoker, H., *Sea Fishing in Dorset* (1972)

Sunter, N., 'Roman-British Industries in Purbeck', DNHAS Mon. no.7 (1987)

Tatchell, L., *The Heritage of Purbeck* (c.1955)

Tatchell, L., *Swanage Congregational Church* (1951)

Taylor, C., *Dorset* (1970)

Thomas, J., *Stone Quarrying* (1998)

Treves, F., *Highways and Byways in Dorset* (1906)

Wallace, E.M., *The First Vaccinator* (1981)

Woodward, I., *In and Around the Isle of Purbeck* (1908)

Woolf, T., *Purbeck Shore* (1973)

Newspapers and printed Periodicals

Dorset County Chronicle

Dorset Life

Dorset Year Book

Illustrated London News

Kelly's Directories

Poole and Dorset Herald

Swanage ADC

Swanage Times

The Times

Tribbett's Wareham Advertiser and Swanage Visitors' List

Ward Lock's Guides

Index

Page numbers printed in **bold** type refer to illustrations